# The InDesign® Effects Book

# The InDesign® Effects Book

Ted LoCascio

Wiley Publishing, Inc.

Acquisitions and Developmental Editor: PETE GAUGHAN

Technical Editor: MICHAEL NINNESS

Production Editor: DARIA MEOLI

Copyeditor: LIZ WELCH

Production Manager: TIM TATE

Vice President & Executive Group Publisher: RICHARD SWADLEY

Vice President and Executive Publisher: JOSEPH B. WIKERT

Vice President and Publisher: DAN BRODNITZ

Compositor and Book Designer: MAUREEN FORYS, HAPPENSTANCE TYPE-O-RAMA

Proofreader: JAMES BROOK

Indexer: TED LAUX

Cover Designer: TED LoCASCIO

## Acknowledgments

First and foremost, I must thank everyone at Sybex for making this book possible. Thanks to publisher Dan Brodnitz and to acquisitions and developmental editor Pete Gaughan for sharing my vision on this project and for being as genuinely enthusiastic about InDesign as I am. Thanks also to Pete for helping me develop this title and paying such close attention to the details, and to Michael Ninness for acting as my technical editor and making sure every shortcut, tip, and step is correct.

Special thanks to my copyeditor, Liz Welch, for making this book read as well as it does. I must also thank my production editor, Daria Meoli, for working with me on the book's schedule and keeping everything on track. I would also like to thank compositor Maureen Forys and her staff at Happenstance Type-O-Rama for doing such a great job of laying out the book. And special thanks to Margaret Rowlands for working with me on the book's cover design.

I must also thank Lynda Weinman, Garo Green, Auriga Bork, and the rest of the wonderful staff at Lynda.com for making me a part of their excellent online instructor team, and for being so much fun to work with.

Thanks also to Photospin.com for allowing me to use their images in this book.

Loving thanks to my wife Jill for being so patient while I was busy writing this book. Thanks also to Mom, Dad, Val, Bob and Evelyn Innocenti, and the rest of my extended family for being so supportive. I must also thank my bandmates in the Threads—Stan Arthur, Michael Hoag, Brian Merrill, and Sonny John Sundstrom.

A big thanks also goes out to my extremely supportive friends: Al Ward, Steve Weiss, Dave Korman, Jeff Wood, Aaron and Colleen Akers, and Finn Walling.

I would also like to thank my cats—Ito, Chloe, Tobias, and Clinton—for forcing me to take breaks from my writing in order play with them.

And of course, thanks to Adobe for making such great software to write about.

*To my wonderful wife, Jill,*
*for her never-ending love and support.*

# About the Author

Ted LoCascio is a professional graphic designer and an expert in InDesign, Photoshop, Illustrator, and QuarkXPress. He served as senior designer at KW Media and the National Association of Photoshop Professionals (NAPP) for several years, and has created layouts and designs for many successful software training books, videos, and magazines. He is the author of *InDesign CS2 at Your Fingertips,* has contributed articles to *Photoshop User* magazine, and has taught at Photoshop World. Ted is also the video author of *InDesign CS2 Essential Training*, available at Lynda.com.

A graphic designer for more than ten years, Ted's designs and illustrations have been featured in several national newsstand and trade magazines, such as *Photoshop User, Mac Design,* Nikon's *Capture User,* PDIA's *Great Output, AAA Going Places,* and *Florida Trend*. Since 2001, he has used Adobe InDesign to create layouts for magazines, books, and various advertising and marketing materials, including brochures, product packaging, posters and signs, and interactive PDFs.

A Chicago native (born a hopeless Cubs fan) and Columbia College alumnus, Ted relocated to the Tampa Bay area in 1994. He currently resides in Tarpon Springs, Florida, with his wife Jill, and four cats.

When he's not designing, writing books, feeding cats, or dodging hurricanes, he writes and records music with his current band, the Threads. A guitar player for over 20 years, Ted has played and recorded with national acts such as Barely Pink (Big Deal records) and Hangtown (Black Dog records). For more info, visit www.tedlukas.com and www.thethreads.us.

# Contents

# Introduction

Okay, I admit it. I've always been a "Photoshop guy." I love creating graphics in Photoshop. And when it comes to creating vector graphics, I've always been an "Illustrator guy." When Adobe first released InDesign, I was hesitant to learn it, simply because I didn't think the world needed another "page layout" application. Luckily, I was working for a very forward-thinking employer at the time, who insisted we start using InDesign soon after it was first released.

Having used QuarkXPress for years, I was less than enthusiastic. But once I started using InDesign, my attitude soon changed. After years of using InDesign, I don't know how I ever used anything else. Indeed, InDesign is truly a designer's tool. The familiar Adobe interface alone is enough to set it apart from other page layout applications and to inspire graphic designers everywhere to expand their print design horizons. Now with the release of CS2, InDesigners can push their creativity through the roof with all of its added functionality.

What I set out to prove with this book is that, as a designer, you can do a lot more with this application than you may realize. It is entirely possible to create graphics in InDesign. Sure, InDesign is a great tool for page layout, but when you dig deeper into the application and start experimenting with all of its added functionality, you'll soon appreciate how much more you can do with it.

*The InDesign Effects Book* does not include any page-size projects such as sample brochures or mock advertisements. Instead, each project is one small piece of the puzzle. Each one is designed to inspire and motivate you to think creatively as you're using InDesign. Once you've tried the different effects described in each chapter, you can then apply them to page layout projects of your own.

With these projects, we'll dive head first into InDesign using layers, transparency effects, nesting, feathering, corner effects, snippets, and the drawing tools—just to name a few. Before you know it, you'll be using InDesign to create placed image effects, type effects, paragraph effects, and shape effects.

My hope is that after reading this book, you will share my opinion of InDesign: that this is by far the coolest page layout program in existence.

## Before You Get Started...

The projects in these chapters assume that you are using the default InDesign application preferences. If you've changed any of the application defaults, some of the steps may not translate properly. You can restore the InDesign default preferences by pressing and holding Shift+Opt+~CM+Control (Mac) or Shift+Ctrl+Alt (Windows) at application launch. When the Delete Preferences dialog appears, click Yes to reset.

In order to provide you with the clearest images, all of the tutorial screen shots were taken with InDesign's Display Performance preference set to High Quality Display. If your system has a fast processor, and you'd like to view your images using High Quality Display, you can choose it as your default under InDesign ▷ Preferences ▷ Display Performance (Mac) or Edit ▷ Preferences ▷ Display Performance (Windows).

**Note:** A lot of the projects in the book require InDesign CS2 because they use snippets as project materials; *snippets* don't work with InDesign CS or InDesign 2. (You can identify snippets by the .inds filename extension.) Also, most of the projects require CS2 dialogs—Drop Shadow, for instance—and various other CS2 nuances.

## The Companion Web Page

All the files you'll need to work through the effects are available from the book's companion web page: www.wiley.com/go/indesignfx.

## How to Contact the Author

Ted LoCascio is always happy to answer any questions that you may have about InDesign CS2. If you can't find the answer in this book, please e-mail your question to indesignquestions@knology.net

# Placed Image Effects

*InDesign offers lots of creative ways to place images into your documents. Although you can't alter the pixels of an image in InDesign like you can in Photoshop, you can control how the image is presented in your layouts. Through the creative use of clipping masks, tables, and InDesign's drawing tools, you can design attention-grabbing frames to hold your images. You can also place images into text objects that have been converted to outlines, colorize grayscale images, and apply effects such as Feather and Drop Shadow to transparent TIFFs and PSDs.*

**Character Outline Frames**

**Clipping Path Frames**

**Popping Out of the Frame**

**Pathfinder Frames**

**Snapshot Frames**

**Filmstrip Frames**

**Table Frames Part 1**

**Table Frames Part 2**

**Transparent Image Outer Glow**

**Duotone CD Art**

# Character Outline Frames

With InDesign, paths can also be containers. This means that images can be placed into frames of all different shapes and sizes, including text characters that have been converted to outlines.

By placing a photo inside a character outline path, you can create a dramatic effect, much like the sky image placed in the word "DREAM" as described in the following steps. Before converting to outlines, you'll want to choose a bold font, set at a large point size, so that the character outlines are wide enough to display an image.

Once you get the hang of placing pictures into character outlines, try experimenting with the effect by using entirely different fonts and images. The more you experiment, the more dramatic the effect can be.

## Placing an Image Inside Text

To re-create this effect using the image shown here, download sky.tif from *The InDesign Effects Book* website, www.wiley.com/go/indesignfx.

**Step 1.**
Create a new document and press T to access the Type tool. Create a text frame and choose a bold condensed font at a large point size (in the example here, it is Compacta at 216pt). Add some logotype.

**Step 2.**
Switch to the Selection tool and click the Formatting Affects Text button at the bottom of the Tools palette. Press the backslash key to apply a fill of None.

**Step 3.**
Press X to bring the Stroke icon to the front and press the comma key (,) to apply a black stroke.

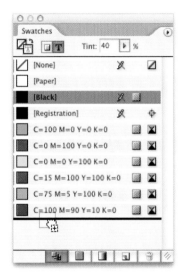

**Step 4.**
Choose Window▷Stroke or press F10 to display the Stroke palette. Enter **2pt** in the Weight field and press Return (Mac) or Enter (Windows). If you prefer, you can also enter this value in the Weight field of the Control palette.

**Step 5.**
Choose Window▷Swatches, or press F5 to display the Swatches palette. Type **40%** in the Tint field and press Return (Mac) or Enter (Windows). Sometimes it's helpful to save a tint build as a swatch, just in case you decide to apply the same tint to other objects in your layout. If you'd like to save the tint as a swatch in the palette, click and drag the Fill Stroke icon into the Swatches palette list.

**Step 6.**
Choose Type▷Create Outlines, or press Shift+⌘+O (Mac) or Shift+Ctrl+O (Windows). Press A to switch to the Direct Selection tool and see the points of the new character outline path.

*continues on next page*

## InDesign Fonts Folder

What if you can't get a certain troublesome font to load properly on your system and appear in the InDesign font menu? Don't panic– there is something you can do to solve this problem. Try placing the problem font in the InDesign Fonts folder.

The Fonts folder is located in the InDesign CS2 application folder. Any fonts in this folder are managed from within InDesign rather than from an outside application or through the operating system.

Fonts that do not load properly through the operating system (such as multiple master fonts in OS X) may work in InDesign if you put them in the Application Fonts folder.

# Character Outline Frames *continued*

## Previewing Applied Fonts

Not sure which font you'd like to use? Well, why don't you try scrolling through the font menu and previewing each one as it's applied to your text selection?

To do this, select a text frame with the Selection tool, then press T to switch to the Type tool and click inside the Font field located in either the Control or Character palette.

To preview available fonts as they are applied to all the text in a selected frame, scroll through the list by pressing the Up/Down arrow keys.

**Step 7.**
Press ⌘+D (Mac) or Ctrl+D (Windows) to display the Place dialog. Locate the sky.tif image on your system and click Open to import the image into the selected character outline.

**Step 8.**
Choose Object ▷ Fitting ▷ Center Content, or press Shift+⌘+E (Mac) or Shift+Ctrl+E (Windows).

**Step 9.**
Choose Object ▷ Drop Shadow. In the dialog that appears, click the Drop Shadow check box to enable the effect, and then turn on the Preview check box to see the shadow applied to your selected object. Enter **50%** for Opacity, **p3** for Blur, and **p3** for the X and Y offsets. Keep the Spread and Noise settings at 0. Click OK to apply.

**Step 10.**

Add some type to complete the logo design. In the example shown here, the word "AIRLINES" is placed underneath the character outline in black, all caps, using 12pt Eurostile Extended 2 with 1840 tracking applied. The words "WE'LL TAKE YOU THERE" above the character outline are set using 10pt Eurostile Extended 2 with 680 tracking applied. They also have a blue fill applied, which was sampled from the sky image with the Eyedropper tool. The thin rules placed on either side of the word "AIRLINES" have a 0.5pt black stroke applied.

**Step 11.**

Here is an example of how this effect can be used with an entirely different photo placed inside the same character outline. The more you experiment with the photos, characters, and colors used in this effect, the more exciting your results will be.

# Find Font

Any time you open an InDesign document that uses fonts not currently loaded on your system, a warning dialog appears letting you know which fonts are unavailable.

If you don't have the fonts, you can replace them with something else. Click the Find Font button in the warning dialog, or if you've already clicked OK, choose Type ▷ Find Font.

The Find Font dialog displays a list of all fonts currently used in the document. Missing fonts appear alphabetically at the top of the list with a warning icon displayed to the right of the window. Click the name of the missing font and choose a replacement font and style from the Font Family and Font Style menus.

Click the Find First button to view the first occurrence of the missing font in the document. Click the Change button to replace it with the selected font. Click the Change All button to replace every occurrence of the missing font in the document. Click Change/Find to locate and replace every occurrence of the missing font with each click of the mouse.

# Clipping Path Frames

You can extract an image from a photograph by creating a clipping path in either InDesign or Photoshop. InDesign paths can be created using the Detect Edges option in the Clipping Path dialog. However, be wary of the InDesign Clipping Path dialog controls. They are clumsy and not very precise. If you need to extract an image from anything more than a simple solid-color background, you may want to create your path in Photoshop instead. A Photoshop path that is embedded in an image can be applied once it is placed in an InDesign document.

Once you create an InDesign clipping path or apply a Photoshop clipping path, you can then convert that path into a frame. The image still appears the same in the document after converting, but who says you need to keep that image in the frame? If you delete its contents, you can then place a totally different image inside the clipping path frame.

## From Clipping Path to Frame with One Click!

To re-create this effect using the images shown here, download violin.tif and music.tif from *The InDesign Effects Book* website.

**Step 1.**

In a new document, press ⌘+D (Mac) or Ctrl+D (Windows) to display the Place dialog. Locate the violin.tif image on your system, check Show Import Options, and click Open.

**Step 2.**

In the Image panel of the Image Import Options dialog, enable the Apply Photoshop Clipping Path option and click OK.

**Step 3.**

Click the loaded place cursor once anywhere on the page to place the image at 100% of its size.

**Step 4.**

Control-click (Mac) or right-click (Windows) the placed image and choose Convert Clipping Path To Frame from the contextual menu.

**Step 5.**

Press A to switch to the Direct Selection tool. Click directly on the violin image to select it from within the new clipping path frame. Press Delete (Mac) or Backspace (Windows). Click the path to select it and enter **2 pt** in the Stroke Weight field of the Control palette.

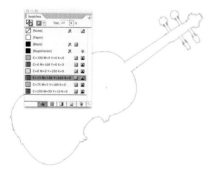

**Step 6.**

Display the Swatches palette by choosing Window▷Swatches (or press F5). Click the red swatch (C=15 M=100 Y=100 K=0), enter a value of **20** in the Tint field, and press Return (Mac) or Enter (Windows).

*continues on next page*

## Converting Clipping Paths to Frames

You can convert a clipping path (applied from Photoshop or created in InDesign) into a graphic frame. To do this, select the image with the Direct Selection tool, Control-click (Mac) or right-click (Windows) to access the contextual menu, and choose Convert Clipping Path To Frame. Once the command is applied, InDesign removes the clipping path and replaces it with a graphic frame of the same shape.

---

**Note:** To open and edit an image in Photoshop, select it and click the Edit Original button at the bottom of the Links palette. Once you save and close the image in Photoshop, InDesign automatically updates it in the InDesign document.

# Clipping Path Frames *continued*

## Detect Edges

To create an InDesign clipping path, select a placed image with either of the selection tools and choose Object ▷ Clipping Path. At the top of the Clipping Path dialog, choose Detect Edges from the Type pop-up menu. You can then adjust the Threshold and Tolerance settings by entering values in the respective fields or dragging the sliders. To see the path as you are applying it, click the Preview check box.

The Threshold slider determines how close a color must be to white before it is removed. Apply lower values to drop a light color background and higher values to drop a dark one. The Tolerance slider determines how close a pixel must be to the Threshold value in order to be removed by the clipping path. Once the Threshold and Tolerance values are set, you can contract the resulting path and remove any black or white edges by entering a value in the Inset Frame field.

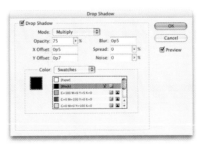

**Step 7.**

Press ⌘+D (Mac) or Ctrl+D (Windows) to display the Place dialog. Locate the music.tif image on your system, uncheck Show Import Options, and click Open. With the Direct Selection tool still chosen, click directly on the image to select it from within the clipping path frame. In the Control palette, enter **27p7** in the X Location field, **17p4** in the Y Location field, and **-51p** in the Rotation Angle field.

**Step 8.**

Click the path again and choose Object ▷ Feather. In the dialog that appears, click the Feather option to enable the effect, and click the Preview check box to see the effect applied to the selected path. Enter **0p7** in the Feather Width field and choose Sharp from the Corners menu. Keep the Noise setting at 0 and click OK to apply the Feather effect.

**Step 9.**

Choose Object ▷ Drop Shadow. In the dialog that appears, click the Drop Shadow option to enable the effect, and click the Preview check box to see the effect applied to the selected path. Choose Multiply from the Mode menu and select the black swatch from the swatches list. Enter **75%** for Opacity, **0p5** for Blur, **0p5** for X Offset, and **0p7** for Y Offset. Keep the Spread and Noise settings at 0. Click OK to apply the Drop Shadow.

**Step 10.**

To create a thick outline around the shape, press V to switch to the Selection tool. Then press ⌘+C (Mac) or Ctrl+C (Windows) to copy the object. Choose Edit▷Paste In Place. Press A to switch to the Direct Selection tool and click directly on the image to select it from within the frame. Press Delete (Mac) or Backspace (Windows). Click the path again and choose Object▷Feather to access the Feather dialog. Uncheck the Feather option and click OK.

**Step 11.**

Now let's add a drop shadow to the outline to give the effect more depth. Choose Object▷Drop Shadow to display the Drop Shadow dialog. Change the Opacity value to **90%**, the Blur amount to **0p3**, the X Offset to **0**, and the Y Offset to **0p3**. Enter **3%** for Spread and keep the Noise setting at 0. Click OK to apply.

**Step 12.**

Display the Transparency palette (choose Window▷Transparency (or press Shift+F10). Choose Hard Light from the Mode menu and then deselect the path. To complete the design, you can add some text as shown here.

# Clipping Path Dialog Options

To allow the clipping path to recognize any areas inside an image as defined by the Threshold and Tolerance settings, enable the Include Inside Edges feature. You can also invert an InDesign path by clicking the Invert check box.

Enabling the Restrict To Frame option limits the clipping path to include only the image areas within the graphic frame and not the areas cropped outside. With this option on, adjusting the crop means re-creating the path. Therefore, in most cases it is best to leave this option off.

You can also edit the path after it has been applied, by using the Clipping Path dialog. To do so, select the image and choose Object ▷ Clipping Path. Using the dialog, you can adjust the settings or turn off the path by choosing None from the Type pop-up menu.

# Popping Out of the Frame

All it takes is the right image and the creative use of a clipping path to add some action to your layout. By applying a Photoshop or InDesign clipping path to an image upon import, or applying/creating a path with the Clipping Path dialog after the image is placed, you can make a portion of the photo "pop" right out of the frame.

With these steps, we'll apply a path to a placed image to make it pop out of the frame behind it. This effect works best with action shots such as the skateboard image shown here, but can also be applied to any image that contains an element you can extract with a clipping path.

Once you get the hang of creating and applying clipping paths in InDesign, try using this effect on some of your own placed images.

## Add Some Action to Your Placed Images!

To re-create this effect using the image shown here, download skater2.tif from *The InDesign Effects Book* website.

**Step 1.**
In a new document, press ⌘+D (Mac) or Ctrl+D (Windows) to display the Place dialog. Locate the skater2.tif image on your system, check Show Import Options, and click Open.

**Step 2.**
In the Image panel of the Image Import Options dialog, enable the Apply Photoshop Clipping Path option and click OK.

**Step 3.**
Click the loaded place cursor once anywhere on the page to place the image at 100% of its size. Deselect the image once it is positioned on the page.

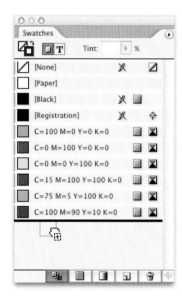

**Step 4.**
Press X to target the Stroke icon and then choose Window▷Swatches (or press F5) to display the Swatches palette. Press I to access the Eyedropper tool and click anywhere in the dark-blue area of the skater image background. In the example here, the sampled color build is C=100, M=89, Y=40, K=44.

**Step 5.**
Although it is not necessary to complete this effect, it's always a good idea to save your custom colors as swatches in the palette. This can be helpful if you should decide to change the color globally (wherever it is applied) in the document later. To do so, click and drag the Stroke icon at the top of the Swatches palette into the swatches list below.

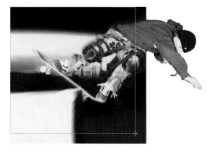

**Step 6.**
Press M to access the Rectangle tool and draw a rectangle that matches the dimensions of the image background.

*continues on next page*

## Frame Tool vs. Shape Tool

The frame/shape relationship can be confusing to new users coming over from QuarkXPress.

By definition, a frame is a container that holds either an image or a body of text. A shape is not intended to be a text or image container, but can be converted into one.

In Quark language, this means that the "box tool" with the "X" in it (the Rectangle Frame tool) is used to draw picture boxes. The box without the "X" (the Rectangle tool) is used for drawing shapes (as you would in Adobe Illustrator). Finally, "text boxes" can be drawn with the Type tool.

In InDesign, both rectangle tools can be used to draw a "picture box" or a "text box." You see, InDesign is extremely liberal. Frames can be shapes and shapes can be frames, and you do not have to draw a "box" first before placing an image!

# Popping Out of the Frame *continued*

## How to Use Frames

A frame is a container that holds either an image or a body of text. If you prefer to draw frames first before placing content in them, you can do so using the Rectangle, Ellipse, or Polygon Frame tool. A newly drawn, empty frame can be assigned as a text or a graphic place-holder using object styles, accessible in both the Control palette and Object Styles palette. Note that an object style can only be applied to an exist-ing frame, not selected beforehand and applied as it is drawn.

If you prefer to paste content first and resize frames later, you can place graphics (or text) using the Place command (Mac: ⌘+D; Windows: Ctrl+D). A frame is automatically drawn for you when you click the loaded cursor anywhere on the page.

A text frame can also contain a "nested" graphic or text frame. "Nesting" allows a text frame to contain an anchored object.

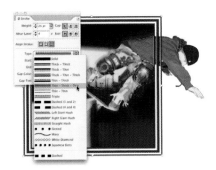

**Step 7.**
Choose Window▷Stroke (or press F10) to display the Stroke palette. Enter 20 in the Weight field and click the Align Stroke To Outside button. Choose Thin: Thick: Thin from the Type pop-up menu.

**Step 8.**
Choose Object▷Arrange▷Send To Back or press Shift+⌘+[ (Mac) or Shift+Ctrl+[ (Windows). Press V to switch to the Selection tool and click the skateboard image to select it.

**Step 9.**
To soften the edges of the clipping path slightly, choose Object▷Feather. In the Feather dialog that appears, click the Feather option to enable the effect and click the Preview check box to see the effect applied to the selected object. Enter 0p1.5 in the Feather Width field and choose Diffused from the Corners pop-up menu. Leave the Noise value at 0 and click OK.

**Step 10.**

Add some type to complete the logo design. In the example shown here, the words "SKATE CORNER" are placed in the lower-left corner in red, using 40pt Helvetica Ultra Compressed with Optical kerning and -30 tracking applied. "THE" is set at 15pt using the same font.

**Step 11.**

Here are some examples of how this effect can be used with different stroke styles and stroke weights applied. The top image uses the Japanese Dots style with a 7pt weight applied. The bottom image uses the Wavy style with a 5pt weight applied. Don't be afraid to experiment—and don't forget that you can also create and apply your own custom stroke styles. You can do this by choosing Stroke Styles from the Stroke palette menu.

# How to Use Shapes

Shapes are drawn using the Rectangle, Ellipse, or Polygon tools. Custom shapes can be drawn using the Pen tools, and freeform shapes can be drawn using the Pencil tools. Assigned shape attributes can be saved as object styles and later applied to other shapes or frames (empty or with content). Note that an object style can be applied to an existing shape or, unlike frames, it can also be selected first and applied to a shape as it is drawn.

Two or more shapes can be combined in various ways using the Pathfinder palette controls. You can also change a selected shape's appearance by selecting the Convert Shape commands on the Object menu, or by clicking the Convert Shape controls in the Pathfinder palette.

To convert a shape or path into a text frame, click inside it with the Type tool. The shape retains any applied object style attributes even after adding text.

# Pathfinder Frames

Similar to the Pathfinder palette in Adobe Illustrator, InDesign's Pathfinder palette also allows you to combine shapes quickly and easily. All you have to do is select two or more shapes and click one of the Pathfinder buttons. Once you create a shape using the Pathfinder palette, you can then place a graphic into it. Creating custom graphic frames has never been easier!

With these steps, we'll create a keyhole shape using the shape tools, the Direct Selection tool, and the Pathfinder palette. We'll then convert the shape into a graphic frame by placing an image into it.

If you like working with Pathfinder commands, try using them to create custom shapes with any combination of paths drawn with the Pen tool, freeform paths drawn with the Pencil tool, and shapes drawn with the Rectangle, Ellipse, and Polygon tools. As you experiment, keep in mind that any shape you create can also be converted into a graphic frame.

## Combine Shapes to Create Custom Frames

To re-create this effect using the image shown here, download eye.tif and woodgrain.tif from *The InDesign Effects Book* website.

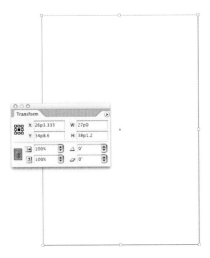

**Step 1.**
In a new document, press M to access the Rectangle tool and draw a shape that is 27p wide and 38p1.2 high. You can enter these values in the Width and Height fields of the Control or Transform palette once the shape is drawn. Alternatively, you can Option-click (Macintosh) or Alt-click (Windows) with the Rectangle tool to display the Rectangle dialog. This allows you to enter in your desired width and height so you end up with the rectangle at the size you want it the first time.

**Step 2.**
Open the Place dialog (press ⌘+D in Mac or Ctrl+D in Windows). Locate the woodgrain.tif image, check Show Import Options, and click Open. Press Shift+⌘+E (Mac) or Shift+Ctrl+E (Windows) to center the image within the frame.

**Step 3.**
Choose Window▷Layers (or press F7) to display the Layers palette. Double-click Layer 1 to display the Layer Options dialog. Name the layer **background** and click OK to close the dialog.

**Step 4.**

Option-click (Mac) or Alt-click (Windows) the Create New Layer button at the bottom of the Layers palette. In the Layer Options dialog, enter a name for the layer (e.g., **key hole frame**) and click OK.

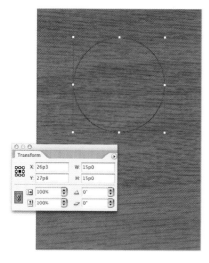

**Step 5.**

Press D to reset the Stroke to default black and the Fill to a default of None. Press L to access the Ellipse tool. Hold down the Shift key to constrain proportions and draw a circle near the center of the rectangle that has a width and height amount of 15p0. You can also enter these values in the Width and Height fields of the Control or Transform palette once the shape is drawn.

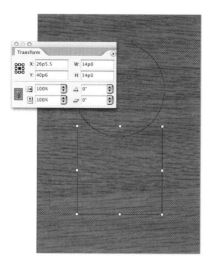

**Step 6.**

Press M to access the Rectangle tool. Hold down the Shift key to constrain proportions and draw a rectangle with a width and height of 14p0, overlapping the bottom edge of the circle as shown.

*continues on next page*

# Aligning and Distributing Objects

You can position multiple selected objects in a document precisely using the Align palette. Simply select two or more objects and click one of the preset buttons located at the top of the palette.

In addition to the alignment controls, the Align palette allows you to precisely distribute multiple selected objects and their spacing both vertically and horizontally. Choose Show Options from the palette fly-out menu to access the Distribute Spacing controls.

To distribute, select two or more objects and click one of the preset buttons located in the palette.

**Note:** You can also select and align or distribute objects that are placed on different layers.

# Pathfinder Frames *continued*

## Moving Objects

To move an object, you must first select it with the Selection tool (by clicking anywhere on it) or with the Direct Selection tool (by clicking its center point). You can then use any one of these methods to reposition it on the page:

- Drag the selected object to a new location.

- Enter new X and Y coordinates in either the Transform or Control palette.

- Access the Move dialog (Object ▷ Transform ▷ Move). Enter values for Position, Distance, and Angle, and then click OK.

- Nudge the object using the arrow keys.

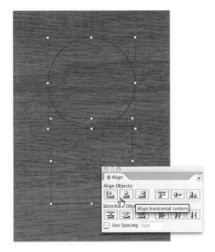

**Step 7.**
Press ⌘+A (Mac) or Ctrl+A (Windows) to select all. Choose Window ▷ Object & Layout Align (or press Shift+F7) to display the Align palette. Click the Align Horizontal Centers button.

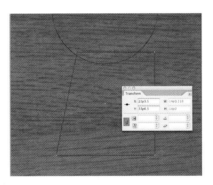

**Step 8.**
Choose Edit ▷ Deselect All (or press Shift+⌘+A [Mac] or Shift+Ctrl+A [Windows]). Press A to access the Direct Selection tool and select the top-left corner node of the rectangle that is positioned under the circle. Type **+3p** next to the current value displayed in the X Location field of the Control or Transform palette. InDesign does the math for you and automatically adds the 3p value to the current value displayed.

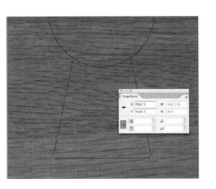

**Step 9.**
Select the top-right corner node of the rectangle that is positioned under the circle. Type **-3p** next to the current value displayed in the X Location field of the Control or Transform palette. InDesign does the math for you and automatically subtracts the 3p value from the current value displayed.

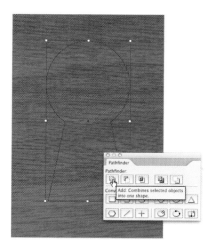

**Step 10.**

Press V to access the Selection tool. Hold down the Shift key and click the circle to add it to your selection. Now with both shapes selected, choose Window ▷ Object & Layout ▷ Pathfinder. Click the Add button in the upper-left corner.

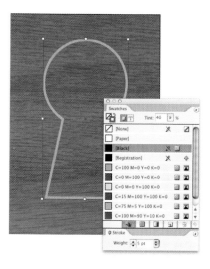

**Step 11.**

Enter **5pt** in the Weight field of the Stroke or Control palette. Press X to bring the stroke icon to the front. Choose Window ▷ Swatches, or press F5 to display the Swatches palette. Type **40%** in the Tint field of the Swatches palette and press Return (Mac) or Enter (Windows).

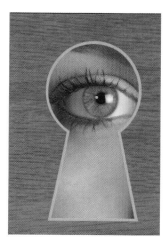

**Step 12.**

Press ⌘+D (Mac) or Ctrl+D (Windows) to display the Place dialog. Locate the eye.tif image on your system and click Open to import it into the pathfinder frame. Press A to switch to the Direct Selection tool and click directly on the eye.tif image to select it from within the frame. Click and drag to position the eye in the center of the keyhole.

# Resizing Objects

To resize an object, you must first select it with the Selection tool and then perform any one of the following actions:

- Drag one of the object's frame nodes with the Selection tool. Press the Shift key to constrain proportions as you drag. To scale an object's contents at the same time, press Shift+⌘ (Mac) or Shift+Ctrl (Windows) as you drag.

- To scale a container and its contents, enter new scale X and Y percentages or new width and height values in either the Transform or Control palette.

- Press S to access the Scale tool, then click and drag. Press the Shift key to constrain proportions or limit the scale to one axis.

- Access the Scale dialog by choosing Object ▷ Transform ▷ Scale. Enter values for Uniform or Non-Uniform scaling and click OK. You can resize the container without its contents by unchecking the Scale Content option.

- Press E to access the Free Transform tool and click and drag. Press the Shift key to constrain proportions.

- Use the keyboard shortcuts:

  **Increase by 1%:** ⌘+> (Mac) / Ctrl+> (Windows)

  **Decrease by 1%:** ⌘+< (Mac) / Ctrl+< (Windows)

  **Increase by 5%:** Opt+⌘+> (Mac) / Alt+Ctrl+> (Windows)

  **Decrease by 5%:** Opt+⌘+< (Mac) / Alt+Ctrl+< (Windows)

# Pathfinder Frames *continued*

## Reference Point

There are several ways to transform objects in InDesign. All of the methods use the reference point selected in the Reference Point icon, located in the Control and Transform palettes. The default reference point is the absolute center of the object; however, you can reposition it by clicking a different square in the Reference Point icon.

The target crosshairs that appears in the center of the object when it is selected with the Rotate, Shear, or Scale tool also indicates the reference point for rotation. You can reposition it anywhere in the document window (even the Pasteboard area) by clicking and dragging.

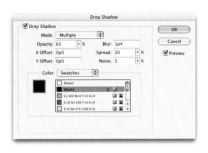

**Step 13.**
Click anywhere on the path of the frame to select it and choose Object ▷ Drop Shadow. In the dialog that appears, click the Drop Shadow option to enable the effect. Choose Multiply from the Mode menu and select the black swatch from the swatches list. Enter **65%** for Opacity, **1p4** for Blur, and 0 for both the X and Y Offset amounts. Enter **20%** for Spread and **5%** for Noise. Click OK to apply.

**Step 14.**
Option-click (Mac) or Alt-click (Windows) the Create New Layer button at the bottom of the Layers palette. In the Layer Options dialog, enter a name for the layer (e.g., **text**) and click OK.

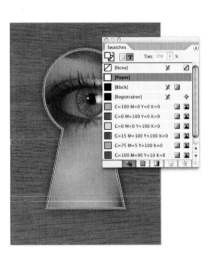

**Step 15.**
Press T to access the Type tool and draw a text frame over the bottom half of the keyhole frame. Click the Fill icon at the top of the Swatches palette to bring it to the front and click the Paper (white) swatch in the palette list.

**Step 16.**

Press Shift+⌘+C (Mac) or Shift+Ctrl+C (Windows) to align to the center. Choose preferred character attributes in either the Control or Character palette. In the example here it is Eurostile Bold Extended 2, set in all caps at 45pt, using 40pt leading, with Optical kerning and tracking set to -10. Enter the words **SNEAK PEEK** in the text frame as shown.

**Step 17.**

Switch to the Selection tool and choose Object ▷ Drop Shadow. In the dialog that appears, click the Drop Shadow option to enable the effect. Choose Multiply from the Mode menu and select the black swatch from the swatches list. Enter **75%** for Opacity, **0p5** for Blur, **-0p1** for X Offset, and **0p6** for Y Offset. Keep the Spread and Noise settings at 0 and click OK to apply.

**Step 18.**

Choose Window ▷ Transparency (or press Shift+F10) to display the Transparency palette and lower the Opacity value to 75%.

# Rotating Objects

To rotate an object, perform any one of the following actions:

- Select the object you would like to rotate by clicking its frame or shape edge with the Rotate tool, then click and drag. Press the Shift key as you drag to constrain rotation angles to 45° increments.

- Select the object you would like to rotate with the Selection tool. Enter a value in the Rotation Angle field located in the Transform or Control palette. You can also select a preset value from the pop-up menu or from the Transform palette menu.

- Access the Rotate dialog by choosing Object ▷ Transform ▷ Rotate. Enter an Angle value and click OK.

- Select the object you would like to rotate by clicking its frame or shape edge with the Free Transform tool. Hover your mouse over one of the corner nodes. When the Left/Right arrow icon appears, click and drag. Press the Shift key as you drag to constrain rotation angles to 45° increments.

# Snapshot Frames

Photo frames can make your placed images pop right off the page (this is a good thing), and believe it or not, you can create them entirely in InDesign. Traditionally, effects such as this were considered a form of photo-realistic illustration, and were usually created in Photoshop and/or Illustrator. However, don't underestimate the drawing tools in InDesign. There's more you can do with them than you may realize.

With these steps, we'll draw a sheared photo frame using the Pen tools, the Direct Selection tool, and compound paths. We'll also take it one step further and add a perspective drop shadow using the Transform palette and InDesign's Feather effect.

To add to the photo-realistic effect, the transparent TIFFs provided for this tutorial contain a slight shear that was applied using Photoshop. If you're familiar with Photoshop and the Shear filter, you may want to try applying a slight shear to your own photos when creating snapshot frames in InDesign.

## How to Draw Realistic Photo Frames in InDesign

To re-create this effect using the images shown here, download Birthday_boy.tif and Birthday_girl.tif from *The InDesign Effects Book* website.

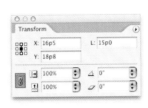

**Step 1.**
In a new document, press D to apply the default colors of black stroke and fill of None. Press the forward slash key (\) to access the Line tool. Holding down the Shift key to constrain, draw a vertical line with a length of 15p. You can enter this value in the Line Length field of the Control or Transform palette once the line is drawn.

**Step 2.**
Press P to switch to the Pen tool. Click directly on the center point to add a point to the line. To move the point, press the Left arrow key 10 times.

**Step 3.**
Hold down Option (Mac) or Alt (Windows) to temporarily access the Convert Direction Point tool. Click and drag the new center point to create a smooth curve, as shown here. You can hold down the Shift key as you drag to constrain the angle of the curve.

**Step 4.**
To create the other side of the frame, press V to access the Selection tool and press Shift+⌘+M (Mac) or Shift+Ctrl+M (Windows). In the Move dialog that appears, enter **14p4** in the Horizontal field and click Copy.

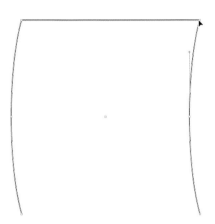

**Step 5.**
Hold down the Shift key and click the left line to add it to the selection. Press P to switch to the Pen tool. Click directly on the top point of the left line, then click directly on the top point of the right line to join the paths.

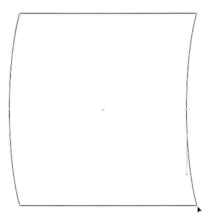

**Step 6.**
Now click directly on the bottom point of the left line, then on the bottom point of the right line to close the path.

*continues on next page*

## Grouping and Ungrouping Objects

To group objects in InDesign, select multiple objects with either selection tool and choose Object ▷ Group or press ⌘+G (Mac) or Ctrl+G (Windows). A dotted rectangle appears around the selected objects, indicating that they are now grouped. You can then apply a transformation to all the objects at once.

To ungroup, select the group with the Selection tool and choose Object ▷ Ungroup or press Shift+⌘+G (Mac) or Shift+Ctrl+G (Windows). The dotted rectangle disappears, allowing you to select the items individually again with the Selection tool.

# Snapshot Frames *continued*

## Selecting Through the Stack

When placing objects on top of one another (called stacking), you may find it challenging to individually select the objects positioned in the lower layers of the stacking order and rearrange them—especially if you are using transparency and can see right through all the objects in the stack! An object may appear to be in front when it is actually in back.

To select through the stacking order, press Command (Mac) or Ctrl (Windows) and click. The first click selects the topmost object and every click afterward selects the next object below. Keep clicking until you get to the object you're trying to select.

**Step 7.**
Choose Window ▷ Layers (or press F7) to display the Layers palette. Double-click Layer 1 to display the Layer Options dialog. Name the layer **picture** and click OK to close the dialog.

**Step 8.**
Option-click (Mac) or Alt-click (Windows) the Create New Layer button at the bottom of the Layers palette. In the Layer Options dialog, enter **frame** in the Name field and click OK.

**Step 9.**
In the Layers palette, Option-click (Mac) or Alt-click (Windows) the small square icon located on the layer below and drag it to the new layer above. Doing so creates a copy of the path and places it on the new layer. (Note: If you don't see a small square icon in the Layers palette, it is because you do not have an object selected.)

**Step 10.**
To add a border effect to the frame, double-click the Scale tool icon in the Tools palette. In the Scale dialog that appears, enable the Uniform option, enter **83%** in the Scale field, and click Copy.

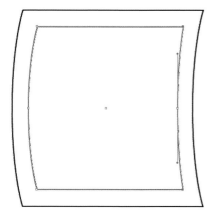

**Step 11.**

Notice that the curve of the right side of the new inner frame does not match the curve of the original. To fix this, you can reposition the points on the path. Press A to switch to the Direct Selection tool. Click directly on the upper-right corner point to select it. Hold down the Shift key and click the bottom-right corner point to add it to the selection. Press the Left arrow key three times to move both points.

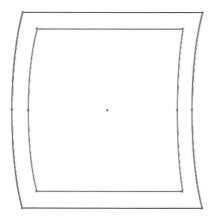

**Step 12.**

Option-click (Mac) or Alt-click (Windows) the "frame" layer to select everything on it. Press ⌘+8 (Mac) or Ctrl+8 (Windows) to convert the selected objects into a single compound path.

*continues on next page*

# Arranging Objects

You can rearrange the order of stacked objects by selecting them and choosing one of the four commands from the Object ▷ Arrange submenu: Bring To Front, Bring Forward, Send Backward, and Send To Back. Or you can use any of the assigned keyboard shortcuts for arranging (listed in the Object ▷ Arrange submenu), or access the commands through the contextual menu (Mac: Control-click; Windows: right-click).

**Note:** The keyboard commands for selecting stacked objects refer to the placed order of all items on the page, and not their visual order. Therefore when using these shortcuts, do not panic if you wind up selecting various page items that are not at all related to the stack you are focusing on. This is not a bug in the application—it is just one of those little InDesign quirks! Also note that you cannot apply the Arrange commands to objects that are placed on different layers.

# Snapshot Frames *continued*

## Locking Objects

To lock an object, select it with either selection tool and choose Object ▷ Lock Position, or press ⌘+L (Mac) or Ctrl+L (Windows). Locking an object prevents you from deleting or transforming it in any way, although you can still select it and edit any text or formatting attributes (stroke, fill color, corner effects, object styles, etc.).

To unlock an object, select it with either selection tool and choose Object ▷ Unlock Position or press Option+⌘ +L (Mac) or Alt+Ctrl+L (Win).

To lock an object even more securely (so that it cannot be selected or edited at all), place it on its own layer and click the Lock toggle icon in the Layers palette.

**Step 13.**
Display the Swatches palette (choose Window ▷ Swatches or press F5), then press X to bring the Stroke icon to the front. From the Swatches palette fly-out menu, choose New Tint Swatch. In the New Tint Swatch dialog, enter **20** in the Tint field and click OK.

**Step 14.**
In the Control palette, enter 0 in the Stroke Weight field.

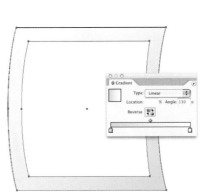

**Step 15.**
Press X to bring the Fill icon to the front. Choose Window ▷ Gradient to display the Gradient palette. In the Gradient palette, choose Linear from the Type pop-up menu. Drag the 20% black tint swatch from the Swatches palette list directly over the left slider. Drag the Paper (white) swatch over the right slider. Enter **130** in the Angle field.

**Step 16.**
Option-click (Mac) or Alt-click (Windows) the "picture" layer to select the path on that layer. In the Control palette, enter 0 in the Stroke Weight field.

**Step 17.**
Hold down ⌘+Option (Mac) or Ctrl+Alt (Windows) and click the Create New Layer button at the bottom of the Layers palette to create a new layer below the "picture" layer. Double-click the new layer to access the Layer Options dialog, change the name to **shadow**, and click OK.

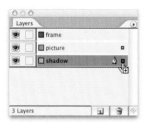

**Step 18.**
To place a duplicate of the path onto the shadow layer, Option-click (Mac) or Alt-click (Windows) the small square icon on the picture layer in the Layers palette and drag it to the shadow layer.

**Step 19.**
Open the Transform palette (choose Window ▷ Object & Layout ▷ Transform or press F9) and choose Flip Both from the palette fly-out menu. Click the Black swatch in the Swatches palette to apply a black fill.

*continues on next page*

# Deleting Objects

In the heat of what I call "design mode" you may find yourself surrounded by the remains of abandoned layout ideas. When this happens, it's time to win back control of your creative mess ... um, I mean kingdom ... and start deleting unused objects.

To delete objects from your InDesign layouts, first use either selection tool to select the object(s) you want to delete, then do one of the following:

- Press the Delete or Backspace key.
- Choose Edit ▷ Clear.
- Drag the selected object(s) to the Trash icon in the Dock (Mac OS X only).

**Note:** Deleting master pages and layers also deletes all objects placed on them—and some of them may still be applied to your document pages. Any time you are about delete a master page or layer containing applied objects, a warning dialog appears. Click Yes *only* if you are sure you want to delete all the objects on the page or layer.

# Snapshot Frames *continued*

## Enabling Layout Adjustment

Unfortunately, in the design world last-minute changes happen more frequently than not. Having to rework a complicated layout to compensate for changes can be a stressful nightmare.

To avoid frustration, try preparing ahead of time and enabling the Layout Adjustment option. It's the best way to protect yourself from having to perform hours of unnecessary extra work. With this option enabled, you can resize a document, apply new margin and column settings, apply totally different master pages, and even change page orientation without reworking anything—InDesign adjusts the page items for you!

You can turn this option on in the Layout Adjustment dialog. Choose Layout ▷ Layout Adjustment and click the Enable Layout Adjustment check box. The other settings in the dialog determine which items you are allowing InDesign to automatically adjust: graphics and groups, ruler guides, and/or locked objects and layers.

**Note:** Layout Adjustment relies on proper guide placement, since it uses margin, column, and ruler guides to calculate how page items are resized and repositioned.

**Step 20.**

Click the center node to select the entire black frame. Reposition it so that is offset underneath the snapshot frame, as shown. Choose Object ▷ Feather. In the dialog that appears, click the Feather option to enable the effect. Enter **1p8** in the Feather Width field and choose Diffused from the Corners pop-up menu. Click OK to apply.

**Step 21.**

Option-c lick (Mac) or Alt-click (Windows) the "picture" layer to select the path on that layer. Press ⌘+D (Mac) or Ctrl+D (Windows) to display the Place dialog. Locate the Birthday_boy.tif image on your system and click Open to place it into the frame. Press A to switch to the Direct Selection tool and click directly on the image to select it. Click and drag to position it nicely within the frame, as shown.

**Step 22.**

Press V to switch to the Selection tool. Press ⌘+A (Mac) or Ctrl+A (Windows) to select all. Press ⌘+G (Mac) or Ctrl+G (Windows) to group the selection. Enter **30°** in the Rotation Angle field of the Control palette.

**Step 23.**

Press ⌘+C (Mac) or Ctrl+C (Windows) to copy the group. Press Option+Shift+⌘+V (Mac) or Alt+Shift+Ctrl+V (Windows) to paste in place. Enter 10° in the Rotation Angle field of the Control palette. Move the duplicate off to the right so that it overlaps the original just slightly, as shown.

**Step 24.**

Press A to switch to the Direct Selection tool and click directly on the image in the offset duplicate group. Press ⌘+D (Mac) or Ctrl+D (Windows) to display the Place dialog. Locate the Birthday_girl.tif image on your system, enable the Replace Selected Item option at the bottom of the dialog, and click Open. Click directly on the image to select it, and drag to position it nicely within the frame, as shown.

**Step 25.**

Add some type to complete the design. In the example shown here, the words "Capture Each Moment" are each placed in separate text frames, below and behind the snapshots, using 55pt Bickley Script Plain with Optical kerning and -10 tracking applied.

## Compound Paths

A compound path is created when two objects are placed on top of each other and merged together, allowing any overlapping areas to become transparent. In basic terms, this means that two overlapping shapes with separate fills can be converted into one shape with a hole in it. When the compound path is placed in front, you can see any underlying objects through the transparent hole.

To create a compound path, select two overlapping frames, shapes, or paths and choose Object ▷ Compound Paths ▷ Make, or press ⌘+8 (Mac) or Ctrl+8 (Windows).

Compound paths can be edited just like any other object. The entire shape can be transformed (moved, scaled, sheared, or rotated) when selected with the Selection tool. In addition, individual points can be selected with the Direct Selection tool and repositioned or deleted.

To revert a compound path, select it and choose Object ▷ Compound Paths ▷ Release or press Option+⌘+8 (Mac) or Alt+Ctrl+8 (Windows). Doing so reverts the shapes back into separate objects but may not include all previously applied attributes (fill color, stroke, etc.).

# Filmstrip Frames

Filmstrip frames are a great way to showcase your placed images in a layout, and they can be created easily in InDesign using basic rectangle shapes and simple black-and-white fills. All you need to do is add some photographs and drop shadows to give your placed images that filmstrip look.

With these steps, we'll create some filmstrip frames using the Rectangle tool, the Step And Repeat command, and the Pathfinder palette. Once you create the filmstrip, you can save it as a template to use over and over again and place any graphic images into it that you like. In fact, you can even save the filmstrip frame as an InDesign Snippet and save it in an InDesign library.

## Use Basic Shapes and Fills to Create Cool Frames

To re-create this effect using the images shown here, download car1.tif and car2.tif from *The InDesign Effects Book* website.

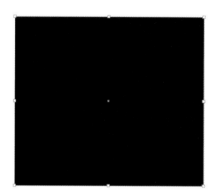

**Step 1.**

In a new document, press D to apply the default colors of black stroke and None fill. Press Shift+X to swap fill and stroke colors. Press M to access the Rectangle tool and draw a rectangle that is 21p wide and 18p high. You can enter these values in the Width and Height fields of the Control or Transform palette once the shape is drawn.

**Step 2.**

Double-click the Scale tool icon in the Tools palette. In the Scale dialog that appears, enable the Non-uniform option and enter **95%** in the Horizontal field and **70%** in the Vertical field. Click Copy to close the dialog.

**Step 3.**

Press the forward slash key (/) to apply a fill of None to the shape copy. Press ⌘+D (Mac) or Ctrl+D (Windows) to display the Place dialog. Locate the car1.tif image on your system and click Open to import it into the frame. Press Shift+⌘+E (Mac) or Shift+Ctrl+E (Windows) to center the image in the rectangle.

**Step 4.**
Deselect the frame and press M to access the Rectangle tool. Choose Window▷Swatches (or press F5) to display the Swatches palette and click the Paper (white) swatch. Then in the upper-left corner of the black frame, draw a small white rectangle above the photo that is 1p wide and 1p2 high. You can enter these values in the Width and Height fields of the Control or Transform palette once the shape is drawn.

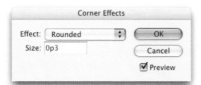

**Step 5.**
Choose Object▷Corner Effects. In the dialog that appears, choose Rounded from the Effect pop-up menu. Enter **0p3** in the Size field and click OK.

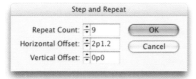

**Step 6.**
Press Option+⌘+U (Mac) or Alt+Ctrl+U (Windows) to display the Step And Repeat dialog. Enter **9** in the Repeat Count field, **2p1.2** in the Horizontal Offset field, and **0** in the Vertical Offset field. Click OK to apply.

**Step 7.**
Press V to access the Selection tool and Shift-click the white boxes to select them all. Press ⌘+G (Mac) or Ctrl+G (Windows) to group the selected objects. To create a duplicate, hold down the Option key (Mac) or the Alt key (Windows), click the selected group, and drag downwards. Hold down the Shift key as you drag to constrain the angle. Position the duplicate group beneath the photo as shown.

*continues on next page*

# Applying Corner Effects

You can apply any one of the six default corner effects to any selected frame, shape, or path. To access the dialog, select the object with either selection tool and choose Object▷Corner Effects. When the dialog opens, choose Fancy, Bevel, Inset, Inverse Rounded, or Rounded from the Effect menu. Enter an amount for Size and check the Preview box to see the effect before applying. When you're ready, click OK to apply the corner effect.

Applying corner effects does not permanently change an object. You can change the size, try a different effect, or turn them off at any time. To turn off corner effects for a selected object, select None from the Corner Effects dialog's Effect menu.

Corner effects generally work best with rectangle frames and shapes. But if you're feeling extra creative, try applying any of these effects to a triangle or polygon shape.

**Note:** A placed photo does not require that its frame container have a stroke placed on it in order to apply corner effects.

# Filmstrip Frames *continued*

## Saving Document Presets

If you think you might want to use the settings you've entered in the New Document dialog more than once, you should save them as a document preset. Before clicking OK to close the dialog and starting work on your new document, click the Save Preset button. When the Save Preset dialog appears, enter a name for it and click OK. The new preset will then appear in the preset menu for all new documents.

You can also save a preset at any time while working on a document by selecting File ▷ Document Presets ▷ Define. When the Document Presets dialog opens, click the New button to launch the New Document Preset dialog and enter your preferred settings. When you're ready, click OK and the preset will be added to the menu list.

**Step 8.**
Select both groups of white boxes and press Shift+⌘+G (Mac) or Shift+Ctrl+G (Windows) to ungroup. Hold down the Shift key and click the black background shape to add it to the selection. Choose Window ▷ Object & Layout ▷ Pathfinder to display the Pathfinder palette and click the Subtract button.

**Step 9.**
Choose Object ▷ Drop Shadow. In the dialog that appears, click the Drop Shadow option to enable the effect. Choose Multiply from the Mode pop-up menu and select the black swatch from the swatches list. Enter **75** for Opacity, **0p4** for Blur, and **0p4** for both X and Y Offset amounts. Keep the Spread and Noise settings at 0 and click OK to apply.

**Step 10.**
Select the photo and press ⌘+C (Mac) or Ctrl+C (Windows) to copy it. Press Option+Shift+⌘+V (Mac) or Alt+Shift+Ctrl+V (Windows) to paste it in place. Press A to switch to the Direct Selection tool. Click the photo to select it from within the frame and press Delete (Mac) or Backspace (Windows). Click in the photo area again to select the empty frame. Press X to bring the Stroke icon to the front and click the Paper swatch in the Swatches palette.

**Step 11.**

Choose Object ▷ Drop Shadow. In the dialog that appears, click the Drop Shadow option to enable the effect. Choose Multiply from the Mode menu and select the black swatch from the swatches list. Enter **80%** for Opacity, **p4** for Blur, and **p0** for both X and Y offset amounts. Enter **40%** for Spread and keep the Noise setting at 0. Click OK to apply.

**Step 12.**

Choose Window ▷ Transparency (or press Shift+F10) to display the Transparency palette. Choose Multiply from the Mode pop-up menu.

*continues on next page*

## Opening InDesign Documents

To open an existing InDesign document or template, choose File ▷ Open, or press ⌘+O (Mac) or Ctrl+O (Windows). When the dialog appears, browse to a compatible file on your system and click the Open button.

At the bottom of the Open A File dialog, you'll find three radio buttons:

- With Open Normal–the default setting–InDesign opens the document in a new window.

- Choosing Open Original allows you to open and edit documents that have been saved as InDesign templates.

- Open Copy allows you to do just that–open a copy of the selected file.

# Filmstrip Frames *continued*

## Opening PageMaker and QuarkXPress Documents

InDesign CS2 can open documents and templates created in QuarkXPress 3.3–4.1 (not Quark 5.*x*–6.*x*) and PageMaker 6.5*x*–7.*x*.

Now, if it just so happens that most of the documents you need to convert are Quark 5 and 6 files, try saving them backward from Quark 6 to Quark 5, then from Quark 5 to Quark 4. You can then open them in InDesign CS2. It works!

Upon opening, InDesign converts these documents to an unsaved .indd format and does not overwrite the original Quark or PageMaker files. You can then save the new InDesign version anywhere on your system.

**Step 13.**
Choose Object ▷ Feather. In the dialog that appears, click the Feather option to enable the effect. Enter **0p3** in the Feather Width field and choose Diffused from the Corners menu. Click OK to apply.

**Step 14.**
Press V to switch to the Selection tool. Press ⌘+A (Mac) or Ctrl+A (Windows) to select all. Press ⌘+G (Mac) or Ctrl+G (Windows) to group the selection.

**Step 15.**
Enter **13** in the Rotation Angle field of the Control or Transform palette.

### Step 16.
Press ⌘+C (Mac) or Ctrl+C (Windows) to copy the group. Press Option+Shift+⌘+V (Mac) or Alt+Shift+Ctrl+V (Windows) to paste in place. Enter -4 in the Rotation Angle field of the Control palette. Move the duplicate off to the right so that it overlaps the original just slightly as shown.

### Step 17.
Press Shift+⌘+G (Mac) or Shift+Ctrl+G (Windows) to ungroup, then choose Edit▷Deselect All. Click the center of the duplicate once, then ⌘-click (Mac) or Ctrl-click (Windows) to select the graphic frame containing the car photo.

### Step 18.
Press ⌘+D (Mac) or Ctrl+D (Windows) to display the Place dialog. Locate the car2.tif image on your system, enable the Replace Selected Item option at the bottom of the dialog, and click Open. Press Shift+⌘+E (Mac) or Shift+Ctrl+E (Windows) to center the content. You can now select and regroup the objects that make up the second filmstrip frame, if you like.

## Converting PageMaker and QuarkXPress Documents

More often than not, you'll find that InDesign does a really good job of converting Quark and PageMaker documents, but there is always something that changes.

After a successful conversion, a Warnings dialog pops up displaying any problem items. Click the Save button if you'd like to refer to these items later; otherwise, click Close. In addition to taking note of everything in this dialog, you should take a close look at the converted InDesign document and compare it to the original Quark or PageMaker file.

Once you make any necessary adjustments to the items that didn't convert quite right, save the document as an InDesign file, and you're good to go. It's a heck of a lot easier than rebuilding pages from scratch, don't you think?

# Table Frames Part 1

One way to showcase your images in a layout is to use tables. Table cells behave like miniature text frames, which means that you can nest graphics inside them. Using the new anchored objects feature in InDesign CS2, you can place graphic frames into table cells and position them precisely. Once you position a graphic frame into a table cell using anchored objects, you can then copy/paste the cell contents into the remaining cells with the Type tool.

With these steps, we'll create a table that showcases four images. Because InDesign tables are flexible and easy to resize, this makes them great for placing multiple images into. Using the Table palette, we'll apply a specific amount of inset cell spacing to position the nested graphics evenly on the page. Once the images are nested, you can move or rotate the text frame containing them all and maintain their even spacing.

## Use Tables to Showcase Your Images

To re-create this effect using the images shown here, download kids1. tif, kids2.tif, kids3.tif, and kids4.tif from *The InDesign Effects Book* website.

### Step 1.
In a new letter-size, landscape-oriented document, press F to access the Rectangle Frame tool and create a frame that is 43p10 wide by 30p10 high. You can enter these values in the Width and Height fields of the Control or Transform palette once the frame is drawn. Press D to apply the default colors of black stroke and None fill.

### Step 2.
Choose Window▷Swatches (or press F5) to display the Swatches palette. Press X to bring the Fill icon to the front and select the blue swatch from the Swatches palette list (C=100, M=90, Y=10, K=0). Choose New Tint Swatch from the Swatches palette fly-out menu. In the dialog that appears, enter **40** in the Tint percent field and click OK.

### Step 3.
Press X to bring the Stroke icon to the front and press the comma key to apply the 40% blue tint swatch to the stroke. Enter **14pt** in the Stroke Weight field of the Control or Stroke palette and choose Dashed from the Stroke Type pop-up menu.

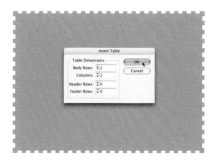

**Step 4.**

Press T to access the Type tool and click inside the frame. Choose Table▷ Insert Table. In the Insert Table dialog that appears, enter an amount of 2 in both the Body Rows and Columns fields.

**Step 5.**

If you don't have them visible already, press ⌘+H (Mac) or Ctrl+H (Windows) to show frame edges. Choose Table▷Table Options▷Table Setup. In the dialog that appears, enter 0 in the Table Border Weight field.

**Step 6.**

Click the Row Strokes button at the top of the dialog to access that panel. Choose Custom Row from the Alternating Pattern pop-up menu, and choose None from both Color pop-up menus.

*continues on next page*

# Resizing Columns Interactively

To resize a column interactively, insert the Type tool anywhere in the table and then position the cursor over the right or left edge of a cell. When the cursor icon changes to display a horizontal, double-headed arrow, click and drag to change the column width.

Note that columns can be expanded beyond the right edge of a text frame, except when the table is right-justified within the text frame.

To resize a column without expanding the table beyond the boundaries of the text frame, hold down the Shift key as you drag.

To change the width of all columns proportionately, hold down the Shift key as you drag the right edge of the table.

# Table Frames Part 1 *continued*

## Resizing Rows Interactively

To resize a row interactively, insert the Type tool anywhere in the table and then position the cursor over the top or bottom of a cell. When the cursor icon changes to display a vertical, double-headed arrow, click and drag to change the row height.

Note that rows can be expanded beyond the bottom edge of a text frame. Any rows that are resized beyond the boundaries of the text frame are stored as overset items.

To change the height of all rows proportionately, hold down the Shift key as you drag the bottom edge of the table.

**Step 7.**
Click the Column Strokes button at the top of the dialog to access that panel. Choose Custom Row from the Alternating Pattern pop-up menu, and choose None from both Color pop-up menus. Click OK to close the dialog.

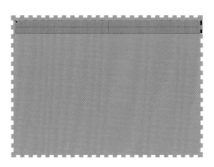

**Step 8.**
Hover the Type tool cursor over the upper-left corner of the table until you see it change to display a diagonal black arrow. Click to select the entire table.

**Step 9.**
Choose Window ▷ Type & Tables ▷ Table (or press Shift+F9) to display the Table palette. Choose At Least from the Row Height pop-up menu and enter **21p4** in the Column Width field.

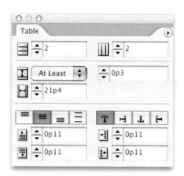

**Step 10.**

In the Table palette, set the cell vertical alignment by clicking the Align Center button. Then enter **0p11** in all four Cell Inset fields. Press Shift+⌘+C (Mac) or Shift+Ctrl+C (Windows) to set the cell horizontal alignment to align center.

**Step 11.**

Insert the Type tool cursor in the upper-left cell and choose Object▷ Anchored Object▷Insert. In the dialog that appears, choose Graphic from the Content pop-up menu and [None] from the Object Style pop-up menu. Enter **12p9** in the Height field and **19p2** in the Width field. Choose Inline or Above Line from the Position pop-up menu and enable the Inline option. Leave the Y Offset amount set to 0 and click OK to apply.

**Step 12.**

Click the Paper (white) swatch in the Swatches palette list. Enter **2** in the Stroke Weight field of the Control or Stroke palette.

*continues on next page*

# Resizing Columns and Rows Numerically

You can resize selected rows and columns numerically using the Cell Options dialog. To do so, choose Cell Options▷ Rows And Columns from the Table menu, the context menu, or the Table palette/Control palette fly-out menus.

Choose At Least or Exactly from the Row Height pop-up menu and enter a measurement value in the field. To apply a maximum row height, enter a value in the Maximum field. To resize selected column widths numerically, enter a measurement value in the Column Width field. You can also apply measurement values by clicking the up/down arrows located next to the Row Height and Column Width fields.

Check the Preview option at the bottom left of the dialog to see the settings applied as you adjust them. When you're ready, click OK to apply.

These settings can also be applied by entering measurement values in the Row Height and Column Width fields located in the Table or Control palette.

# Table Frames Part 1 *continued*

## Cell Spacing

You can apply table cell spacing values using the Cell Options dialog in the same way you would apply text frame inset settings using the Text Frame Options dialog.

To access the dialog, insert the Type tool cursor in a table cell and choose Cell Options ▷ Text from the Table menu or the Table palette menu. The Cell Options dialog is only accessible through the context menu when a cell (or series of cells) is selected.

In the Text panel of the Cell Options dialog, enter top, bottom, left, and right cell inset spacing amounts in the respective fields. You can also enter inset spacing amounts by clicking the up/down arrows located next to each field.

If you prefer palettes to dialogs, you can also enter inset spacing amounts for a selected cell (or series of cells) in the top, bottom, left, and right cell inset fields of the Table palette.

**Step 13.**

Highlight the inline graphic frame with the Type tool and press ⌘+C (Mac) or Ctrl+C (Windows) to copy it to the Clipboard. Press Tab to move to the next cell in the table. Press ⌘+V (Mac) or Ctrl+V (Windows) to paste the frame into the cell. Continue to press Tab and apply the Paste command for the remaining two cells of the table. When you've finished, your table should look like the figure shown here.

**Step 14.**

Switch to the Direct Selection tool and click the graphic frame in the upper-left cell of the table. Press ⌘+D (Mac) or Ctrl+D (Windows) to display the Place dialog. Locate the kids1.tif image on your system and click Open to import it into the frame. Click directly on the image to select it. Click and drag to position it nicely within the frame, as shown.

**Step 15.**

Click the graphic frame in the upper-right cell of the table. Press ⌘+D (Mac) or Ctrl+D (Windows) to display the Place dialog. Locate the kids2.tif image on your system and click Open to import it into the frame. Select and position the photo nicely within the frame, as shown.

**Step 16.**

Click the graphic frame in the lower-left cell of the table. Press ⌘+D (Mac) or Ctrl+D (Windows) to display the Place dialog. Locate the kids3.tif image on your system and click Open to import it into the frame. Select and position the photo nicely within the frame, as shown.

**Step 17.**

Click the graphic frame in the lower-right cell of the table. Press ⌘+D (Mac) or Ctrl+D (Windows) to display the Place dialog. Locate the kids4.tif image on your system and click Open to import it into the frame. Select and position the photo nicely within the frame, as shown.

**Step 18.**

Add some type to complete the effect. In the example shown here, the words "Kid's Korner" are placed in separate text frames and grouped, using the Kid Print font set at 126pt with Optical kerning and zero tracking applied. A drop shadow is applied to each text frame and to the group to make it stand out over the photos. A 4pt white stroke is applied to all the letters. You can use the Eyedropper tool to sample the green and red fill colors from the photos and apply them to the text.

# Vertical Cell Alignment

You can apply vertical cell alignment settings using the Cell Options dialog. Select the table cells and choose Cell Options ▷ Text from the Table menu or the Table palette menu.

To apply vertical alignment settings to the selected cell(s), choose Top, Center, Bottom, or Justify from the Align menu. To apply a limit for paragraph spacing when applying justified vertical alignment, enter a value or click the up/down arrows in the Paragraph Spacing Limit field. This value sets the maximum amount of space allowed between paragraphs in the cell when justified. InDesign adjusts the leading of each line up to the amount entered. Enter higher values to prevent a change in leading.

You can also apply vertical cell alignment settings by clicking one of the vertical alignment buttons located in the Table palette or Control palette. Options include Align Top, Align Bottom, Align Center, or Justify Vertically.

# Table Frames Part 2

As a designer, it is inevitable that at some point you are asked to design a project that uses headshots. When this happens, it can be challenging to come up with a creative layout that contains so many faces. Not only that, but distributing these headshots evenly on the page can also be difficult. Sometimes Step and Repeat or the Distribute Spacing controls in the Align palette are not helpful enough, especially if you are asked to make a change to the layout after the original positioning has been set in place.

This is where tables can come in handy. Tables are easy to resize; therefore, by nesting all the headshots in a table, you gain greater control over their spacing on the page. By using tables, you can make changes to the layout with a minimum amount of hassle.

With these steps we'll use a table to surround some logo-type with several different headshots. Maybe watching too much Brady Bunch has affected my design sense, but, using tables is a creative, effi-cient way to display headshots.

## Having Fun with Headshots

To re-create this effect using the images shown here, download people.zip from *The InDesign Effects Book* website.

**Step 1.**
In a new letter-size, landscape-ori-ented document, press F to access the Rectangle Frame tool and create a frame that is 43p9 width by 31p4 height. You can enter these values in the Width and Height fields of the Control or Transform palette once the frame is drawn. Press D to apply the default colors of black stroke and None fill.

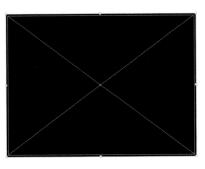

**Step 2.**
Enter **10** in the Stroke Weight field of the Control or Stroke palette. Press X to bring the fill icon to the front and press the comma key to fill the frame with black.

**Step 3.**
Choose Object ▷ Corner Effects. In the dialog that appears, choose Rounded from the Corners pop-up menu. Enter **1p** in the Size field and click OK to apply.

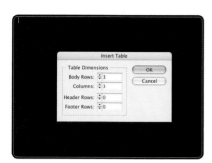

**Step 4.**

Press T to access the Type tool and click inside the frame. Choose Table ▷ Insert Table. In the Insert Table dialog that appears, enter **3** in both the Body Rows and Columns fields.

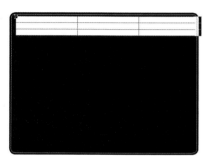

**Step 5.**

If you don't have them visible already, press ⌘+H (Mac) or Ctrl+H (Windows) to show frame edges. Hover the Type tool cursor over the upper-left corner of the table until you see it change to display a diagonal black arrow. Click to select the entire table.

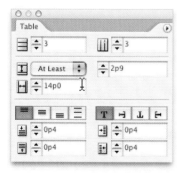

**Step 6.**

Choose Window ▷ Type & Tables ▷ Table (or press Shift+F9) to display the Table palette. Choose At Least from the Row Height pop-up menu. Enter **2p9** in the Row Height field and **14p** in the Column Width field.

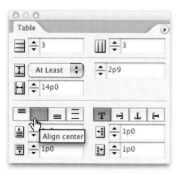

**Step 7.**

In the Table palette, set the cell vertical alignment by clicking the Align Center button, then enter **1p** in all four Cell Inset fields. Press Shift+⌘+C (Mac) or Shift+Ctrl+C (Windows) to set the cell horizontal alignment to align center.

## Setting the Table Border

To set the table border, choose Table Options ▷ Table Setup from the Table menu, the Table palette fly-out menu, or the context menu.

Choose a Stroke Weight, Type, Color, and Tint setting. You can also choose a Gap Color and Tint value when applying an open stroke style. To overprint, enable the Overprint options.

If you have already applied a cell border locally to one or more cells positioned at the top, bottom, right, or left edges of the table using the Cell Options dialog or Control palette, applying a table border using the Table Options dialog overrides it. To maintain local cell formatting, enable the Preserve Local Formatting option.

To apply a table border locally using the Cell Options dialog, select the entire table with the Type tool and choose Cell Options ▷ Strokes And Fills from the Table menu, the Table palette menu, or the context menu. In the center of the cell diagram at the top of the dialog, click the intersecting horizontal and vertical lines. By clicking these lines, you are telling InDesign to apply a stroke to the surrounding edges of the table and not to the interior cell edges.

*continues on next page*

# Table Frames Part 2 *continued*

## Adding Rows and Columns

The four ways to add rows and columns to a table are as follows:

**Insert commands** Select a cell with the Type tool and choose Insert ▷ Row/Column from the context menu, the Table menu, or the Table palette menu.

When the Insert Row/Column dialog appears, enter the number of rows or columns you would like to add in the Number field. At the bottom of the dialog, choose whether to place the new rows above or below (or the new columns to the left or right) of the selected cell. Click OK to add the rows or columns.

**Table palette and Control palette** You can also add rows and columns using the controls located in the Table and Control palettes. The Number Of Rows and Number Of Columns fields each displays the current number of rows and columns in the table. New rows are added at the bottom of the table, and new columns to the right.

**Step 8.**

Insert the Type tool cursor in the upper-left cell and choose Object ▷ Anchored Object ▷ Insert. In the dialog that appears, choose Graphic from the Content pop-up menu and [None] from the Object Style pop-up menu. Enter **7p11** in the Height field and **11p8** in the Width field. Choose Inline or Above Line from the Position pop-up menu and enable the Inline option. Leave the Y Offset amount set to 0 and click OK to apply.

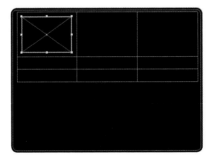

**Step 9.**

Press X to bring the Stroke icon to the front. Click the Paper (white) swatch in the Swatches palette list. Enter **2** in the Stroke Weight field of the Control or Stroke palette.

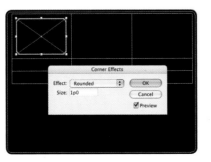

**Step 10.**

Choose Object ▷ Corner Effects. In the dialog that appears, choose Rounded from the Corners pop-up menu. Enter **2** in the Size field and click OK to apply.

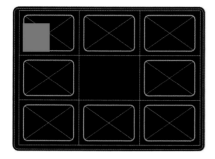

**Step 11.**

Highlight the inline graphic frame with the Type tool and press ⌘+C (Mac) or Ctrl+C (Windows) to copy it to the Clipboard. Press Tab to move to the next cell in the table. Press ⌘+V (Mac) or Ctrl+V (Windows) to paste the frame into the cell. Continue to press Tab and apply the Paste command for the remaining cells of the table, except for the very center cell. When you've finished, your table should look like the figure shown here.

**Step 12.**

Switch to the Direct Selection tool and click the graphic frame in the upper-left cell of the table. Press ⌘+D (Mac) or Ctrl+D (Windows) to display the Place dialog. Locate the people1.tif image on your system and click Open to place it into the frame. Click directly on the image to select it. Click and drag to position it nicely within the frame, as shown.

**Step 13.**

Click the graphic frame in the next cell of the table. Press ⌘+D (Mac) or Ctrl+D (Windows) to display the Place dialog. Locate the people2.tif image on your system and click Open to place it into the frame.

*continues on next page*

## Adding Rows and Columns *continued*

**Option-dragging (Mac) or Alt-dragging (Windows)** Position the Type tool cursor over the top or bottom of a cell, click and hold the mouse button down, then Option/Alt-drag to create a new row or column.

**Table Options dialog** Place the Type tool cursor in a cell and choose Table ▷ Table Options ▷ Table Setup. In the Table Setup panel of the dialog, enter the total number of rows and columns you would like the table to contain in the Body Rows and Columns fields. You can also add rows or columns by clicking the up/down arrows next to the number fields. Rows are added at the bottom of the table, and columns to the right. Check the Preview option at the bottom left of the dialog to see the settings applied as you adjust them. When you're ready, click OK to apply.

**Note:** You can add a single row to the bottom of a table by placing the Type tool cursor in the last cell of the existing bottom row and pressing the Tab key.

# Table Frames Part 2 *continued*

## Deleting Rows and Columns

The three ways to delete rows and columns from a table are as follows:

**Delete commands** Place the Type tool cursor in a cell and choose Delete ▷ Row/Column from the context menu, the Table menu, or the Table palette menu. InDesign immediately deletes the row or column that the cursor is positioned in. You can also select multiple rows or columns and delete them using the Delete command.

**Table Options dialog** Place the Type tool cursor in a cell and choose Table ▷ Table Options ▷ Table Setup. In the Table Setup panel of the dialog, enter the total number of rows and columns you would like the table to contain in the Body Rows and Columns fields. You can also delete rows or columns by clicking the up/down arrows next to the number field. Rows are deleted from the bottom of the table, and columns from the right. Check the Preview option at the bottom left of the dialog to see the settings applied as you adjust them. When you're ready, click OK to apply.

**Step 14.**
Continue filling each nested graphic frame with a different headshot. You can place the headshots in any order that you like. When you've finished, deselect and press ⌘+H (Mac) or Ctrl+H (Windows) to hide the frame edges. Your table should look something like the figure shown here.

**Step 15.**
Press T to access the Type tool and draw a text frame that overlaps the center of the table as shown. Press Shift+⌘+C (Mac) or Shift+Ctrl+C (Windows) to set the text frame horizontal alignment to center.

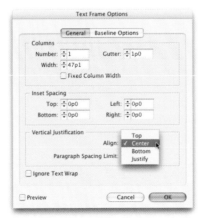

**Step 16.**
Press ⌘+B (Mac) or Ctrl+B (Windows) to display the Text Frame Options dialog. In the General panel, choose Center from the Vertical Justification Align pop-up menu.

**Step 17.**

Add some type to complete the logo design. In the example shown here, the words "The People Connection" are set in all caps, using the Rockwell Regular font at 35pt over 37pt leading, with Optical kerning and 120 tracking applied. An orange fill of C=0, M=81, Y=100, K=0 is applied to the text along with a 1.5pt white stroke.

**Step 18.**

Choose Window ▷ Object & Layout ▷ Align (or press Shift+F7) to display the Align palette. Switch to the Selection tool, hold down Shift, and click the text frame containing the table to add it to the selection. In the Align palette, click the Align Horizontal Centers and Align Vertical Centers buttons.

## Deleting Rows and Columns *continued*

**Table palette and Control palette** The Number Of Rows and Number Of Columns fields each displays the current number of rows and columns in the table. To delete rows or columns, place the Type tool cursor in a cell and enter the total number of rows or columns you would like the table to contain in the Number field. You can also delete rows and columns by clicking the up/down arrows next to the Number field.

InDesign displays a warning dialog whenever new values are entered in the Number Of Rows and Number Of Columns fields. If you are sure you want to delete, click OK. Rows are deleted from the bottom of the table, and columns from the right, regardless of what you may have selected in the table.

# Transparent Image Outer Glow

Normally, an outer glow effect is something you would apply to an image using layer styles in Photoshop. However, let us not forget that you can also save an image that has been extracted from its background in Photoshop and place it as a transparent TIFF into an InDesign document. Once the image is placed in InDesign, you can apply a drop shadow effect, set its Mode option to Screen, and achieve the same outer glow result.

With these steps, we'll place an image of a lightbulb into an InDesign document and apply an outer glow to it. All you need to do is create a path that follows the contour of the lightbulb, place it behind the transparent TIFF, and apply a bright-colored, screen mode drop shadow. In order to see the glow through the bulb, change the image's transparency mode to Multiply. It's just like working in Photoshop!

## Adding an Outer Glow Effect to a Transparent TIFF

To re-create this effect using the image shown here, download light_bulb.tif from *The InDesign Effects Book* website.

**Step 1.**
In a new letter-size, landscape-oriented document, press ⌘+D (Mac) or Ctrl+D (Windows) to display the Place dialog. Locate the light_bulb.tif image on your system and click Open. Click once anywhere on the page to place the image at 100% of its size. Enter **-22** in the Rotation Angle field of the Control or Transform palette.

**Step 2.**
Choose Window▷Layers (or press F7) to display the Layers palette. Double-click Layer 1 to display the Layer Options dialog. Enter a name for the layer (e.g., lightbulb), and click OK to close the dialog.

**Step 3.**
To add a layer underneath the light bulb layer, ⌘+Option-click (Mac) or Ctrl+Alt-click (Windows) the Create New Layer button at the bottom of the Layers palette. Double-click the new layer to display the Layer Options dialog, and enter a name for it (e.g., **outer glow**). Click OK to close the dialog.

### Step 4.

Press D to set the default colors of None fill and black stroke. Press P to access the Pen tool. Proceed to draw a path that follows the contour of the lightbulb. Do not close the path. If you're not comfortable with drawing paths yet, follow the next four steps; otherwise, skip ahead to step 9.

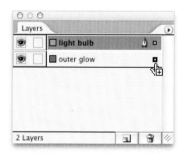

### Step 5.

Press V to switch to the Selection tool and Option-click (Mac) or Alt-click (Windows) the "lightbulb" layer to select its contents. Option-click (Mac) or Alt-click (Windows) the small square icon located on the "lightbulb" layer and drag it to the "outer glow" layer below. Doing so creates a copy of the selection and places it on the new layer.

### Step 6.

In the Layers palette, lock the "lightbulb" layer by clicking the lock toggle. Press A to switch to the Direct Selection tool and click directly on the image to select it. Choose Object ▷ Clipping Path. In the dialog that appears, choose Detect Edges from the Type pop-up menu. Enter an amount of **3** in both the Threshold and Tolerance fields. Check the Preview option to see the path applied as you enter these values. Click OK to apply.

*continues on next page*

## Save vs. Save As

To save an InDesign document, choose File ▷ Save, or press ⌘+S (Mac) or Ctrl+S (Windows). If you're saving the document for the first time, the Save As dialog will appear. Browse to where you'd like to save the file on your system and click the Save button. To update a previously saved document to include any changes or edits you've made, choose File ▷ Save again, or press ⌘/Ctrl+S.

To save an alternate version of an open document without saving over the original, choose File ▷ Save As, or press Shift+⌘+S (Mac) or Shift+Ctrl+S (Windows). Browse to where you'd like to save the file on your system and click Save.

Another way to save an alternate version of an existing document without saving over the original is to create a template to work from. To save a document as a template, choose File ▷ Save As and then choose InDesign CS Template from the Format menu (Mac) or Save As Type menu (Windows).

# Transparent Image Outer Glow *continued*

## Saving Backward with INX Export

When InDesign CS was first introduced, everyone was blown away by all the cool new features–and then we realized that the folks at Adobe forgot to include one really important one: the ability to save files "backward" for use with InDesign 2. Thankfully, they remembered to include it with CS2.

You can now save CS2 files "backward" for use with InDesign CS via the INX export feature. Open the file you want to save backward and then choose File ▷ Export, or press ⌘+E (Mac) or Ctrl+E (Windows). When the Export dialog appears, browse to where you'd like to save the .inx file and then choose InDesign Interchange from the Format menu (Mac) or Save As Type menu (Windows). You can then open the .inx file in InDesign CS.

Keep in mind that when saving backward, the features added in CS2 are not available in CS (object styles, anchored objects, etc.).

### Step 7.
Press Delete (Mac) or Backspace (Windows) to delete the duplicate lightbulb image. Option-click (Mac) or Alt-click (Windows) the "outer glow" layer to select the path. Marquee over all the points beneath the glass area of the bulb as shown and press Delete (Mac) or Backspace (Windows). Press D to apply the default colors of None fill and black stroke.

### Step 8.
Press Delete (Mac) or Backspace (Windows) to delete the duplicate lightbulb image. Option-click (Mac) or Alt-click (Windows) the "outer glow" layer to select the path. Marquee over all the points beneath the glass area of the bulb as shown and press Delete (Mac) or Backspace (Windows). Press D to apply the default colors of None fill and black stroke.

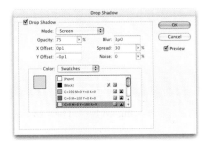

### Step 9.
Choose Object ▷ Drop Shadow. In the dialog that appears, click the Drop Shadow option to enable the effect. Choose Screen from the Mode pop-up menu and select the yellow swatch from the swatches list. Enter **75** for Opacity, **3p0** for Blur, **0p1** for X Offset, and **-0p1** for Y Offset. Enter **30** for Spread and keep the Noise setting at 0. Click OK to apply.

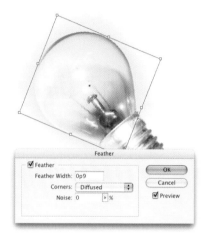

**Step 10.**

Choose Object ▷ Feather. In the dialog that appears, check the Feather option to enable the effect. Enter **0p9** in the Feather Width field and choose Diffused from the Corners pop-up menu. Click OK to apply.

## Adobe InCopy

If your production team includes copy editors as well as designers, you may want to consider purchasing and implementing Adobe InCopy into your workflow. InCopy is designed to work hand-in-hand with InDesign, allowing both editors and designers to work on files at the same time without getting their wires crossed.

With InCopy installed, several new interface items appear in InDesign CS2, including the Assignments and Notes palettes. A Notes menu and Notes tool also appear. The Assignments palettes in both applications allow all users to manage editing duties for specific "stories" (text frames) and graphics in the publication. The Notes features allow users of both applications to communicate with each other right in the document itself—no more e-mails!

**Step 11.**

Unlock the "lightbulb" layer in the Layers palette. Option-click (Mac) or Alt-click (Windows) the "lightbulb" layer to select its contents. Choose Window ▷ Transparency (or press Shift+F10) to display the Transparency palette. Choose Multiply from the Mode pop-up menu and deselect the graphic frame.

**Step 12.**

Add some type to complete the logo design. In the example shown here, the words "IDEA GROUP" are set in black, all caps, using the Huxley Vertical BT Regular font at 102pt over 80pt leading, with Optical kerning and zero tracking applied. The word "THE" is in a separate text frame using 30pt Helvetica Neue 45 Light, with Optical kerning applied, as well as 50% vertical scaling and 80% horizontal scaling.

# Duotone CD Art

With InDesign, you can colorize placed grayscale TIFFs and PSDs. Not only that, but you can also create a duotone effect by colorizing the shadow *and* highlight areas of a grayscale image. And if you're limited to colorizing your grayscale images with spot colors, utilizing InDesign's mixed ink swatches can greatly expand your options.

With these steps, we'll place a layered grayscale TIFF containing a posterized effect into a CD-shaped compound path. We'll then create and apply a mixed-ink swatch in InDesign using a PANTONE spot color and Process Black. Doing so applies the two colors to the various percentages of gray in the shadow areas of the image. Leaving the highlight areas uncolorized means that no ink will be applied in the white areas of the image. This allows the silver surface of the CD to shine through.

## Creating Mixed-Ink Swatch Duotones

To re-create this effect using the images shown here, download CD.inds and CD_art.tif from *The InDesign Effects Book* website.

**Step 1.**
In a new letter-size document, press ⌘+D (Mac) or Ctrl+D (Windows) to display the Place dialog. Locate the CD.inds image on your system and click Open. Click once anywhere on the page to place the InDesign snippet at 100% of its size.

**Step 2.**
Press A to access the Direct Selection tool and click the CD frame to select it. Press ⌘+D (Mac) or Ctrl+D (Windows) to display the Place dialog. Locate the CD_art.tif image on your system and click Open. Click directly on the image to select it from within the frame. Click and drag to position the grayscale image inside the frame as shown.

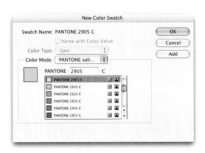

**Step 3.**
Choose Window▷Swatches (or press F5) to display the Swatches palette. Choose New Color Swatch from the Swatches palette fly-out menu. In the dialog that appears, choose Pantone solid coated from the Color Mode pop-up menu. Enter **2905** in the PANTONE field and click OK to add the swatch and close the dialog.

**Step 4.**
Choose New Mixed Ink Swatch from the Swatches palette fly-out menu. In the dialog that appears, click in the left column next to Process Black and PANTONE 2905 in order to include both inks. Leave both ink percentages at 100%. Enter a name for the mixed-ink swatch (e.g., **Black+2905**) and click OK.

**Step 5.**
Click the new mixed-ink swatch in the Swatches palette in order to apply it to the selected image. InDesign applies the two mixed-ink colors to the varying percentages of gray in the image. Any white areas will not use any ink when screen-printed; therefore, the silver of the CD will shine through in all of the white areas.

**Step 6.**
Add some type to complete the design. In the example shown here, the word "threads" is set in all lowercase, Compacta ICG, 43pt, with Optical kerning and -20 tracking applied. The CD title of "don't know what I'm feeling" is set in Helvetica Ultra Compressed, 12pt, with Optical kerning and zero tracking applied. Each line of text is set in its own text frame and is separated by a 1pt white rule, drawn with the Line tool. A white fill is applied to all of the text and a white stroke to the rule, which means that no ink will be applied in those areas, allowing the silver of the CD to shine through.

# Object Layer Options and Placed PSDs

Clipping paths are great for extracting images from placed photographs. The downside is that they can take a long time to draw, and their edges often appear too sharp. To get around this, try extracting your images in Adobe Photoshop and then placing transparent PSDs in InDesign. It's quicker and easier, and produces better-looking images overall. Plus, you can take advantage of InDesign's new Object Layer Options dialog, which allows you to control layer visibility in placed PSDs–including layer comps.

To adjust layer visibility after a PSD is placed, choose Object ▷ Object Layer Options. In the resulting dialog, choose to show or hide different layers or select a different layer comp from the menu. Check the Preview option to view your changes in the document as you make them. When you've finished, click OK to close the dialog and apply your changes.

**Note:** InDesign places an eye icon next to the link's name in the Links palette, indicating that the image now contains layer visibility overrides.

# 2 Type Effects

www.photospin.com © 2005

*InDesign CS2 contains plenty of options that allow you to format text and create styles, but if you look a little deeper into the application, you'll see how easy it is to also create* custom type effects. *Traditionally, these kinds of logo effects are created in such programs as Illustrator or Photoshop and placed as graphic links into an InDesign document. However, by applying InDesign's built-in effects to type—such as feather, drop shadow, transparency, and the blending modes—you can create some really cool type effects right in your document without having to go outside of InDesign.*

Outer Glow

Inner Glow

Perspective Type Shadow

Grunge Type

Metal Gradient

Put Your Logo in Lights

"Gel-ly" Type

Neon Type

Spray Stencil

Type Around the World

# Outer Glow

InDesign CS2 doesn't come with a built-in outer glow effect like Illustrator or Photoshop, but that doesn't mean we can't still create one! Instead, we'll use what we do have—the Drop Shadow effect. Believe it or not, you can create an outer glow effect by experimenting with the drop shadow dialog settings, including the drop shadow blending modes, X and Y offsets, and the opacity, blur, and spread values.

An outer glow effect can make your type pop right off the page. Creating the effect is simple, but its success depends on which fonts and colors you choose to work with. In this example, to simulate the real-life glow of digital text on a computer screen, I chose the Digital font with a bright green fill applied and placed it over a black background. Keep in mind that using different fonts and colors with this effect can produce entirely different results, but the more you experiment, the more creative you can get!

## Drop Shadow: Not Just for Shadows

Don't be fooled by the name. There's a lot you can do with InDesign's Drop Shadow effect. In these steps, we'll learn how you can use it to apply an outer glow to some type.

**Step 1.**
Start out by drawing a rectangle with the Rectangle tool and filling it with black. If your print project is a four-color (CMYK) job, you might want to consider using a "black build" or a "rich black"—that is, a black that is made up of percentages of all four inks rather than just black ink. You can use this as a background for the effect.

**Step 2.**
Display the Layers palette (choose Window ▷ Layers or press F7). Double-click Layer 1 to display the Layer Options dialog. Enter a name for the background layer, check the Lock Layer option, and click OK to close the dialog.

**Step 3.**
Option-click (Mac) or Alt-click (Windows) the Create New Layer button at the bottom of the Layers palette. In the Layer Options dialog, enter a name for the layer (e.g., **outer glow text**) and click OK. Press D to apply the document default colors of None fill and black stroke. Display the Swatches palette (by choosing Window ▷ Swatches or pressing F5).

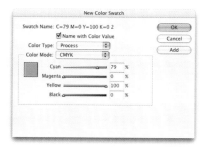

### Step 4.

Press / (forward slash key) to apply a stroke of None, then press X to bring the fill icon to the forefront. Choose New Color Swatch from the Swatches palette fly-out menu. In the dialog that appears, choose Process from the Color Type pop-up menu and CMYK from the Color Mode pop-up menu. Enter **79–0–100–0** into the C-M-Y-K percentage fields (as shown) to create a bright green color swatch, and click OK.

### Step 5.

Press T to access the Type tool. Create a text frame and then press ⌘+Option+7 / Alt+Ctrl+7 to access the control palette Character Formatting controls, and choose a font and point size (in the example here, it is the Digital font at 66pt). Add some logo type. Switch to the Selection tool and choose Object▷Drop Shadow.

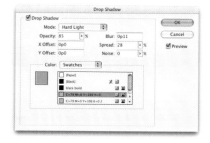

### Step 6.

Now let's add a green glow effect to the type. In the Drop Shadow dialog, check the Drop Shadow option (at the top) to enable the effect and the Preview option (to the right) to see the settings applied as you enter them. To make the glow color really "pop," choose Hard Light from the Mode pop-up menu and Swatches from the Color pop-up menu. From the Swatches list, select the green swatch you created in step 4. To soften the glow, enter these settings: 85% for Opacity, 0p11 for Blur, 28% for Spread, 0p0 for X and Y Offsets, and 0p0 for Noise.

## Working with Layers

The Layers palette allows you to separate various objects in a layout by placing them on different layers. By toggling layer visibility on or off, you can view different design compositions and create PDFs of them using the Export Adobe PDF feature.

By default, new layers always appear at the top of the list in the Layers palette. However, if you'd like to create a new layer directly underneath the layer you currently have selected, press ⌘+Option (Mac) or Ctrl+Alt (Windows) and click the Create New Layer icon or choose New Layer Below from the palette fly-out menu. To create a new layer directly above the one you currently have selected, ⌘-click / Ctrl-click the Create New Layer icon at the bottom of the Layers palette.

Every layer you create has an assigned color. These colors are applied to the outline frames of all of your selections to indicate which layers the objects are placed on. You can change a layer's color by double-clicking the layer name to open the Layer Options dialog.

*continues on next page*

# Outer Glow *continued*

## Sampling Drop Shadows

You can sample and apply your favorite drop shadow settings to multiple objects in a document by using the Eyedropper tool.

1. Show frame edges in the document by pressing ⌘+H / Ctrl+H.

2. Select the objects you would like to apply the drop shadow to with the Selection tool.

3. Press I to switch to the Eyedropper tool and click directly on the frame edge of the object containing the drop shadow you'd like to sample.

4. InDesign places the sampled drop shadow on all of the selected objects at once—and you don't have to reenter any dialog settings!

**Step 7.**
Click OK to close the dialog and admire your new outer glow effect—but wait, there's more! As long as we're at it, let's create another outer glow effect that is slightly different.

**Step 8.**
To create an alternate version of the effect on a separate layer, choose Duplicate Layer from the Layers palette menu.

**Step 9.**
Enter a name for the layer in the Duplicate Layer dialog (e.g., **outer glow outline**), and click OK. In the Layers palette, turn off the outer glow text layer's visibility by clicking the eye icon in the far-left column, next to the layer name.

**Step 10.**

Select the text frame with the Selection tool and choose Type▷Create Outlines. Click the fill icon at the top of the Swatches palette and select black (or black build, if you created one) from the swatches list.

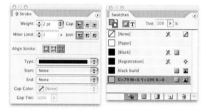

**Step 11.**

Press X to bring the stroke icon to the forefront and select the green swatch from the swatches list. Display the Stroke palette (choose Window▷ Stroke or press F10) and enter **2p** in the Weight field. Click the Align Stroke To Outside button and enter **1** in the Miter Limit field.

**Step 12.**

And there you have it ... an alternate version of the text glow effect. You can view each version of the effect by toggling layer visibility. To do so, just click the eye icon in the far-left column of the Layers palette, next to each layer's name.

## Adding Strokes to Text

You can apply a color or gradient stroke to editable text. To do so, bring the Stroke swatch to the forefront. You can then enter a stroke weight in either the Control palette or the Stroke palette.

To apply a color or gradient stroke to all editable text in a story, select any text frame (or frames) with either selection tool, and click the Formatting Affects Text button. To apply a stroke to specific characters within a story, highlight them with the Type tool.

Once the characters are selected, use any one of the five following methods to apply a color or gradient to the stroke:

- Click directly on a color or gradient swatch name in the Swatches palette.

- Create a color or gradient using their respective palettes.

- Choose a color using the Color Picker and click OK.

- Choose and apply a sampled color or gradient stroke with the Eyedropper tool (this also samples all other style attributes applied).

- Click the Apply (Last Used) Color or Gradient button located at the bottom of the Tools palette, or press the comma key (color) or period key (gradient).

**Note:** Applying a stroke color or gradient does not automatically add it to the Swatches palette.

# Inner Glow

An inner glow effect is something you would normally create using layer styles in Photoshop. However, by duplicating text layers in InDesign and applying different blending modes, you can create an effect similar to Photoshop's Inner Glow layer style. Granted, you won't have as much control over the effect as you would in Photoshop, but the fact that you can even simulate this effect at all in a "page layout" program is pretty amazing. Of course, we know better than to refer to InDesign as merely a "page layout" program.

As with outer glows, the success of the inner glow depends on which font and background color you choose to work with. The effect works best with thick, bold typefaces, set at very large point sizes, and placed over brightly colored backgrounds. When you apply transparent blend modes to feathered text layers, they interact with the background color underneath to create the effect.

## Sharp Feathers and Blending Modes

"Sharp Feather" sounds like a contradiction, but in InDesign there actually is such a thing. You can use it along with layers and transparent blend modes to create an effect similar to Photoshop's Inner Glow.

**Step 1.**
Start out by drawing a rectangle with the Rectangle tool and filling it with red (e.g., C=15 M=100 Y=100 K=0). You can use this as a background for the effect.

**Step 2.**
Choose Window ▷ Layers (or press F7) to display the Layers palette. Double-click Layer 1 to display the Layer Options dialog. Enter a name for the background layer, check the Lock Layer option, and click OK to close the dialog.

**Step 3.**
Option-click (Mac) or Alt-click (Windows) the Create New Layer button at the bottom of the Layers palette. In the Layer Options dialog, enter a name for the new layer (e.g., **sharp feather**) and click OK.

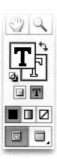

**Step 4.**

Press T to access the Type tool and click the Formatting Affects Text button (at the bottom of the Tools palette). Press D to apply the document default colors (None fill and black stroke). Press X to bring the fill icon to the forefront and the comma key to fill with black. If they are not visible already, press ⌘+Option+7 / Ctrl+Alt+7 to access the Control palette Character Formatting controls.

**Step 5.**

Enter an amount of 1.5pt in the stroke weight field of the Control palette. Create a text frame and choose a bold font and large point size (in the example here, it is Eurostile Bold Extended 2 at 80pt). Add some logo type in all caps.

**Step 6.**

Switch to the Selection tool and choose Object ▷ Feather. In the dialog that appears, check the Feather option (at the top) to enable the effect, and the Preview option (to the right) to see the settings applied as you enter them. Enter **3p0** in the Feather Width field and choose Sharp from the Corners pop-up menu. Keep the Noise setting at **0p0**. Click OK to apply.

*continues on next page*

## What Are Blend Modes?

InDesign allows you to apply blending modes to selected objects, similar to the blending modes found in Photoshop and Illustrator. Applying blending modes allows you to control how transparent objects blend with the colors underneath:

**Normal**  At 100% opacity, a selected object's color does not blend with the colors of the objects underneath.

**Multiply**  Darkens a selected object's color by multiplying its values with the values of the colors underneath. White colors are not affected.

**Screen**  Lightens a selected object's color by multiplying the inverse of the base and blend colors. Screening lighter colors produces greater changes; black is not affected.

**Overlay**  Darkens (multiplies) or lightens (screens) a selected object's color while preserving luminosity. Contrasting colors produce greater changes; black, white, and 50% gray are not affected.

*continues on next page*

# Inner Glow *continued*

## What Are Blend Modes? *continued*

**Soft Light** Darkens (multiplies) or lightens (screens) a selected object's color without preserving highlight and shadow values. Blend colors above 50% darken the base color; blend colors below 50% lighten the base color. Black, white, and 50% gray are not affected.

**Hard Light** Produces the same effect as Soft Light but with more contrast.

**Color Dodge** A selected object's pixels are colorized using the hue of the pixels underneath. Color Dodge has a greater effect on lighter colors.

**Color Burn** A selected object's pixels are colorized using the hue of the pixels underneath. Color Burn has a greater effect on darker colors.

**Darken** When a selected object's color is lighter than the colors underneath, the darker color is applied.

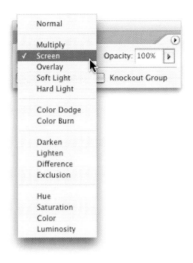

**Step 7.**
Choose Window ▷ Transparency (or press Shift+F10) to display the Transparency palette. Choose Screen from the Blending Mode pop-up menu.

**Step 8.**
Now create a new layer underneath the one you're working on. You can do this by holding down ⌘+Option / Ctrl+Alt and clicking the Create New Layer button at the bottom of the Layers palette. Double-click the new layer to access the Layer Options dialog and enter a name for it (e.g., **shadow**). Click OK to close the dialog.

**Step 9.**
In the Layers palette, Option-click (Mac) or Alt-click (Windows) the small square icon located on the right of the layer above and drag it to the new layer underneath (shown here, from the sharp feather layer to the shadow layer). Doing so creates a copy of the text frame and places it on the new layer.

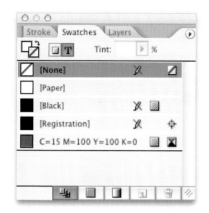

**Step 10.**
Choose Window ▷ Swatches (or press F5) to display the Swatches palette and click the Formatting Affects Text button located at the top. Select Paper from the swatches list to apply a white fill. Press X to bring the stroke icon to the forefront and the forward slash key (/) to apply a stroke of None.

**Step 11.**
Click the Formatting Affects Container button located at the top of the Swatches palette. Choose Object ▷ Feather to access the Feather dialog. Uncheck the Feather option and click OK. Press ⌘+Option+M / Ctrl+Alt+M to display the Drop Shadow dialog.

**Step 12.**
In the Drop Shadow dialog, check the Drop Shadow option (at the top) to enable the effect and the Preview option (to the right) to see the settings applied as you enter them. Choose Multiply from the Mode pop-up menu and Swatches from the Color pop-up menu. From the Swatches list, select black. Enter these settings: 75% for Opacity, 0p5 for Blur, and 0p4 for X and Y Offsets. Keep the Spread and Noise settings at 0p0. Click OK to apply.

*continues on next page*

## What Are Blend Modes? *continued*

**Lighten** When a selected object's color is darker than the colors underneath, the lighter color is applied.

**Difference** Applies the color that results when blend and base colors are subtracted from each other. White inverts the base color; black has no effect.

**Exclusion** Produces the same effect as Difference but with less contrast.

**Hue** Applies the hue of the blend color to the luminance and saturation of the base color.

**Saturation** Applies the saturation of the blend color to the luminance and hue of the base color.

**Color** Applies the hue and saturation of the blend color to the luminance of the base color.

**Luminosity** Applies the luminance of the blend color to the hue and saturation of the base color.

# Inner Glow *continued*

## Feathered Corners

InDesign allows you to apply a soft edge (referred to as a feather) to any selected object, including imported graphics, shapes, and editable text. To create a feathered edge using the Feather dialog, select an object and choose Object ▷ Feather.

Check the Feather option in the upper left of the dialog, then enter a value in the Feather Width field. Larger values produce softer edges. To see the settings applied as you enter them, check the Preview option on the right.

Choose a corner option from the pop-up menu. Options include:

**Sharp** Applies the feather along the outline of the path.

**Rounded** Applies the feather along the outline of the path, but "rounds" the edges of the feather around sharp corners.

**Diffused** Applies a transparent fade from the center of the object rather than along the outline of the path.

**Note:** To apply a feather to editable text characters, the text frame must have a fill of None applied. When a fill color (other than None) is applied, a feather is added to the text frame rather than the text.

**Step 13.**
In the Transparency palette, choose Multiply from the Blending Mode pop-up menu.

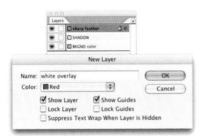

**Step 14.**
Option-click (Mac) or Alt-click (Windows) the Create New Layer button located at the bottom of the Layers palette. In the Layer Options dialog, enter a name for it (e.g., white overlay) and click OK.

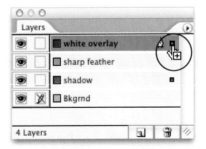

**Step 15.**
Copy the text frame by Option-clicking (Mac) or Alt-clicking (Windows) the small square icon located on the shadow layer and dragging it to the new "white overlay" layer.

**Step 16.**

Choose Object ▷ Drop Shadow (or press ⌘+Option+M / Ctrl+Alt+M) to display the Drop Shadow dialog. Uncheck the Drop Shadow option (at the top) to disable the effect.

**Step 17.**

In the Transparency palette, choose Overlay from the Blending Mode pop-up menu. Press Shift+⌘+A / Shift+Ctrl+A to deselect all. That's all there is to it! You just created an inner glow effect in InDesign.

**Don't stop now—customize the effect:** experimenting with entirely different fonts and background colors. Here is an example that uses a lowercase bold italic font (Futura) over a dark green background. Remember that saturated background colors can produce the best results.

## Drop Shadows

You can apply drop shadows to imported graphics, shapes, lines, tables, text frames, and editable text characters. One of the great things about InDesign drop shadows is that they are not permanent effects. You can turn them on or off at any time.

To apply a drop shadow in InDesign, select an object with either selection tool and choose Object ▷ Drop Shadow. InDesign launches the Drop Shadow dialog.

Check the Drop Shadow option in the upper left of the dialog. Enter an Opacity value, Blur amount, and X and Y Offset amount. You can also apply Spread and Noise percentages. To see the settings applied as you enter them, check the Preview option. Select a color to apply to the drop shadow from the swatches list (the default is Black). To view and edit the color build of a chosen swatch, choose RGB, CMYK, or Lab from the Color menu. Note that adjusting the color build of a chosen swatch does not change its color build in the Swatches palette.

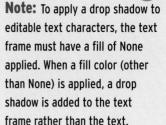

**Note:** To apply a drop shadow to editable text characters, the text frame must have a fill of None applied. When a fill color (other than None) is applied, a drop shadow is added to the text frame rather than the text.

# Perspective Type Shadow

Drop shadows are cool, but let's face it, perspective drop shadows are even cooler. Technically this would fall under the category of "photo-realistic" effects, which is pretty hard to pull off in a "page layout" program. But as we now know, InDesign is much more than just a "page layout" application. In fact, by shearing and scaling a duplicate text frame and then applying a gradient fill and a feather effect, you can simulate a perspective type shadow.

In this example, the type is placed over a blank white page, which makes it easier to create the highlight effect in the final steps. However, if you'd like to create this effect over a color, you can do so by nesting the highlight shape inside a character outline—a masking technique that we cover in greater detail in the next effect, Grunge Type.

## Put Your Type in Perspective

Sometimes a little perspective is all you need. In these steps, we'll learn how to create a perspective type shadow entirely in InDesign.

**Step 1.**
Press T to access the Type tool and create a text frame. If they're not showing already, press ⌘+Option+7 / Ctrl+Alt+7 to access the Control palette Character Formatting controls. Choose a bold font and large point size (in the example here, it's Friz Quadrata Bold at 72pt). You can also enter these settings in the Character palette.

**Step 2.**
Add some logo type in all caps. Choose Window ▷ Swatches (or press F5) to display the Swatches palette.

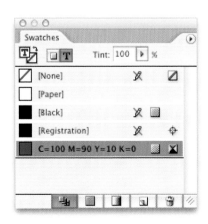

**Step 3.**
Switch to the Selection tool and click the Formatting Affects Text button at the top of the Swatches palette. Create a color to apply to the text using the Color palette, or select an existing color from the Swatches palette list (or select one using the Color Picker). In the example here it's a dark blue build of C=100 M=90 Y=10 K=0.

**Step 4.**

Choose Window ▷ Layers (or press F7) to display the Layers palette. Double-click Layer 1 to display the Layer Options dialog. Enter a name for the layer (e.g., **type layer**), and click OK to close the dialog.

**Step 5.**

Now create a new layer underneath the one you're working on. You can do this by holding down ⌘+Option or Ctrl+Alt and clicking the Create New Layer button at the bottom of the Layers palette. Double-click the new layer to access the Layer Options dialog and enter a name for it (e.g., **shadow layer**). Click OK to close the dialog.

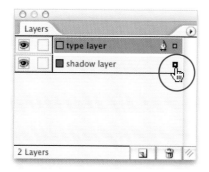

**Step 6.**

In the Layers palette, Option-click (Mac) or Alt-click (Windows) the small square icon located on the "type" layer above and drag it to the new "shadow" layer underneath. Doing so creates a copy of the text frame and places it on the new layer.

*continues on next page*

# Adding Swatches with Color Picker

InDesign now features a Color Picker. To open the Color Picker, double-click the Stroke or Fill swatches located at the bottom of the Tools palette or in the Color palette. When the dialog opens, you can click anywhere in the color field to locate a specific RGB, CMYK, or Lab build.

To change the color spectrum displayed in the Color Picker, click a letter: R (red), G (green), or B (blue); or L (luminance), a (green-red axis), or b (blue-yellow axis).

To add the chosen color to the Swatches palette, click the Add RGB Swatch or Add Lab Swatch button (depending on which color spectrum is currently displayed in the Color Picker). Click inside any of the RGB, Lab, or CMYK percentage fields to display the Add RGB, Lab, or CMYK Swatch button.

Click OK to display the chosen color in the Fill or Stroke swatch (whichever is placed in front) and apply it to any selected objects.

# Perspective Type Shadow *continued*

## Changing Case

To change the text case in InDesign, highlight some text with the Type tool, then either choose Type ▷ Change Case or Control/right-click and select the command from the contextual menu. Select Uppercase, Lowercase, Title Case, or Sentence Case from the submenu. Title Case capitalizes the first letter of every word, and Sentence Case capitalizes the first letter of every sentence.

To change case of all text in a story (including overset text) that has only one text frame, select the frame with either selection tool and apply the Change Case command.

If the selected frame is part of a threaded series, you cannot change case for an entire story using this method. To change case for an entire story that is contained in a series of threaded frames, place the Type tool cursor in any one of the threaded frames and choose Edit ▷ Select All, and then apply the command.

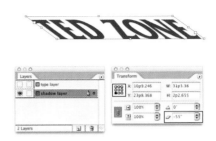

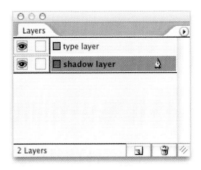

**Step 7.**
In the Layers palette, turn off layer visibility for the type layer by clicking the eye icon in the left column. Then in the Control palette (or Transform palette), click the bottom-left square of the reference point icon. Enter the angle (here, -55°) in the Shear X Angle field. The shadow's angle can face any direction, so don't be afraid to experiment with this setting.

**Step 8.**
Turn layer visibility back on for the type layer. Now hold down the ⌘ key (Mac) or the Ctrl key (Windows) and drag the top-center frame node down to the vertical center of the forefront text as shown.

**Step 9.**
Deselect the text frame. Select the color that is applied to the text from the Swatches palette list and lower the Tint value to 80%. Drag the Fill icon in the upper left of the palette into the swatches list to create a new tint swatch. Lower the Tint value again, this time to 5%, and drag the fill icon into the list to create a second tint swatch.

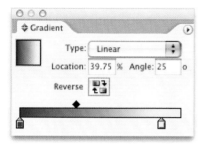

### Step 10.

Now let's simulate real-world lighting conditions by creating and applying a gradient. Choose Window ⊳ Gradient to display the Gradient palette. Select the sheared text frame and click the Formatting Affects Text button at the top of the Swatches palette. In the Gradient palette, choose Linear from the Type pop-up menu. Drag the 80% tint swatch from the Swatches palette list directly over the left slider in the Gradient palette. Enter **0p0** in the Location field. Drag the 5% tint swatch from the Swatches palette over the right slider in the Gradient palette and enter **88.47** in the Location field. Click the top-center slider and enter **3Step 9.75** in the Location field. Enter **25** in the Angle field. Note that these gradient settings work best with the color and angle chosen for this shadow. If you choose a different color and angle for your shadow, your settings can be very different. Feel free to experiment, and don't forget that you can also use the Gradient tool to apply the gradient.

### Step 11.

Click the Formatting Affects Container button at the top of the Swatches palette. Choose Object ⊳ Feather. In the dialog that appears, check the Feather option (at the top) to enable the effect. Enter **0p4** in the Feather Width field and choose Diffused from the Corners pop-up menu. Keep the Noise setting at **0p0**. Click OK to apply.

*continues on next page*

## Shearing Objects

Any time you shear an object, you must choose a reference point from the icon located in the Control or Transform palette. The default reference point is the absolute center of the object; however, you can reposition it by clicking a different square in the icon.

To shear an object, perform any one of the following actions:

- Select the object by clicking its frame or shape edge with the Shear tool, then click and drag. Press the Shift key as you drag to constrain along the horizontal axis.

- Select the object with the Selection tool, and enter a value in the Shear X angle field located in the Transform or Control palette. You can also select a preset value from the pop-up menu.

- Select the object with the Selection tool. Access the Shear dialog by choosing Object Transform  Shear and enter a value for Shear Angle. Choose an axis (Horizontal, Vertical, or specified Angle) and click OK.

- Select the object by clicking its frame or shape edge with the Free Transform tool. As you begin to click and drag a side node, hold down Option+⌘ (Mac) or Ctrl+Alt (Windows). Press the Shift key as you drag to constrain vertically or horizontally.

# Perspective Type Shadow *continued*

## Converting Text to Outlines

To convert all of the text characters in a selected frame into editable paths, select the text frame with either selection tool and choose Type ▷ Create Outlines. InDesign instantly converts all the characters in the frame and groups them. Characters such as "O" and "D" are automatically converted into compound paths.

To convert individual selected characters in a text frame into editable paths, highlight them with the Type tool and choose Type ▷ Create Outlines. InDesign converts the selected characters into outlines and treats them as nested inline objects.

Just like with any other custom shape, you can edit a character outline by selecting and repositioning points on the path with the Direct Selection tool. You can also add, delete, or convert points using the various Pen tools; add points using the Pencil tool; erase points using the Erase tool; cut points and line segments using the Scissors tool; and smooth points using the Smooth tool.

**Step 12.**
Option-click (Mac) or Alt-click (Windows) the Create New Layer button located at the bottom of the Layers palette. In the Layer Options dialog, enter a name for it (e.g., **highlight**) and click OK.

**Step 13.**
Deselect the text frame and press L to access the Ellipse tool. Click the Paper swatch in the Swatches palette and draw an oval shape that overlaps the bottom right of the type and shadow layers as shown.

**Step 14.**
Choose Object ▷ Feather to display the Feather dialog. Check the Feather option (at the top) to enable the effect. Enter **2p10** in the Feather Width field and choose Diffused from the Corners pop-up menu. To break up the shadow a bit and give it more of a real-world photographic quality, enter an amount of 2% in the Noise field. Click OK to apply.

**Step 15.**

Choose Window ▷ Transparency (or press Shift+F10) to display the Transparency palette. Choose Screen from the Blending Mode pop-up menu and lower the Opacity value to 80%. Deselect the ellipse.

## Snapping to the Document Grid

You can align objects evenly on the page by snapping to the document grid. The document grid displays a series of both vertical and horizontal lines on the page, resulting in what looks like transparent graph paper placed over the top of your layout. When made visible, the grid can be very distracting to work with—even when placed in back with a lighter color applied to it. Thankfully, you can still snap to the document grid even when it is hidden.

Document Grid color settings and gridline options are accessible in Grids Preferences. To align graphic frames and other objects to the top and bottom lines of paragraph text, enter gridline subdivision values that coincide with the baseline grid.

Select View ▷ Grids & Guides ▷ Snap To Document Grid, or Control/right-click anywhere on the Pasteboard and select it from the contextual menu.

**Step 16.**

To put a finishing touch on this logo, I selected the type layer from the Layers palette and added the word "THE" in a much smaller font (16pt). Press Shift+⌘+A / Shift+Ctrl+A to deselect all. You're done!

**Don't stop now—customize the effect:**
Now try experimenting with this effect by using different fonts and applying alternate colors to the type and shadow. Here is an example that uses a much flashier font (Haulnhouse by House Industries). To make this work over a colored background, duplicate the text, convert it to outlines, and paste the white highlight shape inside the characters (a masking technique called "nesting"). To add to the effect, try applying a gradient stroke to the text that uses the same angle as the perspective shadow, and change the white highlight shape's blending mode to 100% Overlay as shown here.

# Grunge Type

The "grunge" look is in. It's used just about everywhere, but especially in movie posters, DVD covers, and advertisements. Typically, this is an effect you would create using Adobe Photoshop, but what you may not realize is that you can also create grunge type right in InDesign. By nesting a textured grayscale image into a character outline frame (similar to a clipping mask in Photoshop or Illustrator) and applying colors and transparent blending modes, you can get that "grungy" look.

"Grunge" requires textures, and I encourage you to create your own using natural media such as spray paint or chalk on textured material. By scanning them in and saving them as grayscale TIFFs or PSDs, you can place your textures in InDesign and colorize them. You can also use textures created in Adobe Photoshop—or better yet—Corel Painter.

As with most type effects, this one works best when applied to a thick, bold typeface set at a very large point size.

## Create Your Own Texture

To create this effect, I sprayed some paint onto a white matte board and scanned in the texture, saving it as a grayscale PSD. You can download the file (texture1.psd) from the *InDesign Effects Book* website: www.wiley.com/go/indesignfx

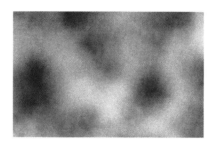

**Step 1.**
Press V to access the Selection tool. Using the Place command (⌘+D / Ctrl+D), import a Grayscale TIFF or PSD of a texture. Deselect the graphic once it is placed in the document.

**Step 2.**
Display the Layers palette (choose Window▷Layers or press F7). Double-click Layer 1 to display the Layer Options dialog. Enter a name for the layer (e.g., **background layer**), and click OK to close the dialog.

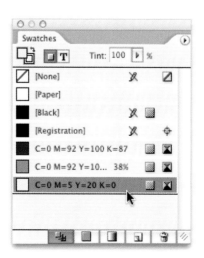

**Step 3.**
Display the Swatches palette (choose Window▷Swatches or press F5). Create a new color swatch to apply to the texture (e.g., C=0 M=92 Y=100 K=87). Now create a tint swatch by lowering the Tint slider to 38% and drag the fill or stroke icon (whichever is in front) into the swatches list. Finally, create a second color swatch using a much lighter color (e.g., C=0 M=5 Y=20 K=0).

**Step 4.**

Select the placed graphic with the Selection tool. Drag the 38% tint swatch on top of the texture to colorize the shadow areas. Then select the light tint swatch (e.g., C=0 M=5 Y=20 K=0) from the Swatches palette list (don't drag it onto the image—just select it in the palette) to colorize the highlight areas.

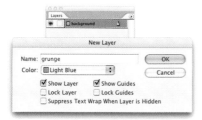

**Step 5.**

Option-click / Alt-click the Create New Layer button located at the bottom of the Layers palette. In the Layer Options dialog, enter a name for it (e.g., **grunge**) and click OK.

**Step 6.**

Press T to access the Type tool. Choose a bold font and large point size from the Control or Character palette (in the example here, it's Futura Extra Bold at 94pt). Create a text frame and enter some text. Switch to the Selection tool and choose Type ▷ Create Outlines. Apply a fill of None and a 0.75pt white (Paper) stroke to the character outline.

*continues on next page*

## Colorizing Placed Graphics

You can colorize a placed grayscale TIFF or PSD by selecting it with the Direct Selection tool and applying a color with the Swatches or Color palette, Color Picker, or Eyedropper tool.

To create a duotone effect in InDesign, select a placed grayscale TIFF or PSD with the Selection tool (not the Direct Selection tool) and drag in a color from the Swatches palette. This colorizes the shadow areas of the image. To colorize the highlight areas, click a second swatch in the palette (but don't drag it onto the image).

**Note:** Duotones are generally used for spot-color print jobs, but you can still use the effect when designing for process-color output. You do not have to use spot colors when colorizing a grayscale image.

# Grunge Type *continued*

## Creating a Mixed-Ink Swatch

InDesign allows you to create a single "mixed-ink" swatch by combining varying percentages of two different spot colors. You can use these colors to jazz up those boring old two- and three-color designs.

To create a mixed-ink swatch, choose New Mixed Ink Swatch from the Swatches palette menu. You must have at least one spot color saved in the Swatches palette to access the New Mixed Ink Swatch dialog.

In the dialog, choose a color to add to the mixed-ink swatch by clicking the box to the left of its name. You can then indicate what ink percentage to use by dragging the slider left or right or entering a value in the percentage field. As you add colors, refer to the preview swatch in the upper left.

Enter a name for the mixed-ink swatch and click OK to save it.

**Step 7.**

Press A to switch to the Direct Selection tool and click on the colorized background texture. Press ⌘+C / Ctrl+C to copy, then press V to switch back to the Selection tool. Select the character outline and choose Edit ▷ Paste Into. Press Shift+⌘+E / Shift+Ctrl+E to center the content.

**Step 8.**

Press A to switch to the Direct Selection tool and click anywhere inside the character outline frame to select its contents. Select the first color you created in the Swatches palette (e.g., C=0 M=92 Y=100 K=87). Choose Window ▷ Transparency (or press Shift+F10) to display the Transparency palette, and choose Multiply from the Blending Mode pop-up menu.

**Step 9.**

Option-click (Mac) or Alt-click (Windows) the Create New Layer button located at the bottom of the Layers palette. In the Layer Options dialog, enter a name for it (e.g., **color burn**) and click OK. Press V to switch to the Selection tool and Option-click (Mac) or Alt-click the grunge layer to select the character outline.

**Step 10.**

In the Layers palette, Option-click (Mac) or Alt-click (Windows) the small square icon located on the grunge layer and drag it to the new color burn layer above. Doing so creates a copy of the character outline and places it on the new layer.

**Step 11.**

Press A to switch to the Direct Selection tool and click anywhere inside the character outline frame to select its contents. Choose New Color Swatch from the Swatches palette fly-out menu and create a complementary color (e.g., C=50 M=14 Y=81 K=14). Finally, click on any character path segment and choose Color Burn from the Transparency palette Blending Mode pop-up menu.

**Step 12.**

Option-click (Mac) or Alt-click (Windows) the grunge layer in the Layers palette to select the original character outline. Choose Object ▷ Drop Shadow. In the dialog that appears, check the Drop Shadow option (at the top) to enable the effect. Choose Multiply from the Mode pop-up menu and Swatches from the Color pop-up menu. From the swatches list, select black. Enter **82%** for Opacity, **0p5** for Blur, and **0p7** for X and Y Offsets. Enter **10%** for Spread and **3%** for Noise. Click OK to apply.

## Creating a Mixed-Ink Group

To create a mixed-ink group, choose New Mixed Ink Group from the Swatches palette menu.

In the dialog, choose which colors to add by clicking the boxes to the left. You must include at least two colors and at least one spot color. It's also possible to include process colors (Cyan, Magenta, Yellow, and Black).

For each color, enter an Initial Tint percentage, Repeat amount, and Increment percentage in the respective fields.

The Initial Tint value tells InDesign what percentage of ink you'd like to start out with for each color in the group. The Repeat value indicates how many swatches InDesign should create. The Increment value tells InDesign how much ink to add with each repeat.

Click the Preview Swatches button to display a list of mixed-ink swatches that InDesign can generate using these settings. Enter a name for the group and click OK to add all the swatches in the group to the Swatches palette.

*continues on next page*

# Grunge Type *continued*

## Nesting Objects

Objects can be nested inside one another to create interesting design and logo effects. Objects can be nested as deep as you like, but multiple objects cannot be nested without grouping them first.

You can create a nested object by copy/pasting a graphic frame, text frame, or path into another graphic frame, text frame, or path.

Select an object with the Selection tool (graphic frame, text frame, or path) and copy or cut it to the Clipboard (Edit ▷ Cut or Edit ▷ Copy). Then select another object and choose Edit ▷ Paste Into for the object to appear nested inside the frame or path.

To select an object after it has been pasted into another frame or path, click the nested object's frame edge with the Direct Selection tool and then press V to switch to the Selection tool. You can then resize the frame, move it, or nudge it with the arrow keys. Switch back to the Direct Selection tool to resize, move, or nudge the nested components. Switch to the Type tool to select and edit nested text.

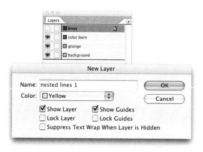

**Step 13.**
Option-click (Mac) or Alt-click (Windows) the Create New Layer button located at the bottom of the Layers palette. In the Layer Options dialog, enter a name for it (e.g., **lines**) and click OK. Press Shift+⌘+A / Shift+Ctrl+A to deselect all.

**Step 14.**
Press the backslash key (\) to access the Line tool. Set the Fill color to None and Stroke color to Paper (white). Proceed to draw random white lines over the text using various thin stroke weights (e.g., 0.25pt, 0.5pt, 0.75pt). When you've finished drawing, Option-click (Mac) or Alt-click (Windows) the lines layer to select all. Press V to switch to the Selection tool and ⌘+G / Ctrl+G to group the lines.

**Step 15.**
In the Layers palette, turn off visibility for the lines layer by clicking the eye icon in the left column. Then Option-click (Mac) or Alt-click (Windows) the Create New Layer button. In the Layer Options dialog, enter a name for it (e.g., **nested lines 1**) and click OK.

**Step 16.**
Option-click (Mac) or Alt-click (Windows) the color burn layer to select the duplicate character outline frame. Then drag the small square icon located on the color burn layer up to the new nested lines 1 layer above. Doing so creates a copy of the character outline and places it on the new layer.

**Step 17.**
Press A to switch to the Direct Selection tool and click anywhere inside the character outline frame to select its contents. Then press Delete (Mac) or Backspace (Windows). Turn visibility back on for the lines layer and Option-click (Mac) or Alt-click (Windows) the layer to select the group of white lines. Press ⌘+C / Ctrl+C to copy the lines to the Clipboard.

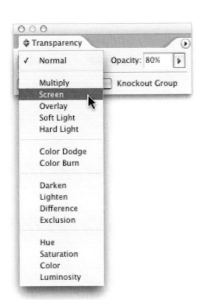

**Step 18.**
Toggle visibility off again for the lines layer. Option-click (Mac) or Alt-click (Windows) the nested lines layer and choose Edit ▷ Paste Into. Press Shift+⌘+E / Shift+Ctrl+E to center the content. Finally, choose Screen from the Transparency palette Blending Mode pop-up menu and set the Opacity to 80%.

*continues on next page*

# Nesting Grouped Objects

Grouping allows you to nest more than one object at a time. This is great for creating custom, editable logos and icons much as you would in programs such as Adobe Illustrator or Macromedia FreeHand. To give this a try, follow these simple steps:

1. Select multiple items and choose Object ▷ Group or press ⌘+G / Ctrl+G.

2. Copy the group to the Clipboard by choosing Edit ▷ Copy or pressing ⌘+C / Ctrl+C.

3. Select the object you would like to paste the group into with the Selection tool and choose Edit ▷ Paste Into.

4. Option/Alt-click the nested group with the Direct Selection tool (aka the Group Selection tool) and move, resize, or transform it within its new object container. You can also select and transform individual objects in the nested group with the Group Selection tool.

# Grunge Type *continued*

## Selecting Objects Within a Group

To select an object that is part of a group, click directly on a path segment with the Direct Selection tool. Shift-click to select multiple objects in the group.

To move, resize, or transform the object, you must select the entire path by clicking directly on its center point or Option/Alt-clicking on a path segment with the Direct Selection tool (also referred to as the Group Selection tool). You will know that the entire path is selected when all of the points of the path appear solid rather than hollow.

Once an object in a group is selected with the Direct Selection tool, press V to select it with the Selection tool and change its shape by dragging any of its nodes. You can move the grouped object with the Selection tool by clicking its center point and dragging.

To place a graphic into a grouped object, select it with the Direct Selection tool and choose File ▷ Place, or press ⌘+D / Ctrl+D. You can select the contents of a grouped object by clicking directly on it with the Direct Selection tool.

**Step 19.**

Option-click (Mac) or Alt-click (Windows) the Create New Layer button. In the Layer Options dialog, enter a name for it (e.g., **nested lines 2**) and click OK.

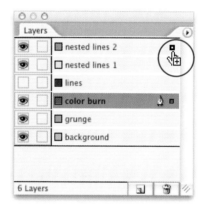

**Step 20.**

Option-click (Mac) or Alt-click (Windows) the color burn layer again to select the character outline frame. Then make another duplicate by dragging the small square icon located on the color burn layer to the new nested lines 2 layer above.

**Step 21.**

Turn visibility back on for the lines layer and Option-click (Mac) or Alt-click (Windows) the layer to select the group of white lines. Choose Window ▷ Object & Layout ▷ Transform (or press F9) to display the Transform palette and choose Flip Both from the fly-out menu (make sure the center square is chosen in the reference point icon). Press ⌘+C / Ctrl+C to copy the lines to the Clipboard. Toggle visibility off again for the lines layer.

**Step 22.**
Option/Alt-click the nested lines 2 layer to select the character outline. Click anywhere inside the frame to select its contents. Then press Delete or Backspace. Option/Alt-click the layer again and choose Edit ▷ Paste Into. Press Shift+⌘+E / Shift+Ctrl+E to center the content. Finally, choose Overlay from the Transparency palette Blending Mode pop-up menu.

**Step 23.**
Create a new layer and add some type to complete the logo design. Now try experimenting with this effect by using different fonts and applying alternate colors to the grayscale texture and nested lines.

# Flipping Objects

There are several ways to flip objects in InDesign. Each method flips objects using the reference point selected in the icon, located in the Control or Transform palette. The default reference point is the absolute center of the object; however, you can reposition it by clicking a different square in the icon.

To flip an object, perform any one of the following actions:

- Click the Transform palette menu button and choose Flip Horizontal, Flip Vertical, or Flip Both.

- Enter a negative Scale X or Scale Y Percentage value in the Transform or Control palette.

- Select one of the object's frame nodes with the Selection tool and drag it past the opposite side.

- Press A to switch to the Direct Selection tool and drag one of the object's line segments past the opposite side.

- Select the object by clicking its frame or shape edge with the Free Transform tool. Drag one of the object's frame nodes past the opposite side.

# Metal Gradient

Metal textures are commonly used in logos and advertisements (I'm sure you've seen the "Built Ford Tough" logo). There is no doubt that the best way to re-create this effect is in Photoshop, where it's easy to simulate brushed metal. However, if you are limited to using InDesign, you can create a metal effect without using textures at all. Instead you can use a combination of layers, different blending modes, and gradients.

InDesign allows you to apply gradients to the fills and strokes of editable text characters, as well as to shapes and paths. You can create gradients and save them in the Swatches palette. To have more control over the way gradients are applied to selected objects and text, try using the Gradient tool.

By blending shades of gray with some color, you can simulate a metal effect and apply it to some type. The trick is all in the gradients you use and how they interact with each other when various transparency blending modes are applied.

## Gradient Power

With these steps, we'll use gradients, layers, and blending modes to simulate a metal surface. We'll also apply some drop shadows to add some depth.

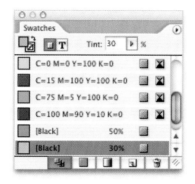

### Step 1.
Choose Window ▷ Swatches (or press F5) to display the Swatches palette. Press D to set the default colors of None fill and black stroke. Select Black from the swatches list and lower the Tint slider to 50%. Drag the stroke icon (or fill icon, whichever is in front) into the swatches list to create a tint swatch. Now lower the Tint slider to 30% and create another tint swatch.

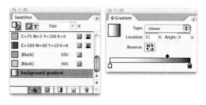

### Step 2.
Choose Window ▷ Gradient to display the Gradient palette. Choose Linear from the Gradient Type pop-up menu. Select the top-center slider and enter **72%** in the Location field. Drag the gradient icon in the upper-left corner of the Gradient palette into the Swatches palette, then double-click on the new swatch. In the Gradient Options dialog that appears, enter **background gradient** in the Swatch Name field and click OK.

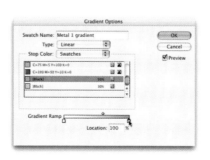

### Step 3.
Choose Duplicate Swatch from the Swatches palette fly-out menu. Double-click the background gradient copy swatch to display the Swatch Options dialog. Enter **Metal 1 gradient** in the Swatch Name field. Select the top-center slider and enter **60%** in the Location field. Select the bottom-right slider and click the 50% black swatch from the swatches list. Click OK.

**Step 4.**
Press M to access the Rectangle tool and draw a large rectangle to use as a background for the type effect. Fill it with the background gradient swatch and apply a stroke of None. Then choose Object ▷ Feather. In the dialog that appears, check the Feather option (at the top) to enable the effect. Enter **8p6** in the Feather Width field and choose Diffused from the Corners pop-up menu. Enter **2%** in the Noise field and click OK to apply.

**Step 5.**
Chose Window ▷ Layers (or press F7) to display the Layers palette. Double-click Layer 1 to display the Layer Options dialog. Enter a name for the layer (e.g., **background layer**), check the Lock Layer option, and click OK to close the dialog.

**Step 6.**
Option-click (Mac) or Alt-click (Windows) the Create New Layer button located at the bottom of the Layers palette. In the Layer Options dialog, enter a name for it (e.g., **Metal 1**) and click OK.

*continues on next page*

# The Gradient Palette

The Gradient palette lets you apply various gradient styles to selected items within your layout. This palette works closely with the Gradient tool and Swatches palette, allowing you to apply gradients to both fills and strokes on selected frames, shapes, paths, and even editable text.

To create or edit a gradient, click one of the color sliders found at the bottom of the palette. Then drag directly on top of it a color from one of these locations: from the Swatches palette list, from either swatch at the bottom of the Tools palette, or from either swatch at the top of the Swatches palette. Alternatively, you can also drag and drop a swatch anywhere on the gradient line to add a slider. Drag the gradient and color sliders left or right to alter the gradient blend. You can delete a color from the gradient by dragging its slider off the palette; however, you must always have at least two colors present.

You can save any gradients you create by dragging the gradient palette swatch directly into the Swatches palette list.

# Metal Gradient *continued*

## Filling with Gradients

To apply a gradient fill, you must first bring the Fill swatch to the forefront by clicking it in one of three places: at the bottom of the Tools palette, at the top of the Swatches palette, or in the Color palette. Then with either selection tool, proceed to select any frame, shape, or path and apply the gradient fill using any one of the following methods:

- Click directly on a gradient swatch name in the Swatches palette.

- Create a gradient using the Gradient palette.

- Choose and apply a sampled gradient with the Eyedropper tool (this also samples and applies all other object style attributes).

- Click the Apply (Last Used) Gradient button located at the bottom of the Tools palette, or press the period key.

- Apply a gradient chosen from the Swatches palette or created in the Gradient palette by clicking and dragging with the Gradient tool.

In every instance except the last, the chosen gradient fill is applied to all selected objects separately. To apply the same gradient across multiple selected objects, use the Gradient tool method described in the last bullet.

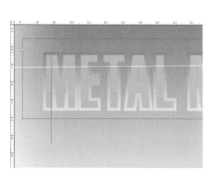

**Step 7.**

Press T to access the Type tool. Choose a bold font and large point size from the Control or Character palette (in the example here, it's Helvetica Ultra Compressed at 100pt). Create a text frame and enter some text in all caps.

**Step 8.**

Switch to the Selection tool and click the Formatting Affects Text button at the top of the Swatches palette. Click the fill icon at the top of the Swatches palette to bring it to the front and click the 30% black tint swatch. Click the stroke icon to bring it to the front and select Metal 1 gradient from the swatches list. Enter **4pt** in the Stroke Weight field of the Control palette. Enter **90°** in the Angle field of the Gradient palette.

**Step 9.**

Press G to access the Gradient tool. From about 4 picas below the bottom of the letters (see the graphic), click and drag up to the very top of the letters. Hold down the Shift key to constrain as you drag.

**Step 10.**
Click the Formatting Affects Container button and choose Object ▷ Drop Shadow. In the dialog that appears, check the Drop Shadow option (at the top) to enable the effect, and the Preview option (to the right) to see the settings applied as you enter them. Choose Multiply from the Mode pop-up menu and Swatches from the Color pop-up menu. From the Swatches list, select black. Enter **85%** for Opacity, **0p5** for Blur, and **0p7** for X and Y Offsets. Keep the Spread and Noise settings at **0p0**. Click OK to apply.

**Step 11.**
Choose Duplicate Layer Metal 1 from the Layers palette fly-out menu. In the Duplicate Layer dialog that appears, enter **Metal 2** in the Name field and click OK. Option-click (Mac) or Alt-click (Windows) the new layer to select the text frame. Choose Object ▷ Drop Shadow and uncheck the Drop Shadow option to disable the effect.

**Step 12.**
Choose Window ▷ Transparency (or press Shift+F10) to display the Transparency palette and select Color Burn from the Blending Mode pop-up menu. Lower the Opacity level to 65%.

*continues on next page*

# Applying Gradient Text Fills

To apply a gradient fill to editable text, bring the Fill swatch to the forefront by clicking it in one of three places: at the bottom of the Tools palette, at the top of the Swatches palette, or in the Color palette.

How the gradient is applied depends on how the text is selected. To apply a gradient to all editable text in the story, select any text frame (or frames) with either selection tool, and click the Formatting Affects Text button located at the bottom of the Tools palette, at the top of the Swatches palette, or in the Color palette. To apply a gradient fill to specific characters within a story, highlight them with the Type tool cursor.

Once the characters are selected, use any one of the following methods to apply a fill color:

- Click directly on a gradient swatch name in the Swatches palette.

- Create a gradient using the Gradient palette.

- Choose and apply a sampled gradient fill with the Eyedropper tool (this also samples and applies all other object style attributes).

- Click the Apply (Last Used) Gradient button located at the bottom of the Tools palette, or press the period key.

# Metal Gradient *continued*

## Applying Strokes to Objects

To apply a color or gradient stroke to a selected frame, shape, or path, bring the Stroke swatch to the forefront by clicking it in one of three places: at the bottom of the Tools palette, at the top of the Swatches palette, or in the Color palette.

Choose a stroke style and weight in either the Control or Stroke palette. Other stroke options, including alignment, start/end styles, and gap color, can be set only in the Stroke palette.

With either selection tool, proceed to select any frame, shape, or path and apply a color or gradient to the stroke using any one of the five following methods:

- Click directly on a color or gradient swatch name in the Swatches palette.

- Create a color or gradient using its palette.

- Choose a color using the Color Picker and click OK.

- Choose and apply a sampled color or gradient stroke with the Eyedropper tool (this also samples and applies all other object style attributes).

- Click the Apply (Last Used) Color or Gradient button located at the bottom of the Tools palette, or press the comma key (color) or period key (gradient).

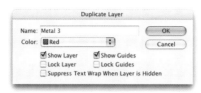

**Step 13.**
Choose Duplicate Layer Metal 2 from the Layers palette fly-out menu. In the Duplicate Layer dialog that appears, enter Metal 3 in the Name field and click OK. Option-click (Mac) or Alt-click (Windows) the new Metal 3 layer to select the text frame.

**Step 14.**
Click the Formatting Affects Text button and change the Fill and Stroke color to 100% black. Click the Formatting Affects Container button and select Overlay from the Transparency palette Blending Mode pop-up menu. Lower the Opacity level to 75%.

**Step 15.**
Choose Duplicate Layer Metal 3 from the Layers palette menu. In the Duplicate Layer dialog that appears, enter **Metal 4** in the Name field and click OK. Option-click (Mac) or Alt-click (Windows) the Metal 4 layer to select the text frame. Click the Formatting Affects Text button and click the fill icon to bring it to the front.

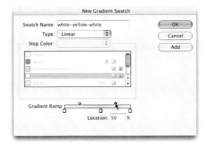

**Step 16.**

Choose New Gradient Swatch from the Swatches palette fly-out menu. Enter **white-yellow-white** in the Swatch Name field and choose Linear from the Type pop-up menu. Click on the center of the Gradient Ramp at the bottom to add another color stop. Choose Swatches from the Stop Color pop-up menu and select Yellow from the Swatches list. Enter **55%** in the Location field. Click the far-right color stop on the Gradient Ramp and choose the Paper swatch from the list. Click the top-left mid-point slider and enter **42%** in the Location field. Click the top-right mid-point slider and enter **50%** in the Location field and click OK.

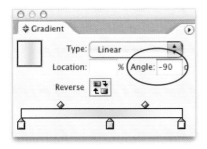

**Step 17.**

Enter **-90°** in the Angle field of the Gradient palette. Click the stroke icon in the Swatches palette to bring it to the front, then select 100% Cyan from the Swatches palette list.

*continues on next page*

## Applying Gradient Strokes to Text

To apply a gradient stroke to editable text, bring the Stroke swatch to the forefront by clicking on it in one of three places: at the bottom of the Tools palette, at the top of the Swatches palette, or in the Color palette. Enter a stroke weight in either the Control or Stroke palette.

How the gradient is applied to the stroke depends on how the text is selected. To apply a gradient stroke to all editable text in a story, select any text frame (or frames) with either selection tool, and click the Formatting Affects Text button located at the bottom of the Tools palette, at the top of the Swatches palette, or in the Color palette. To apply a stroke to specific characters within a story, highlight them with the Type tool.

Once the characters are selected, use any one of the following methods to apply a gradient to the stroke:

- Click directly on a gradient swatch name in the Swatches palette.

- Create a gradient using the Gradient palette.

- Choose and apply a sampled gradient stroke with the Eyedropper tool (this also samples all other object style attributes applied).

- Click the Apply (Last Used) Gradient button located at the bottom of the Tools palette, or press the period key (gradient).

# Metal Gradient *continued*

## Duplicating Objects

To duplicate an object, you must first select it with either selection tool, and then perform any one of the following actions:

- Copy the selected item to the Clipboard by choosing Edit ▷ Copy or pressing ⌘+C / Ctrl+C. You can then paste the object by choosing Edit ▷ Paste or pressing ⌘+V / Ctrl+V. By default, the object is placed in the center of the page, unless you choose Edit ▷ Paste In Place, which places the copy directly in front of the original.

- Choose Edit ▷ Duplicate to copy/paste a selected object all in one step. For placement, the Duplicate command uses the current Horizontal Offset and Vertical Offset values set in the Step And Repeat dialog. To duplicate and distribute several copies of a selected object, choose Edit ▷ Step And Repeat. When the dialog opens, enter settings for Repeat Count and Horizontal/Vertical Offset. Click OK to duplicate and distribute.

**Note:** As an alternative method of pasting in place, try setting the Horizontal/Vertical Offset amounts to 0p0 in the Step And Repeat dialog. This allows you to paste the duplicated object directly in front of the original when using the Duplicate command.

**Step 18.**

Click the Formatting Affects Container button in the Swatches palette, then choose Multiply from the Blending Mode pop-up menu in the Transparency palette. Change the Opacity level to 40%.

**Step 19.**

Choose Duplicate Layer Metal 4 from the Layers palette fly-out menu. In the Duplicate Layer dialog that appears, enter **white outline** in the Name field and click OK. Option-click (Mac) or Alt-click (Windows) the new layer to select the text frame.

**Step 20.**

Click the Formatting Affects Text button in the Swatches palette and apply a fill of None. Enter **1pt** in the Stroke Weight field of the Stroke palette. Click the stroke icon in the Swatches palette and choose Paper (white) from the Swatches list. Click the Formatting Affects Container button in the Swatches palette, then choose Normal from the Blending Mode pop-up menu in the Transparency palette. Change the Opacity value to 100%.

### Step 21.

Choose Object ▷ Drop Shadow. In the dialog that appears, check the Drop Shadow option (at the top) to enable the effect. Choose Multiply from the Mode pop-up menu and Swatches from the Color pop-up menu. From the Swatches list, select Black. Enter **80%** for Opacity, **0p1** for Blur, and **0p1** for X and Y Offsets. Keep the Spread and Noise settings at **0p0**. Click OK to apply.

### Step 22.

To make the metal effect look even more realistic, create a new layer and draw a small circular rivet with the Ellipse tool. Apply a 0.75pt 20% cyan stroke and a None fill. Add a Drop Shadow effect to the rivet, using the same drop shadow settings you applied to the white outline. Then duplicate the circle several times and position the circles at various points over the letters as shown in the figure.

### Step 23.

That's all there is to it! It's amazing how creative you can get just by experimenting with different gradient fills and strokes in InDesign. And the great part is that the text is still all entirely editable. You do not have to convert to outlines to apply gradient fills or strokes. Just note that if you do edit the text at this point, you'll need to reposition the rivets.

## Duplicating Objects *continued*

- Hold down the Option/Alt key and drag a selected object or objects. It doesn't get any easier than this!

- Enter a transformation value in one of the move, scale, shear, or rotation fields located in the Transform or Control palette and press Option+Return (Mac) or Alt+Enter (Windows). This transforms a copy of the original.

- You can also transform and copy through the Move, Scale, Shear, or Rotate dialogs. Access the dialog and enter your preferred settings, then click the Copy button.

- To transform and copy multiple times sequentially, make your initial transformation, and then choose Object ▷ Transform ▷ Transform Again or press Option+⌘+3 / Alt+Ctrl+3. Continue to apply the command as many times as needed.

# Put Your Logo in Lights

The next time one of your clients wants the superstar treatment (don't they all?), try using this effect. By creating a custom dotted-stroke style and applying it to several layers of text in contrasting colors, you can place your logo in lights—just like on the Vegas strip.

Stroke styles are somewhat of a hidden feature in InDesign. You can access the Stroke Styles dialog from the Stroke palette fly-out menu. From this dialog you can create custom striped, dashed, or dotted strokes. Every stroke style you create appears in the Stroke Type pop-up menu. You can then apply custom stroke styles to selected frames, shapes, paths, or text objects.

This type effect works best when applied to large, bold typefaces, just as you would see on a real marquee. The glow of the lights can be created using contrasting colors, layers, gradients, and feather and drop shadow effects.

## The Stroke Style Lighting Effect

With these steps we'll create a custom dotted stroke style and use it along with layers and contrasting colors to simulate a Vegas-style marquee lighting effect.

**Step 1.**
Choose Window ▷ Swatches (or press F5) to display the Swatches palette. Click the fill icon to bring it to the front. Choose New Color Swatch from the Swatches palette fly-out menu. Choose Process from the Color Type pop-up menu and CMYK from the Color Mode pop-up menu. Create a dark blue color (e.g., C=100 M=98 Y=27 K=49). Click OK to add the swatch and close the dialog.

**Step 2.**
Press M to access the Rectangle tool. Draw a large rectangle to use as a background for the effect.

**Step 3.**
Choose Window ▷ Layers (or press F7) to display the Layers palette. Double-click Layer 1 to display the Layer Options dialog. Enter a name for the layer (e.g., **background**), check the Lock Layer option, and click OK to close the dialog.

### Step 4.
Option-click (Mac) or Alt-click (Windows) the Create New Layer button located at the bottom of the Layers palette. In the Layer Options dialog, enter a name for it (e.g., **color layer**) and click OK.

### Step 5.
Press T to access the Type tool and create a text frame. Click the Paper (white) swatch in the Swatches palette list. Choose a bold font and large point size from the Control or Character palette (in the example here, it's Futura Extra Bold Condensed at 92pt). Enter some text in all caps. Choose Optical Kerning and a Tracking amount of 40, then choose Type ▷ Create Outlines.

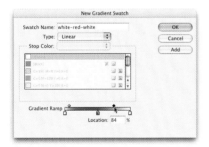

### Step 6.
Choose New Gradient Swatch from the Swatches palette fly-out menu. Enter **white-red-white** in the Swatch Name field and choose Linear from the Type pop-up menu. Click on the center of the Gradient Ramp to add another color stop and enter the setting C=15 M=100 Y=100 K=0. Enter **50%** in the Location field. Click the far-right color stop on the Gradient Ramp and choose the Paper swatch from the list. Click the top-left mid-point slider and enter **13%** in the Location field. Click the top-right mid-point slider, enter **84%** in the Location field, and click OK.

## Optical vs. Metrics Kerning

InDesign offers two different types of auto kerning: Metrics and Optical. You can choose either method from the fly-out menu located in the Character or Control palette. (Note: Character and Paragraph attributes can only be accessed in the Control palette when working with the Type tool.)

Metrics kerning relies on paired values built into the font by the font's designer. Depending on how well the font's designer prepared the built-in paired kerning values, Metrics may or may not be the most effective method of auto kerning. More often than not, you'll find that the font's designer could have done a much better job.

Optical kerning applies spacing amounts based on character outlines. In general, this results in much more even character spacing than Metrics kerning.

To apply either auto-kerning method, select all of the text in the story with the Type tool and choose Metrics or Optical from the Kerning pop-up menu in the Character or Control palette. You can also apply auto-kerning to all of the text in a single, unthreaded text frame by selecting the frame with either selection tool and choosing Metrics or Optical.

*continues on next page*

# Put Your Logo in Lights *continued*

## Stroke Styles

One of the hidden features of InDesign is the ability to create, save, and apply custom stroke styles.

To create a custom stripe, dash, or dotted stroke, choose Stroke Styles from the Stroke palette fly-out menu. The Stroke Styles dialog appears and displays a list of noneditable default stroke styles. Click the New button to create a whole new stroke style.

When the New Stroke Style dialog opens, click the Stroke Type pop-up menu and choose Stripe, Dash, or Dotted. Each one has its own set of controls, which displays in the dialog once selected.

The Type and Preview sections of the dialog change when a selection is made from the Stroke Type pop-up menu. Enter the preferred settings and refer to the window below for a preview of how the stroke will look once applied. To save your style, enter a name for it and click the Add button.

InDesign displays your new styles at the bottom of the Stroke Styles dialog Styles list. When you've finished creating and editing, click OK.

To apply your new stroke style, select any frame, shape, or path with either selection tool and choose it from the Stroke Type pop-up menu in the Stroke palette.

**Step 7.**
Press G to access the Gradient tool, hold down the Shift key, and click and drag along the vertical height of the letters as shown.

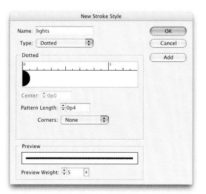

**Step 8.**
Choose Window ▷ Stroke (or press F10) to display the Stroke palette. Choose Stroke Styles from the Stroke palette fly-out menu. In the Stroke Styles dialog, click New. Enter lights in the Name field and choose Dotted from the Stroke Type pop-up menu. Enter **0p4** into the Pattern Length field and choose None from the Corners pop-up menu. Click OK to add the stroke style and close the dialog. Click OK to close the Stroke Styles dialog.

**Step 9.**
Press X to bring the stroke icon to the front. In the Stroke palette, enter **6pt** in the Weight field, and choose lights from the Stroke Type pop-up menu. Click the 100% yellow swatch in the Swatches palette.

**Step 10.**

Choose Object ▷ Feather. In the dialog that appears, check the Feather option (at the top) to enable the effect. Enter 0p10 in the Feather Width field and choose Diffused from the Corners pop-up menu. Keep the Noise setting at 0p0 and click OK to apply.

**Step 11.**

Choose Object ▷ Drop Shadow. In the dialog that appears, check the Drop Shadow option (at the top) to enable the effect and the Preview option (to the right) to see the settings applied as you enter them. Choose Hard Light from the Mode pop-up menu and Swatches from the Color pop-up menu. Select 100% yellow from the Swatches list. Enter **70%** for Opacity, **0p10** for Blur, and **0p0** for X and Y Offsets. Enter **30%** for Spread and keep the Noise setting at **0p0**. Click OK to apply.

**Step 12.**

Choose Duplicate Layer color layer from the Layers palette fly-out menu. In the Duplicate Layer dialog that appears, enter **shadow** in the Name field and click OK. Option-click (Mac) or Alt-click (Windows) the new layer to select the character outline.

# Gap Color and Open Stroke Styles

Open stroke styles contain gaps between stripes, dashes, or dots. These gaps can be filled with solid colors, tints, or gradients. Try playing around with this some and you'll find that combining gap color with stroke color can create some interesting effects.

To apply a gap color to an open stroke style, select the stroked object with either selection tool and choose a color or gradient from the Gap Color pop-up menu located in the Stroke palette. The Gap Color pop-up menu contains the same colors and gradients as the Swatches palette. Once chosen, the color or gradient is applied immediately.

To apply a tint to a chosen gap color, enter a value in the Gap Tint field located at the bottom of the Stroke palette or use the slider control. A tint can only be applied to solid colors and not gradients.

**Note:** It is also possible to apply a gradient swatch to an open stroke's gap color.

*continues on next page*

# Put Your Logo in Lights *continued*

## Stroked Path Start and End Styles

To apply a stroke start and end style to a selected line or path, open the Stroke palette and choose options from the Start and/or End pop-up menus. The chosen style is immediately applied. You can apply a start style without an end style and vice versa–or apply both–so have fun experimenting with different combinations.

Start and end styles can be applied with any chosen stroke type, but cannot be saved as part of a stroke style. However, to make up for it, they can be saved as part of an object style.

Keep in mind that stroke path start and end styles can be applied to any open custom and freeform drawn paths and lines, which makes it possible to get really creative with your design elements.

**Note:** Start and end styles can only be applied to lines and open paths–not closed paths, frames, and shapes.

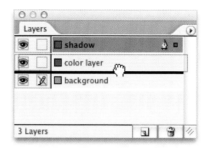

**Step 13.**
In the Layers palette, position the shadow layer underneath the color layer. Then apply a fill color of None and a stroke color of Paper (white).

**Step 14.**
Choose Object ▷ Drop Shadow. In the dialog, choose Multiply from the Mode pop-up menu and change the Opacity level to 100%. Choose black from the swatches list and enter **0p4** for Blur, and **0p3** for X and Y Offsets. Enter **0p0** for both the Spread and Noise settings and click OK to apply.

**Step 15.**
Press V to access the Selection tool. Using the Arrow keys, nudge the character outline 3 increments down and to the right. Choose Object ▷ Feather. In the dialog that appears, enter **2p3** in the Feather Width field and click OK to apply.

### Step 16.

In the Layers palette, select the color layer. Choose Duplicate Layer color layer from the Layers palette fly-out menu. In the Duplicate Layer dialog that appears, enter **lights** in the Name field and click OK. Option-click (Mac) or Alt-click (Windows) the new layer to select the character outline.

### Step 17.

In the Control or Stroke palette, enter **4pt** in the Stroke Weight field and choose lights from the Stroke Type pop-up menu. Apply a stroke color of Paper (white). That's all there is to it! Your logo is now in lights.

## Using Default Object Styles

Every document contains three default object styles: Basic Graphics Frame, Basic Text Frame, and None. By default, the Basic Text Frame style is applied to any new text frame created with the Type tool; the Basic Graphics Frame style is applied to any new shapes drawn with the Shape, Pen, and Pencil tools; and the None style is applied to any new frame drawn with the Frame tools.

To change the object style defaults, choose Default Text/Graphic Frame Style from the Object Styles palette fly-out menu and select a different style from the list. You can also change defaults by dragging the object type icon (text or graphics) from the current default style in the palette to another.

To set the default Object Style for text or graphics, select a style from the Object Style palette with nothing selected in the document.

The Basic Graphics Frame and Basic Text Frame object styles can be edited but not deleted. The None style cannot be edited or deleted.

# "Gel-ly" Type

The "gel" effect has been around for a while. Gel buttons are a popular web graphic effect, and if you're a Mac user, you've no doubt seen it used as part of the OS X interface. "Gel-ly" effects are definitely "in" and can also be used with type.

Gel effects can be created in Photoshop using layer styles, gradients, blur effects, and blending modes. Similarly, they can also be created in InDesign using layers, feather and drop shadow effects, and blending modes. In order to get that toothpaste (or liquid gel) look and feel, try applying this effect to a rounded typeface.

You'll also want to use bright colors. In the example here it's 100% cyan over a white background. Because we are working with transparent blending modes with this effect, using different background and text-fill colors can produce entirely different results. However, don't be afraid to experiment. You might come up with a winning combination!

## Toothpaste, Cold Medicine, and Your Logo

With these steps, we'll create "gel-ly" type using layers, feather and drop shadow effects, and blending modes.

**Step 1.**

Press T to access the Type tool and create a text frame. Choose Window ▷ Swatches (or press F5) to display the Swatches palette. Click the fill icon to bring it to the front and then click the 100% Cyan swatch in the Swatches palette list. Press X to bring the stroke icon to the front and press the forward slash key (/) to apply None. Choose a bold font and large point size from the Control or Character palette (in the example here, it's VAG Rounded Black at 82pt).

**Step 2.**

Enter some text in all caps. Choose Optical kerning and a tracking amount of 1Step 20. Place a paragraph return between the two words and enter a Leading amount of 78 in the Control or Character palette.

**Step 3.**

Switch to the Selection tool. Choose Object ▷ Drop Shadow. In the dialog that appears, check the Drop Shadow option to enable the effect. Choose Multiply from the Mode pop-up menu and set the Opacity level to 100%. Choose 100% cyan from the Swatches list and enter 0p7 for Blur. Enter 0p0 for X Offset and 0p5 for Y Offset. Enter 14% for Spread and 4% for Noise. Click OK to apply.

**Step 4.**

Choose Window ▷ Layers (or press F7) to display the Layers palette. Double-click Layer 1 to display the Layer Options dialog. Enter a name for the layer (e.g., **blue shadow**). Click OK to close the dialog.

**Step 5.**

Choose Duplicate Layer blue shadow from the Layers palette fly-out menu. In the Duplicate Layer dialog that appears, enter **white screen** in the Name field and click OK. Option-click (Mac) or Alt-click (Windows) the new layer to select the text frame.

**Step 6.**

Click the Formatting Affects Text button at the top of the Swatches palette. Press X to bring the fill icon to the front and click Paper (white) in the Swatches palette list to apply a white fill. Click the Formatting Affects Container button and choose Object ▷ Drop Shadow. In the dialog that appears, deselect the Drop Shadow option to disable the effect.

*continues on next page*

## Adjusting Leading

Leading reflects the vertical space between baselines of a paragraph (the imaginary lines that each row of characters sits on top of). Increasing the leading pushes baselines farther away from each other and decreasing it brings them closer together.

Unlike QuarkXPress, InDesign treats leading as a character attribute and not as a paragraph attribute. However, you can tell InDesign to treat leading as a paragraph attribute (as it would in Quark) by enabling the Apply Leading To Entire Paragraphs option from the Type Preferences dialog. Enabling this option applies the same leading value to all characters in a paragraph. To get the best of both worlds with this option, keep it enabled and only turn it off to make leading adjustments to individual lines. When you turn the option back on in Type Preferences, the newly applied leading values do not reset.

# "Gel-ly" Type *continued*

## Auto Leading

When you choose Auto from the Leading fly-out menu, InDesign applies a leading value based on a percentage of the largest character on a line. This can often result in uneven leading amounts that appear awkward in your layout. Therefore, it is best to avoid using the Auto Leading feature. (When Auto Leading is being used, the leading value appears in parentheses in the Character and Control palettes.)

**Step 7.**
Choose Object ▷ Feather. In the dialog that appears, check the Feather option (at the top) to enable the effect. Enter **0p6** in the Feather Width field and choose Diffused from the Corners pop-up menu. Enter **2%** in the Noise field and click OK to apply.

**Step 8.**
Choose Window ▷ Transparency (or press Shift+F10) to display the Transparency palette. Choose Screen from the Blending Mode pop-up menu and lower the Opacity value to 95%.

**Step 9.**
Choose Duplicate Layer white screen from the Layers palette fly-out menu. In the Duplicate Layer dialog that appears, enter **blue overlay** in the Name field and click OK. Option-click (Mac) or Alt-click (Windows) the new layer to select the text frame.

**Step 10.**
Click the Formatting Affects Text button at the bottom of the Tools palette and press the comma key (,) to apply a fill color of 100% cyan.

## Baseline Shift

There may be times when you need to select and move individual characters above or below the baseline. Examples include centering a large lead-in character, such as a bullet point, or repositioning a drop cap that uses an ornate script font.

To shift the baseline of an individual character, select it with the Type tool and enter a value in the Baseline Shift field in the Character palette and Control palette. Entering a positive value positions the selected character farther above the baseline and entering a negative value positions it farther below.

**Step 11.**
Choose Object ▷ Feather. In the dialog that appears, change the Feather Width amount to **1p9** and choose Sharp from the Corners pop-up menu. Click OK to apply. In the Transparency palette, choose Color Burn from the Blending Mode pop-up menu and increase the Opacity value back up to 100%.

**Note:** You can set the default keyboard increment amount for baseline shift in the Units & Increments panel of the Preferences dialog.

**Step 12.**
Choose Duplicate Layer blue overlay from the Layers palette fly-out menu. In the Duplicate Layer dialog that appears, enter **outer glow** in the Name field and click OK. Option-click (Mac) or Alt-click (Windows) the new layer to select the text frame.

*continues on next page*

# "Gel-ly" Type *continued*

## Accessing Colors Stored in Libraries

You can access colors stored in swatch libraries (such as Pantone colors) through the Color Mode pop-up menu of the New Color Swatch dialog. To access the dialog, choose New Color Swatch from the Swatches palette fly-out menu.

From the Color Mode pop-up menu, choose a swatch library to display. To save a library color in the Swatches palette and close the dialog, select it from the list and click OK. To save the color in the Swatches palette without closing the dialog, click the Add button. You can then continue selecting library swatches and adding them to the palette.

If you know the number of a specific library swatch that you'd like to locate and use, enter it in the search field and let InDesign select it for you. Hover the cursor over any swatch name in the library list and a tooltip displays its color build.

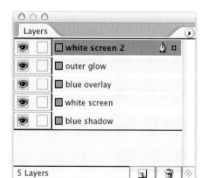

**Step 13.**
Click the Formatting Affects Text button at the bottom of the Tools palette and press the forward slash key (/) to apply a fill of None. Press X to bring the stroke icon to the front and press the comma key (,) to apply a stroke color of 100% cyan. Enter **5pt** in the Stroke Weight field of the Control palette.

**Step 14.**
Click the Formatting Affects Container button at the bottom of the Tools palette and choose Object ▷ Feather. In the dialog that appears, change the Feather Width amount to 0p8 and choose Diffused from the Corners pop-up menu. Click OK to apply. Choose Difference from the Transparency palette Blending Mode pop-up menu and lower the Opacity level to 30%.

**Step 15.**
In the Layers palette, select the white screen layer and choose Duplicate Layer from the Layer palette fly-out menu. In the Duplicate Layer dialog that appears, enter **white screen 2** in the Name field and click OK. Position the new white screen 2 layer at the top of the layer list. Option-click (Mac) or Alt-click (Windows) the new layer to select the text frame.

**Step 16.**

Choose Object ▷ Feather. In the dialog that appears, change the Feather Width amount to 1pStep 1. Click OK to apply.

**Step 17.**

Choose Object ▷ Drop Shadow. In the dialog that appears, check the Drop Shadow option to enable the effect. Choose Overlay from the Mode pop-up menu and set the Opacity level to 50%. Choose Paper (white) from the Swatches list and enter **0p3** for Blur. Enter **0p0** for both the X and Y Offsets. Keep the Spread and Noise settings at **0p0** and click OK to apply.

**Step 18.**

Create a new layer and add some type to complete the design.

## Converting Spot Colors to Process

You can convert spot colors to process using the Ink Manager, or by changing a selected color's mode and type settings in the Swatch Options dialog.

The Ink Manager converts spot colors to process during output without changing the color swatch definitions in the document. To convert spot colors to process using the Ink Manager, choose Ink Manager from the Swatches palette fly-out menu. Locate a spot color from the list and click its color mode icon in the far-left column to toggle from spot to process. To convert all spot colors in the document to process, check the All Spots to Process option in the bottom left of the dialog.

Unlike with the Ink Manager, converting a spot color to process using the Swatch Options dialog actually alters the swatch definition in the document. To convert a spot color to process using the Swatch Options dialog, select a spot color from the Swatches palette and choose Swatch Options from the palette menu. Choose CMYK from the Color Mode pop-up menu and Process from the Color Type pop-up menu. Click OK to convert the color and close the dialog.

# Neon Type

In Adobe Photoshop, you can re-create the glow of neon using photo-realistic illustration techniques. Even though InDesign does not offer as many illustration tools and effects as Photoshop, you can still create a neon glow and apply it to type. Using multiple layers of brightly colored type over a dark background and applying feather effects and blending modes, you can make type glow on your page just like a neon sign.

In order to get that neon look and feel, try applying this effect to a rounded, sans-serif typeface, such as VAG rounded or OCRA. Also, be sure to increase the tracking amount in order to create extra space between the letters, just as on a real neon sign.

This effect also works best when placed over a background color of 100% rich black. You can choose to preview and output 100% black as rich black under Preferences ▷ Appearance Of Black.

## Boldly Glow Where No One Has Gone Before ...

... at least not in InDesign! With these steps, we'll create neon type using layers, feather and drop shadow effects, and blending modes.

**Step 1.**
Start out by drawing a rectangle with the Rectangle tool and filling it with 100% black. You can use this as a background for the effect.

**Step 2.**
Choose Window ▷ Layers (or press F7) to display the Layers palette. Double-click Layer 1 to display the Layer Options dialog. Enter a name for the layer (e.g., **black background**). Check the Lock Layer option and click OK to close the dialog.

**Step 3.**
Option-click (Mac) or Alt-click (Windows) the Create New Layer button at the bottom of the Layers palette. In the Layer Options dialog, enter a name for the layer (e.g., **outer glow**) and click OK.

**Step 4.**

Press T to access the Type tool and create a text frame. In the Swatches palette, click the fill icon to bring it to the front and then click the green swatch in the Swatches list. Press X to bring the stroke icon to the front and click the green swatch again. Choose a bold font and large point size from the Control or Character palette (in the example here, it's OCRA Standard Medium at 92pt).

**Step 5.**

Press ⌘+Shift+C / Ctrl+Shift+C to align center and enter some text in all caps (e.g., **ALIEN DREAMS**). Choose Optical Kerning and a Tracking amount of 1Step 20. Place a paragraph return between the two words and enter a Leading amount of **103** in the Control or Character palette. Enter a large stroke weight in the Stroke Weight field of the Control or Stroke palette (the example uses 16pt). Be careful not to apply a stroke that is too thick for the chosen font, as it could potentially ruin the effect.

**Step 6.**

Switch to the Selection tool and choose Object ▷ Feather. In the dialog that appears, check the Feather option to enable the effect. Enter **6p4** in the Feather Width field and choose Sharp from the Corners pop-up menu. Click OK to apply. Choose Window ▷ Transparency (or press Shift+F10) to display the Transparency palette, and choose Screen from the Blending Mode pop-up menu.

*continues on next page*

## Check Spelling

To check spelling with the Check Spelling palette, choose Edit ▷ Spelling ▷ Check Spelling or press ⌘+I / Ctrl+I.

At the bottom of the palette, you can choose to search for misspelled words in a selected story, document, word selection, to the end of a selected story, or in all open documents (if you have more than one open). You can also select from a list of user dictionaries that appears at the top of the palette. The palette also checks the spelling of any overset text when searching a story or document.

In the Change To data field, enter the correct spelling or choose from the list of suggested corrections (if available). Click the Change button to correct the word in the document and continue the spelling check. To correct every occurrence of the word within the search parameters, click Change All.

You can also add words to a chosen user dictionary so that they do not come up in future spelling checks. To do so, click Add.

# Neon Type *continued*

## Dynamic Spelling and Autocorrect

It is also possible to enable the Dynamic Spelling feature, which underlines any found spelling check errors in assigned colors as you type, or upon text import. You can turn this option on or off under Edit  Spelling  Dynamic Spelling or in Spelling Preferences.

To automatically correct misspelled words as you type, enable the Autocorrect feature under Edit ▷ Spelling ▷ Autocorrect or in Autocorrect Preferences. Autocorrect only fixes misspelled words that are added to the list in Autocorrect Preferences.

When enabled, Autocorrect fixes capitalization errors for all words located in the default and user dictionaries, not just for words that are added to the Autocorrect Preferences list.

**Note:** Unlike the Dynamic Spelling feature, Autocorrect only works as you type and not upon text import.

**Step 7.**
Choose Duplicate Layer outer glow from the Layers palette menu. In the Duplicate Layer dialog that appears, enter **inner glow** in the Name field and click OK. Option-click (Mac) or Alt-click (Windows) the new inner glow layer to select the text frame.

**Step 8.**
Click the Formatting Affects Text button at the top of the Swatches palette. Change the Stroke Weight size to 6pt. Click the Formatting Affects Container button and choose Object ▷ Feather. In the dialog that appears, change the Feather Width amount to 1pStep 10. Click OK to apply.

**Step 9.**
Choose Object ▷ Drop Shadow. In the dialog that appears, check the Drop Shadow option to enable the effect. Choose Screen from the Mode pop-up menu and set the Opacity level to 90%. Choose Paper (white) from the Swatches list and enter **0p9** for Blur. Enter **0p0** for the X and Y Offsets. Keep the Spread and Noise settings at **0p0** and click OK to apply. In the Transparency palette, change the blending mode to Hard Light.

### Step 10.

Choose Duplicate Layer inner glow from the Layers palette menu. In the Duplicate Layer dialog that appears, enter **green overlay** in the Name field and click OK. Option-click (Mac) or Alt-click (Windows) the new green overlay layer to select the text frame.

### Step 11.

Choose Object ▷ Drop Shadow. In the dialog that appears, deselect the Drop Shadow option to disable the effect. Click OK to apply.

### Step 12.

Choose Duplicate Layer green overlay from the Layers palette menu. In the Duplicate Layer dialog that appears, enter **color dodge** in the Name field and click OK. Option-click (Mac) or Alt-click (Windows) the new color dodge layer to select the text frame.

*continues on next page*

# Editing the Dictionary

Proper names, technical terms, abbreviations, and various other slang words are not included in InDesign's default dictionary. To avoid having these words show up repeatedly when running a spelling check, try adding them to a saved user dictionary.

You can add words to user dictionaries as you're running a spelling check. To add words as the Check Spelling palette locates them, select a user dictionary from the Add To menu and click the Add button. To access and edit user dictionaries with the Dictionary palette while spell checking, click the Dictionary button.

Choose a dictionary to edit from the Target menu located at the top of the Dictionary palette. You must also choose a language to edit with from the Language menu. From the Dictionary List menu, choose to display Added Words, Removed Words, or Ignored Words.

Dynamic Spelling and the Check Spelling palette cannot locate Added Words unless they are spelled incorrectly. Removed Words are erased from the dictionary but can always be added back. Ignored Words are still in the dictionary, but go unnoticed by the Check Spelling palette or Dynamic Spelling.

# Neon Type *continued*

## Using the Dictionary with Foreign Languages

With InDesign, it is not only possible to use more than one language in a document—you can even mix languages in the same paragraph! There are 28 languages to choose from in the built-in user dictionary. To apply any other languages you must purchase a special language edition of InDesign CS2.

InDesign sees applied languages as a character attribute, unlike QuarkXPress Passport, which considers language a paragraph attribute. You can choose a language to apply to selected text from the Character palette (you must show all options in the palette to access the Language menu) or from the Control palette (when working with the Type tool).

You can then check spelling for multiple languages in the same paragraph. The Check Spelling palette refers to all available dictionaries when different languages have been applied.

You can select a default language for the document under Dictionary Preferences. It is also possible to edit foreign dictionaries using the Dictionary palette.

**Step 13.**
Click the Formatting Affects Text button at the top of the Swatches palette. Change the Stroke Weight size to 3pt. Click the Formatting Affects Container button and choose Object ▷ Feather. In the dialog that appears, deselect the Feather option to disable and click OK to apply. In the Transparency palette, change the blending mode to Color Dodge.

**Step 14.**
Choose Duplicate Layer color dodge from the Layers palette menu. In the Duplicate Layer dialog that appears, enter **soft light** in the Name field and click OK. Option-click (Mac) or Alt-click (Windows) the new soft light layer to select the text frame.

**Step 15.**
In the Transparency palette, change the blending mode to Soft Light and set the Opacity level to 60%.

**Step 16.**
Choose Duplicate Layer soft light from the Layers palette menu. In the Duplicate Layer dialog that appears, enter **white overlay** in the Name field and click OK. Option-click (Mac) or Alt-click (Windows) the new soft light layer to select the text frame.

**Step 17.**
Click the Formatting Affects Text button at the top of the Swatches palette. Change the Stroke color to Paper (white) and the Fill color to None. Click the Formatting Affects Container button and, in the Transparency palette, change the blending mode to Overlay and set the Opacity level to 100%.

**Step 18.**
To add to the neon logo, create a duplicate of the text frame on a separate layer. Select the duplicate and choose Type ▷ Create Outlines. Draw some white lines with the Line or Pen tool, then group and nest them into the character outline (see the Grunge Type tutorial earlier in this chapter for more on nesting). Set the blending mode of the new layer to Screen in the Transparency palette. As a last step, add an ellipse by drawing one with the Ellipse tool. Add a Step 1.5 white stroke and a None fill. Press R to access the Rotate tool and rotate the ellipse 23°.

## The Font Menu

You can apply any font loaded on your system to selected text through the Type ▷ Font submenu or the Character or Control palette Font pop-up menus. To access the Font menu in the Control palette, you must first access the Type tool from the Tools palette.

Select a font family and accompanying type style (if available) from the respective menus. Unlike in QuarkXPress, no bold or italic type style controls are available in the Character or Control palette. You can only apply a bold or italic type style if it is part of a chosen font family.

The Font menu list also displays a PostScript, TrueType, or Open Type icon before each font name as well as a sample preview. You can choose to display sample previews at small, medium, or large sizes under Type Preferences.

# Spray Stencil

Even though there are no brush tools in InDesign—like the ones found in Photoshop, Illustrator, and Corel Painter—you can still create paintlike effects. We won't let a little thing like not having any brush tools stop us from painting—we'll make our own instead!

By applying noise to InDesign's feather and drop shadow effects, you can simulate the look and feel of spray paint. The effect works especially well when applied to the Stencil typeface. To add smudges, highlights, and ink spots, you can use object styles as brush settings and paint with the Pencil tool.

This effect works great on type that is placed over a colored background. However, don't be afraid to experiment with the blend mode, noise, and opacity settings and apply it to type that is placed over an image (such as a wood texture).

## Painting with Noise and Object Styles

With these steps, we'll use layers, feathers and drop shadows, blending modes, objects styles, and the Pencil tool to create a stencil spray paint effect.

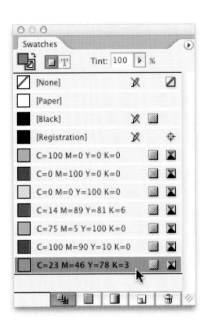

**Step 1.**
Choose Window ▷ Swatches (or press F5) to display the Swatches palette. Click the fill icon to bring it to the front. Choose New Color Swatch from the Swatches palette fly-out menu. Choose Process from the Color Type pop-up menu and CMYK from the Color Mode pop-up menu. Create a brown color (e.g., C=23 M=46 Y=78 K=3). Click OK to add the swatch and close the dialog.

**Step 2.**
Press M to access the Rectangle tool. Draw a large rectangle to use as a background for the effect.

**Step 3.**
Choose Window ▷ Layers (or press F7) to display the Layers palette. Double-click Layer 1 to display the Layer Options dialog. Enter a name for the layer (e.g., **background**), check the Lock Layer option, and click OK to close the dialog.

**Step 4.**
Option-click (Mac) or Alt-click (Windows) the Create New Layer button located at the bottom of the Layers palette. In the Layer Options dialog, enter a name for it (e.g., **spray paint 1**) and click OK.

**Step 5.**
Press T to access the Type tool. Create a large text frame and click the brown swatch in the Swatches palette list. Press X to bring the stroke icon to the front and click the red swatch. Enter **0.5pt** in the Stroke Weight field of the Control palette. Choose a bold font and large point size from the Control or Character palette (in the example here, I used Stencil at 87pt). Enter some text in all caps. Choose Optical Kerning and a Tracking amount of **200**.

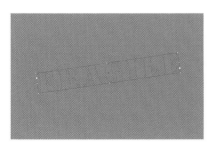

**Step 6.**
Enter a setting of 8° in the Rotation field of the Control or Transform palette.

# Selecting Type

To select editable type characters, you must use the Type tool. Click an insertion point in any text frame with the cursor, and then highlight the characters by clicking and dragging over them.

You can also select editable text by clicking with the mouse:

- Double-clicking selects a single word.

- Triple-clicking selects a line if the Triple Click To Select A Line option is enabled in Type Preferences; otherwise it selects the entire paragraph.

- Clicking four times selects the entire paragraph if the Triple Click To Select A Line option is enabled; otherwise it selects the entire story.

- Clicking five times selects the entire story when the Triple Click To Select A Line option is enabled in Type Preferences. It's also a surefire way to trash your mouse hand. Therefore, you may want to try using ⌘+A / Ctrl+A—a better and faster way to select the entire story.

*continues on next page*

# Spray Stencil *continued*

## Selecting Multiple Objects

To select multiple objects, access either of the selection tools and Shift-click the items on the page, or hold down the Shift key and marquee over an area that includes the objects you would like to select. You can tell that the objects are selected when the boundary nodes of the frame or shape appear. Shift-click again to deselect.

You can select the contents of multiple frames by Shift-clicking with the Direct Selection tool. You can also add other objects to a selection, such as text frames, shapes, and lines, by continuing to hold down Shift as you click.

Once selected, multiple objects (including points on a path) can be moved simultaneously by dragging the mouse or pressing the arrow keys. To resize the selected objects, press S to switch to the Scale tool, then click and drag. You can also rotate, shear, and free transform multiple selected objects.

**Step 7.**

Switch to the Selection tool and choose Object ▷ Drop Shadow. In the dialog that appears, check the Drop Shadow option to enable the effect. Choose Multiply from the Mode pop-up menu and set the Opacity level to 75%. Choose the red swatch from the Swatches list and enter **1p** for Blur. Enter **0p0** for the X and Y Offsets. Enter **35%** for Spread and **5%** for Noise, and click OK to apply.

**Step 8.**

Choose Object ▷ Feather. In the dialog that appears, check the Feather option to enable the effect. Enter **1p1** in the Feather Width field and choose Sharp from the Corners pop-up menu. Enter **10%** in the Noise field and click OK to apply. Choose Window ▷ Transparency (or press Shift+F10) to display the Transparency palette, and choose Overlay from the Blending Mode pop-up menu.

**Step 9.**

Choose Duplicate Layer spray paint 1 from the Layers palette menu. In the Duplicate Layer dialog that appears, enter **spray paint 2** in the Name field and click OK. Option-click (Mac) or Alt-click (Windows) the new spray paint 2 layer to select the text frame.

**Step 10.**

In the Transparency palette, choose Normal from the Blending Mode pop-up menu.

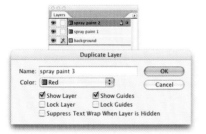

**Step 11.**

Choose Duplicate Layer spray paint 2 from the Layers palette menu. In the Duplicate Layer dialog that appears, enter **spray paint 3** in the Name field and click OK. Option-click (Mac) or Alt-click (Windows) the new spray paint 3 layer to select the text frame.

**Step 12.**

Choose Object ▷ Drop Shadow. In the dialog that appears, change the Opacity level to 40% and click OK to apply. In the Transparency palette, choose Soft Light from the Blending Mode pop-up menu and lower the Opacity level to 60%. Our logo is starting to look like spray-painted stencil, but it's still too perfect—let's dirty it up some.

*continues on next page*

## Drawing Freeform Shapes

To create a freeform shape using the Pencil tool, press N to access it from the Tools palette and begin drawing. As you draw, InDesign calculates where the points fall on the path and places them for you. You can then switch to the Pen toolset and adjust the placed points, or use the Smooth and Erase tools to edit.

Entering specific settings in the Pencil tool Preferences dialog before you begin drawing can eliminate the need for editing and smoothing of points later. To access the dialog, double-click the Pencil tool icon in the Tools palette.

Lower Fidelity and Smoothness values result in jagged paths. Higher Fidelity and Smoothness values result in cleaner paths.

The Smooth tool has a similar set of preferences that you can access by double-clicking the Smooth tool icon in the Tools palette.

# Spray Stencil *continued*

## Creating Object Styles

There are three ways to set up an object style: from scratch, by basing the new style on an object you've selected, or by basing it on an existing style:

- To create an object style from scratch–with no attributes already set–make sure that no object is selected and no style is highlighted in the palette, then Option/Alt-click the Create New Style button at the bottom of the Object Styles palette or choose New Object Style from the palette menu.

- To create an object style and have it start out inheriting all the attributes of another style, make sure that no object is selected, highlight the existing style in the Object Styles palette, then click the Create New Style button or choose New Object Style from the palette menu.

- To create an object style and have it start out using all the attributes of an object that has already been formatted locally, select the object or text frame with either selection tool, then Option/Alt-click the Create New Style button. This is probably the easiest way to create a new style.

**Step 13.**
Option-click (Mac) or Alt-click (Windows) the Create New Layer button at the bottom of the Layers palette. In the Layer Options dialog, enter **smudges** in the Name field and click OK. Choose Edit ▷ Deselect All.

**Step 14.**
Choose Window ▷ Object Styles (or press ⌘+F7 / Ctrl+F7) to display the Object Styles palette. Choose New Object Style from the palette fly-out menu. In the dialog that appears, enter **spray paint brown** in the Style Name field. Choose None from the Based On pop-up menu. From the list on the left, select the first five options (Fill through Drop Shadow & Feather) and deselect the rest. To edit the settings for a category, click on the category name. By clicking on the respective categories, apply a Fill of None and an 8pt brown Stroke. In the Transparency panel, set the Opacity level to 85%. In the Drop Shadow & Feather panel, check the Feather option to enable the effect and enter **1p9** in the Feather Width field. Choose Sharp from the Corners pop-up menu and enter **10%** in the Noise field. Click OK to close the dialog.

**Step 15.**

Double-click the Pencil tool icon in the Tools palette to display the Pencil tool Preferences dialog. Enter a setting of **10** pixels in the Fidelity field and **71%** in the Smoothness field.

**Step 16.**

Select the spray paint brown object style from the Object Styles palette and proceed to draw random smudge marks over the stencil letters like those shown in the figure.

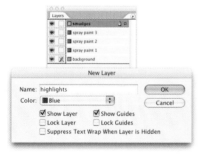

**Step 17.**

Option-click (Mac) or Alt-click (Windows) the Create New Layer button at the bottom of the Layers palette. In the Layer Options dialog, enter **highlights** in the Name field and click OK. Choose Edit ⊳ Deselect All.

*continues on next page*

## The New Object Style Dialog

Any time you create a new object style, you're presented with the New Object Style dialog, where you can enter your preferred settings. Each of this dialog's panels mirror the formatting controls located in the corresponding palette or dialog. You can access a panel by clicking its name in the menu to the left.

Type a name for the style and add or remove any formatting using the different panels of the options dialog or by checking/unchecking any of the attribute options listed in the menu. Click the category arrows in the Style Settings portion of the General panel to display a summary of applied attributes.

Click OK when you've finished defining the style to add it to the Object Styles palette list.

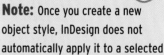

**Note:** Once you create a new object style, InDesign does not automatically apply it to a selected object. You must do so manually.

# Spray Stencil *continued*

## Applying Object Styles

To apply an object style, select an object, frame, or group with either selection tool and click the style name in the Object Styles palette or choose one from the Control palette menu. Hovering over the style name in the palette displays a tooltip containing a list of applied attributes.

You can also drag and drop the style from the palette onto the selection. When you apply an object style to a group, the style is applied to every object in the group.

Once applied, the style is linked to the object and can only be removed by clicking None in the Object Styles palette or choosing Break Link To Style from the palette menu. You can also choose None from the Object Style menu located in the Control palette.

When you break an object style link, stylized attributes become local and are not removed from the object. To remove the style and its applied attributes, change the Object Style to None rather than break the link.

**Step 18.**
From the Object Styles palette fly-out menu, choose Duplicate Object Style. Enter **spray paint bright red** in the Name field. In the Stroke panel, change the stroke weight to 10pt and the color to red. In the Transparency panel, choose Overlay from the Mode pop-up menu and set the Opacity level to 40%. In the Drop Shadow & Feather panel, change the Feather Width amount to 1p3. Click OK to close the dialog.

**Step 19.**
Select the spray paint bright red object style from the Object Styles palette and proceed to draw random highlights over the stencil letters.

**Step 20.**
Option-click (Mac) or Alt-click (Windows) the Create New Layer button at the bottom of the Layers palette. In the Layer Options dialog, enter **spots** in the Name field and click OK. Choose Edit▷Deselect All.

**Step 21.**

From the Object Styles palette menu, choose Duplicate Object Style. Enter **spray paint dark** in the Name field. In the Transparency panel, choose Darken from the Mode pop-up menu and set the Opacity level to 80%. Click OK to close the dialog.

**Step 22.**

Select the spray paint dark object style from the Object Styles palette and proceed to draw random small circles over the stencil letters.

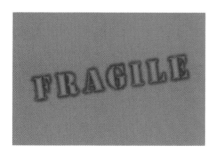

**Step 23.**

Choose Edit ▷ Deselect All and admire you new spray stencil type effect. Not bad for a page layout program, eh?

## Object Style Overrides

You may be wondering why a plus sign occasionally appears next to the selected style name in the Object Styles palette. When the plus sign appears, it means that the applied style has been overridden.

Overrides are handled a little differently with object styles than with character and paragraph styles. With object styles, overrides are not displayed unless they are part of the style. Therefore, any formatting added outside of the style is not considered an override, and is not removed by clicking the Clear Overrides button. To remove all added formatting, you must click the Clear Attributes Not Defined By Style button located in the Control palette or at the bottom of the Object Styles palette. Clicking this button also resets any disabled categories in the style to None.

**Note:** You can identify what object style attributes have been overridden by hovering your mouse over the style name in the palette; the tooltip lists them for you.

# Type Around the World

The InDesign Type On A Path tool is so cool that you'll find yourself looking for reasons to use it. I personally try to use it as much as possible (admittedly, I am a type-on-a-path addict). It's great for adding logotype effects to placed images, as in the example shown here.

The Type On A Path tool allows you to place editable type along the contour of any open or closed path. As with all other editable text, you can select type on a path with the Type tool, format it, apply styles to it, and even edit it with the Story Editor.

The Type On A Path tool also contains its own set of effects that you can apply to any text path object. You can access these effects, including Rainbow, Skew, 3D Ribbon, Stair Step, and Gravity, in the Type On A Path Options dialog. The dialog also contains options for aligning the type to the path and to the stroke of the path (if it has one applied).

## Skewed Type on a Path

With these steps, we'll use the type on a path skew effect to wrap some type around a sphere. To re-create this effect using the image shown here, download bowling_ball.tiff from *The InDesign Effects Book* website: www.wiley.com/go/indesignfx.

**Step 1.**
Press ⌘+D / Ctrl+D to display the Place dialog. Import the bowling_ball.tiff image into a new document.

**Step 2.**
Press L to access the Ellipse tool and create an oval that extends across the horizontal center of the image as shown. Then press R to access the Rotate tool and rotate the oval counterclockwise about 15°.

**Step 3.**
Proceed to apply a fill and stroke of None to the oval. Press ⌘+H / Ctrl+H to show frame edges.

**Step 4.**

Press Shift+T to access the Type On A Path tool and click and drag along the top half of the oval path. This defines the area to which you would like to add text.

**Step 5.**

Choose Window ▷ Swatches (or press F5) to display the Swatches palette. Click the fill icon at the top of the palette to bring it to the front. Select the red swatch from the palette list. Press X to bring the stroke icon to the front and select the Paper (white) swatch. Choose Window ▷ Stroke (or press F10) to display the Stroke palette and enter **2pt** in the Stroke Weight field.

**Step 6.**

Next, select a bold font from the Control or Character palette Font menu (e.g., Helvetica Ultra Compressed) and add some text in all caps (e.g., **BOWL-A-RAMA**). You can then apply any character formatting attributes such as Size, Kerning, Tracking, and Horizontal/Vertical Scale (in the example, it's 100pt type, with a Tracking amount of 20, and Optical Kerning applied). Press ⌘+Shift+C / Ctrl+Shift+C to center the type along the path.

## Type on a Path

To create type on a path, press Shift+T to access the Type On A Path tool, and position the cursor over any open or closed path. When the cursor changes to display a plus sign, you can place it by clicking the path.

Clicking once positions the cursor using the default document paragraph alignment. To define the area of the path you'd like to add text to, click and drag with the tool. As you type, the added text follows the contour of the path.

You can also add text to the path by pasting from the Clipboard, or importing with the Place command. InDesign also lets you thread type on a path objects using the available in and out ports. Any text that does not fit is stored as overset text.

To change the position of type on a path, select the Start or End indicator with the Selection tool, hold down the mouse button, and drag it along the path. Release the mouse button to reposition the text.

To flip the type, select the Flip indicator located in the center of the text, hold down the mouse button, and drag it to the other side of the path. Release the mouse button to flip the text.

*continues on next page*

# Type Around the World *continued*

## Object-Level Display Settings

InDesign allows you to apply settings from the Display Performance sub-menu not only to an entire document, but to individual objects as well. This means that you can override document-level display settings by applying the Fast Display, Typical Display, or High Quality Display setting to selected objects.

For example, if working with High Quality Display enabled slows down your computer, you may want to consider switching to Typical Display and then applying High Quality Display overrides to specific objects as needed.

To do this, you must enable the Allow Object-Level Display Settings option in the View ▷ Display Performance submenu. With the document display set to Typical Display, select an object (or objects) with either selection tool and choose Object ▷ Display Performance ▷ High Quality Display.

To clear local display settings for a selected object (or objects), choose Use View Setting. To clear all object-level display overrides and display all images in the document with the chosen View setting, select View ▷ Display Performance ▷ Clear Object-Level Display Settings.

**Step 7.**
Double-click the Type On A Path tool icon on the Tools palette to access the Type On A Path Tool Options dialog. Choose Skew from the Effect pop-up menu, and choose Center from the Align and To Path pop-up menus. To open up the letter spacing a bit around the curves of the path, enter an amount of 2 in the Spacing field. Check the dialog Preview option to see the settings applied as you enter them. Click OK to apply.

**Step 8.**
To add more curve to the path, access the Selection tool and open up the oval by clicking and dragging the bottom-center node downward.

**Step 9.**
If you need to center the type after adjusting the curve, hover the cursor over the Flip icon located at the bottom center of the text. When you see the cursor change to display what looks like an upside down "T," drag the type to the center of the oval.

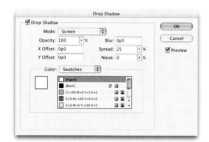

**Step 10.**

To create a white glow around the type, choose Object ▷ Drop Shadow to display the Drop Shadow dialog. Check the Drop Shadow option to enable the effect, and click the dialog Preview option to see the settings applied as you enter them. Choose Swatches from the Color pop-up menu and select Paper (white) from the Swatches list. Select Screen from the Mode pop-up menu and enter an amount of **100%** in the Opacity field. Enter **0p0** for the X and Y Offsets and **0p5** for Blur. Enter **25%** for Spread and **0p0** for Noise. Click OK to apply.

**Step 11.**

Apply any manual kerning, if needed; otherwise hide your frame edges (⌘+H / Ctrl+H) to view the skewed type on a path effect.

# Type On A Path Options Dialog

Access the Type On A Path Options dialog by selecting any path text object and choosing Type ▷ Type On A Path ▷ Options. The dialog allows you to apply specific type effects to selected type on a path. It also lets you change character alignment and spacing, flip the type, or delete it.

To apply a type effect to a selected path text object, simply choose one from the dialog's Effect menu. Options include Rainbow, Skew, 3D Ribbon, Stair Step, and Gravity. Check the Preview option to see the effect as it is applied.

The Align menu lets you choose a method for aligning the type to the path. Use the To Path menu to choose a method for aligning the type to the stroke of the path.

Enter a point value in the Spacing field to control the amount of character spacing applied to the type around the curves of the path.

To flip the type, check the Flip option located in the center of the dialog.

# 3 Paragraph Effects

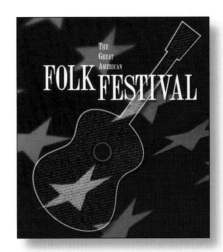

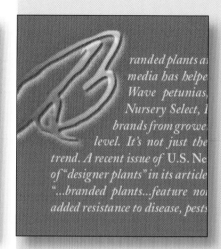

Sure, type effects are cool, but did you know that it's also possible to create these kinds of effects using an entire body of text? It's true! By applying InDesign's type on a path effects, blend modes, and various other formatting tricks to an entire paragraph, you can take type effects to a whole other dimension. In this chapter, paragraphs become design elements, such as a background that fades to none, or a frame that surrounds a placed graphic. You can even place text inside of text!

Skewed Text Path

Gradient Text Mask

Text Inside Text

Inverted Text Wrap

Angled Margins

Paragraph Rule Frames

Vertical Side Heads

Feathered Drop Cap

Text Path Frame

# Skewed Text Path

You can add type to any path, regardless of whether you created it with one of the Frame or Shape tools, or the Pen or Pencil tool. If you're feeling extra creative, you can use the Type On A Path tool Skew option to create type that twists and turns around the contour of any freeform drawn path.

With these steps, I'll show you how to apply a paragraph list of coffee flavors along a freeform path in order to make it look like steam rising from a coffee cup. All we have to do is create a curved path with the Pencil tool, import some text, and apply a gradient.

You can create some really interesting curved paths using the Pencil tool, especially if you draw them using higher Fidelity and Smoothness preference settings. To get even better curves as you draw, try using a graphics pen and tablet. Before you add text to your curved path, you can use the Direct Selection tool and Pen toolset to fine-tune it.

## Create Type That Twists and Turns

To re-create this effect using the images and text shown here, download coffee.psd and flavors.txt from *The InDesign Effects Book* website.

www.photospin.com © 2005

**Step 1.**
Create a new document. Press ⌘+D / Ctrl+D to display the Place dialog. Import the coffee.psd image into the document.

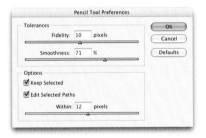

**Step 2.**
Double-click the Pencil tool icon in the Tools palette to display the Pencil Tool Preferences dialog. Enter **10** (pixels) in the Fidelity field and **71%** in the Smoothness field. Using these settings creates smoother freeform curves than the default settings and adds fewer points to the path. Click OK to close the dialog.

**Step 3.**
Choose a fill and stroke color of None. Then draw a curved path above the placed coffee cup image as shown here. If you need to, you can adjust the points and curves of the path using the Direct Selection tool and Pen toolset.

**Step 4.**
Press Shift+T to access the Type On A Path tool and hover the cursor over the path. When you see the + symbol appear, click and drag along the path to define the area you would like to add type to. Or if you prefer, you can also click once at the beginning of the path. Press ⌘+D / Ctrl+D to display the Place dialog. Browse to the flavors.txt file and click Open. Click the Paragraph Formatting Controls icon in the Control palette, or press ⌘+Option+7 / Ctrl+Alt+7, then click the Align Left button.

**Step 5.**
Press ⌘+A / Ctrl+A to select all of the text on the path. Click the Character Formatting Controls icon in the Control palette, or press ⌘+Option+7 / Ctrl+Alt+7 and enter your preferred text settings. You can also enter these settings in the Character palette. In the example shown here, the settings are Adobe Garamond Bold at 26pt, with Optical Kerning applied.

**Step 6.**
Double-click the Type On A Path tool icon in the Tools palette to display the Type On A Path Options dialog. Choose Skew from the Effect pop-up menu and Center from the Align pop-up menu. Click OK to close the dialog.

*continues on next page*

## Importing a Graphic Image

You can import graphics using the File▷Place command (Mac: ⌘+D, Windows: Ctrl+D). When the Place dialog opens, browse to a graphic image on your system and click the Open button. With the loaded place cursor, you can then click on an existing frame, draw a frame, or click once anywhere on the page for InDesign to draw a frame for you. In all three scenarios, the image is automatically placed in the frame.

To import a graphic image as you would in QuarkXPress, select an existing frame and choose the Place command. In the resulting dialog, browse to the image and click the Open button. The image appears at 100% of its size in the graphic frame. You can then resize the image or apply one of the fitting commands, from the Object▷Fitting submenu.

It is also possible to import graphic images by dragging and dropping them from a folder on your system into a document window. You can even drag an image onto an existing frame to place it inside the frame.

# Skewed Text Path *continued*

## Image Import Options

InDesign accepts all graphic file formats used for prepress, including TIFF, EPS, PDF, and DCS, as well as native file formats such as AI (Adobe Illustrator format) and PSD (Photoshop document).

To access additional import options, click Show Import Options in the Place dialog, or press Shift as you click Open. Import options vary depending on selected file types. PDF and EPS files have their own options dialogs, while all other file types use the Image Import Options dialog.

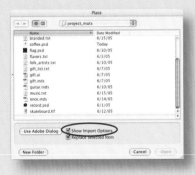

**Step 7.**

Press Shift+⌘+A / Shift+Ctrl+A to deselect all. Choose Window▷Swatches (or press F5) to display the Swatches palette, and then choose New Color Swatch from the Swatches palette fly-out menu. Create two gray builds, one dark (C=51, M=63, Y=52, K=25), and one very dark (C=65, M=65, Y=56, K=47). Click the Add button to add each swatch to the palette list. Click OK to close the dialog.

**Step 8.**

Press A to switch to the Direct Selection tool. Select the text path and click the Formatting Affects Text button at the bottom of the Tools palette. Press X to bring the fill icon to the front.

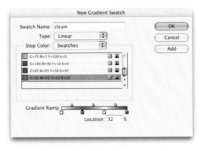

**Step 9.**

Choose New Gradient Swatch from the Swatches palette fly-out menu. Enter **steam** in the Swatch Name field and choose Linear from the Type pop-up menu. Create a gradient that blends from white to dark gray to white to very dark gray, as shown here. Click OK to close the dialog. The gradient should already be applied to your text path selection. Choose Window▷Gradient to display the Gradient palette and enter **Step 11. 42°** in the Angle field.

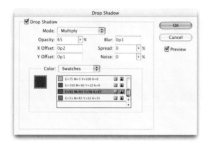

**Step 10.**
Now let's add a drop shadow to enhance the text "steam" effect. Click the Formatting Affects Container button and choose Object ▷ Drop Shadow. In the dialog that appears, click the Drop Shadow check box to enable the effect. Choose Multiply from the Mode pop-up menu and select the very dark gray swatch from the swatches list. Enter **65%** for Opacity, **0p3** for Blur, **0p2** for X Offset, and **0p1** for Y Offset. Keep the Spread and Noise settings at **0%**, and click OK.

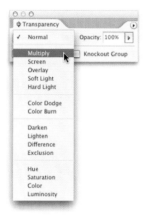

**Step 11.**
Choose Window ▷ Transparency (or press Shift+F10) to display the Transparency palette, and choose Multiply from the Mode pop-up menu. Doing so adds transparency to the text so that you can see through it to the cup behind (just like with real steam from a hot coffee mug).

## Applying Photoshop Paths and Channels at Image Import

Clipping paths and alpha channels allow you to extract an image from a photograph. If the image you are importing contains a Photoshop clipping path or alpha channel, the Image panel of the Image Import Options dialog allows you to apply and edit the path in InDesign.

To do so, check the Apply Photoshop Clipping Path box or choose an alpha channel from the menu. You can always apply this option later in the Clipping Path dialog if you decide to leave it off during import.

**Step 12.**
To complete the design, add some thin rules and some text underneath and behind the coffee cup image.

# Gradient Text Mask

Unfortunately, there is no foreground-to-transparent gradient option in InDesign like there is in Photoshop. InDesign is also lacking any layer masking capabilities like those in Photoshop and Illustrator. Despite these limitations, we can still create the illusion of fading to "none" (or transparent) right here in InDesign.

One thing you can do in InDesign is apply gradients to editable text. With these steps, we will import a body of a text and apply a gradient to it that blends from white to the chosen background color. Doing so creates the illusion of fading to transparent. The great thing is that the text remains entirely editable. You can change any of the character or paragraph formatting attributes at any time while the pseudo-text mask gradient is applied.

Feel free to experiment with this effect using different fonts and colors. Remember, you can't apply the None color swatch to a gradient color stop, but you can always gradate to the same color as the chosen background, even if it is white.

## Using Text as a Background

To re-create this effect using the images and text that are shown here, download gift.inds and gift_list.txt from *The InDesign Effects Book* website.

**Step 1.**
In a new document, draw a rectangle with the Rectangle tool (press M on your keyboard to access the tool quickly) and fill it with red. You can use this as a background to nest some text into later.

**Step 2.**
Deselect the rectangle and press ⌘+D / Ctrl+D to display the Place dialog. Browse to the gift_list.txt file and click Open. Draw a frame with the loaded place cursor that extends out beyond the dimensions of the rectangle underneath.

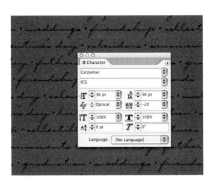

**Step 3.**
Press T to access the Type tool. In the Character Formatting Controls of the Control palette (or the Character palette), choose a fancy script font set at a large point size. In the example shown here, I used Carpenter ICG at 36pt over 36pt leading, with Optical Kerning and -20 Tracking applied.

**Step 4.**

Press ⌘+Shift+F / Ctrl+Shift+F to force-justify all lines of text in the frame. Then press V to access the Selection tool and enter **15°** in the Rotation Angle field of the Control palette. Click the Formatting Affects Text button at the bottom of the Tools palette.

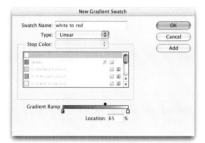

**Step 5.**

Choose Window ▷ Swatches (or press F5) to display the Swatches palette and choose New Gradient Swatch from the Swatches palette fly-out menu. Enter a name in the Swatch Name field (e.g., **white to red**) and choose Linear from the Type pop-up menu. Click the left color stop icon and choose red from the swatches list. Click the right color stop icon and choose Paper (white) from the swatches list. Click the midpoint slider icon and enter **65%** in the Location field. Click OK to close the dialog.

**Step 6.**

Choose Window ▷ Gradient to display the Gradient palette and enter **90°** in the Angle field. Press Return or Enter, and the Angle field displays 105° because of the 15° rotation already applied. If you prefer, you can also use the Gradient tool to apply an angle to the gradient. To do so, press G to access the tool, and then click and drag in the direction shown here to apply the gradient.

## The Image Import Options Layers Panel

The Layers panel only appears when importing a native Photoshop PSD. In the Show Layers section of the dialog, an eye icon appears next to each layer's name; click the icon to turn a layer's visibility on or off. If the image contains Photoshop layer comps, you can choose to display one in InDesign by selecting it from the Layer Comp drop-down menu.

When editing a placed PSD in Photoshop and then updating it in InDesign, you have the option to keep the layer visibility overrides chosen upon import, or to view layers as they are saved in the PSD; select either option from the When Updating Link drop-down menu.

*continues on next page*

# Gradient Text Mask *continued*

## EPS Import Options Dialog

The EPS Import Options dialog has fewer options than the PDF and Image Import Options dialogs. There are only three options that allow you to read embedded OPI image links, apply Photoshop clipping paths, and choose an option for proxy generation.

**Read Embedded OPI Image Links** An Open Prepress Interface (OPI) workflow allows you to place low-res EPS images that are used to reference high-res versions from an OPI server during output. Enable this option to allow InDesign to act as an OPI server.

**Apply Photoshop Clipping Path** If the EPS image you are importing contains a Photoshop clipping path, the EPS Import Options dialog allows you to apply it in InDesign. Unlike with a clipping path applied to a TIFF or PSD, you cannot edit a Photoshop path applied to an EPS file in InDesign.

**Proxy Generation** To use the preview embedded in the EPS image, select Use TIFF or PICT Preview. To create a preview in InDesign, select Rasterize The PostScript.

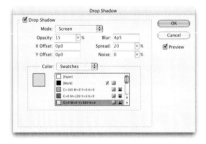

**Step 7.**
Press ⌘+X / Ctrl+X to cut the text frame to the Clipboard and delete it from the page. Click the red rectangle and choose Edit ▷ Paste Into or press Option+⌘+V / Alt+Ctrl+V.

**Step 8.**
Press ⌘+D / Ctrl+D to display the Place dialog. Browse to the gift.inds file (an InDesign CS2 snippet) and click Open. Click once in the center of the document to place the image at 100% of its size.

**Step 9.**
To add a soft outer glow to the shape, choose Object ▷ Drop Shadow. In the dialog that appears, click the Drop Shadow check box to enable the effect. Choose Screen from the Mode pop-up menu and select the yellow swatch from the swatches list. Enter **15%** for Opacity, **4p5** for Blur, and **0p0** for X and Y Offsets. Enter **20%** for Spread and keep the Noise setting at 0%. Click OK to apply.

**Step 10.**

Now let's add some transparency to the gift shape so that we can see through it to the gradient words underneath. Choose Window ▷ Transparency (or press Shift+F10) to display the Transparency palette and choose Screen from the Mode pop-up menu.

**Step 11.**

To complete the design, add some text on top of the gift image. The example here uses the words "the gift shop" in all lowercase white letters, using the Bodoni Book font. To make the type stand out even more, apply a slight drop shadow effect, as shown here.

## PDF Import Options

The General panel of the Place PDF dialog allows you to import a specific page, all pages, or a range of pages from a PDF document into InDesign. It is also possible to select which page you would like to import by entering a page number or clicking the left/right arrows under the preview window and selecting the Previewed Page option.

You can also choose how much of the page you would like to import. From the Crop To drop-down menu, select Bounding Box, Art, Crop, Trim, Bleed, or Media.

Enable the Transparent Background option to allow imported PDFs containing transparent backgrounds to remain transparent in InDesign.

With the exception of layer comps, the Layers panel of the Place PDF dialog has the same functionality as the Layers panel of the Image Import Options dialog.

# Text Inside Text

InDesign allows you to convert text characters into outlined paths. You can then place graphics or text, or even nest frames inside the character outlines. By nesting a text frame in a character outline, you can create an effect similar to applying a clipping mask in Photoshop or Illustrator. The nested paragraph takes the shape of the outlined characters, and in a few easy steps, you have text inside text!

With these steps, we'll import an InDesign snippet of a character outline path originally created in Adobe Illustrator and then copied and pasted into an InDesign CS2 document. We'll duplicate this path onto several different layers, and apply different fills, strokes, and blend modes to create some depth. We'll also apply a gradient to the editable characters in the nested text frame.

InDesign also allows you to apply different blend modes to nested frames and their containers. We'll use this to our advantage with this effect.

## Character Outlines Can Be Frames Too!

To re-create this effect using the images and text that are shown here, download bookswap.inds and booklist.txt from *The InDesign Effects Book* website.

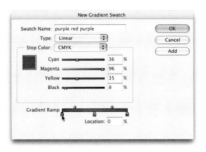

**Step 1.**
Press M to access the Rectangle tool and draw a rectangle to use as a background. Choose Window ▷ Swatches (or press F5) to display the Swatches palette and choose New Gradient from the Swatches palette fly-out menu. Enter a name into the Swatch Name field (e.g., **purple red purple**) and choose Linear from the Type pop-up menu. Choose CMYK from the Stop Color pop-up menu. Click the left color stop icon and create a purple build using C=36, M=96, Y=35, K=Step 8. Click the right color stop icon and use the same purple build. Click in the center of the Gradient Ramp to add another color stop icon and create a red build using C=12, M=83, Y=100, K=3. Enter 50% in the Location field. Click the upper-left midpoint slider and enter 40% in the Location field. Click the upper-right midpoint slider and enter 55%. Click OK to close the dialog.

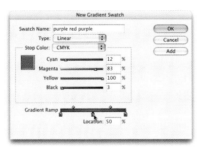

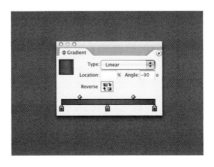

**Step 2.**
Choose Window ▷ Gradient to display the Gradient palette and enter **–90°** in the Angle field. If you prefer, you can also use the Gradient tool to apply an angle to the gradient.

**Step 3.**

Choose Window ▷ Layers (or press F7) to display the Layers palette. Double-click Layer 1 to display the Layer Options dialog. Enter a name for the layer (e.g., **background**), check the Lock Layer option, and click OK to close the dialog.

**Step 4.**

Option-click / Alt-click the Create New Layer button at the bottom of the Layers palette. In the Layer Options dialog, enter a name for it (e.g., **inner color layer**) and click OK.

**Step 5.**

Press ⌘+D / Ctrl+D to display the Place dialog. Browse to the bookswap.inds file and click Open. When the snippet appears in the center of your document, select it with the Selection tool. Choose Window ▷ Transparency (or press Shift+F10) to display the Transparency palette and choose Soft Light from the Mode pop-up menu. Changing the blend mode to Soft Light allows you to see through the letters to the gradient underneath. Notice how the colors of the letters now blend with the gradient.

*continues on next page*

## Copying To and From Adobe Illustrator

In addition to placing native AI (Adobe Illustrator format) files, you can copy/paste or drag-and-drop Illustrator objects into an InDesign document. With the proper settings enabled, it is possible to edit simple objects in InDesign that have been copied from Illustrator, and vice versa.

To edit Illustrator objects in InDesign, you must enable the AICB option–Adobe Illustrator Clipboard–in Illustrator's File Handling & Clipboard preferences, and disable the Prefer PDF When Pasting option in InDesign's File Handling preferences. Once these preferences are set, you can edit Illustrator paths using InDesign's drawing tools.

When you're copying-and-pasting or dragging-and-dropping an Illustrator graphic into InDesign, paths are automatically grouped. Ungroup to edit them with InDesign's drawing tools.

Note that InDesign converts any editable text copied from Illustrator into objects that can be transformed but not edited with the Type tool. InDesign also does not accept compound shapes or applied transparency such as blend modes and drop shadows.

To copy-and-paste or drag-and-drop editable paths from InDesign into Illustrator, enable the Copy PDF To Clipboard option in the File Handling panel of InDesign's preferences.

# Text Inside Text *continued*

## Embedding Images

When you embed an image it becomes part of the document, thereby eliminating the need to refer to a separate file on your system. However, embedding images also adds to a document's file size, which is why it is best to only embed small graphics such as end mark icons and small vector graphics.

To embed an image, select it in the document or click the link name in the Links palette and choose Embed File from the palette menu. You can also select and embed several links at once.

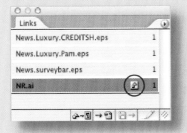

Once you embed a file, an Embedded icon appears in the palette next to the link name.

**Step 6.**

Choose Duplicate Layer inner color layer from the Layers palette fly-out menu. In the Duplicate Layer dialog that appears, enter **outline/shadow** in the Name field and click OK. Option-click / Alt-click the new outline/shadow layer to select the character outline.

**Step 7.**

In the Transparency palette, select Normal from the Mode pop-up menu. Then in the Control palette, enter **4pt** in the Stroke Weight field. Press X to bring the stroke icon to the front and choose New Color Swatch from the Swatches palette fly-out menu. In the dialog that appears, create a green build using C=81, M=43, Y=100, K=46. Click OK to close the dialog. Choose New Tint Swatch from the Swatches palette fly-out menu and enter **75%** in the Tint field. Again, click OK to close the dialog. Press X to bring the fill icon to the front and click the None swatch in the palette.

**Step 8.**

Choose Object ▷ Drop Shadow. In the dialog that appears, click the Drop Shadow check box to enable the effect. Choose Multiply from the Mode pop-up menu and select the black swatch from the swatches list. Enter **100%** for Opacity, **0p4** for Blur, and **0p2** for X and Y Offsets. Keep the Spread and Noise settings at 0%. Click OK to apply.

**Step 9.**

Choose Duplicate Layer outline/ shadow from the Layers palette fly-out menu. In the Duplicate Layer dialog that appears, enter **nested text** in the Name field and click OK. Option-click / Alt-click the new nested text layer to select the character outline. In the Control palette, enter **5pt** in the Stroke Weight field. Choose Object ⊳ Drop Shadow. In the dialog that appears, uncheck the Drop Shadow check box to disable the effect.

**Step 10.**

Deselect the character outline and press ⌘+D / Ctrl+D to display the Place dialog. Browse to the booklist.txt file and click Open. Draw a frame with the loaded place cursor that extends out beyond the dimensions of the character outline.

**Step 11.**

Press T to access the Type tool. In the Character Formatting Controls of the Control palette (or the Character palette), choose a light san serif font set at a smaller point size. In the example shown here, I chose Gill Sans Light at 12pt over 14pt leading, with Optical Kerning.

## Relinking Embedded Images

To relink an embedded file, select it and choose Unembed File from the palette menu. As with embedding, you can also select and unembed several links at once.

After choosing the Unembed File command, InDesign displays a dialog asking if you'd like to relink to the original file or create a new file. Click Yes to relink to the original and No if you'd like InDesign to create a new file.

Unless the file has been moved to a new location on your system, InDesign remembers the original file location when relinking. When creating a new file, you must select a file location from the Choose A Folder (Mac) or Browse For Folder (Windows) dialog and click the Choose button.

*continues on next page*

# Text Inside Text *continued*

## InDesign Snippets

A snippet is a type of XML file used to export and import page content. Snippets are based on the InDesign Interchange format and use the .inds extension.

To export snippets, select one or more objects and choose File ▷ Export. At the bottom of the dialog, choose InDesign Snippet from the Format menu (Mac) or the Save As Type menu (Windows). Enter a name for the snippet file and choose where you'd like to save it on your system, then click Save.

You can also drag the selected objects (or items selected from the Structure menu) to your desktop. A snippet file is automatically created when dragging from the document. Snippets can also be imported into an InDesign document by using the Place command or by dragging.

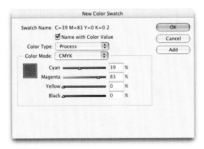

**Step 12.**

Press ⌘+Shift+F / Ctrl+Shift+F to force-justify all lines of text in the frame. Then press V to access the Selection tool and enter **12. 5**° in the Rotation Angle field of the Control palette. Deselect the text frame.

**Step 13.**

Choose Window ▷ Swatches (or press F5) to display the Swatches palette and choose New Color Swatch from the Swatches palette fly-out menu. In the dialog that appears, choose Linear from the Type pop-up menu. Create a purple build using C=39, M=83, Y=0, K=0. Click OK to close the dialog. Choose New Tint Swatch from the Swatches palette fly-out menu and in the dialog, enter **15%** in the Tint field. Click OK to close the dialog.

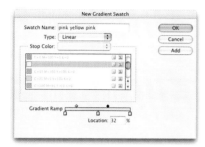

**Step 14.**

Select the text frame and click the Formatting Affects Text Button at the top of the Swatches palette. Then choose New Gradient Swatch from the Swatches palette fly-out menu. Enter a name in the Swatch Name field (e.g., **pink yellow pink**) and choose Linear from the Type pop-up menu. Click the left color stop icon and choose the 15% purple tint swatch the swatches list. Click the right color stop icon and choose the 15% purple tint swatch again. Click in the center of the Gradient Ramp to add another color stop icon and choose yellow from the swatches list. Enter **50%** in the Location field. Click the upper-left midpoint slider and enter **34%** in the Location field. Click the upper-right midpoint slider and enter **62%**. Click OK to close the dialog. Press G to access the Gradient tool and click and drag from the top of the letters to the bottom. Hold down Shift to constrain the angle as you draw.

**Step 15.**

Press ⌘+X / Ctrl+X to cut the text frame to the Clipboard and delete it from the page. Option-click / Alt-click the nested text layer to select the character outline and choose Edit▷Paste Into or press Option+⌘+V / Alt+Ctrl+V. Press Shift+⌘+E / Shift+Ctrl+E to center the contents.

*continues on next page*

## Preflighting Fonts

Any time you run an InDesign pre-flight check on a document (choose File▷Preflight), a dialog appears displaying a summary of what it found.

The Preflight dialog contains six panels: Summary, Fonts, Links And Images, Colors And Inks, Print Settings, and External Plug-ins. The Summary panel displays a brief description of what is found for each category. When a potential output problem exists, InDesign places a warning icon next to the category in the summary.

Click the Fonts category on the left to display the panel in the Preflight dialog. Click to select from the list of fonts used in the document. InDesign displays more information about the font in the Current Font section of the panel, including where the font is located on your system, the full font name, and where it is first used in the document.

Check the Show Problems Only option to display missing fonts exclusively. Click the Find Font button to relink or replace any missing fonts using the Find Font dialog.

# Text Inside Text *continued*

## Preflighting Links and Images

When a potential output problem exists regarding links and images, InDesign places a warning icon next to that category in the Preflight summary panel.

Click the Links And Images category on the left to display the panel in the Preflight dialog. In the center of the panel, click to select from the list of links placed in the document. InDesign displays more information about the link/image in the Current Link/Image section of the panel, including where it is located on your system, its full name and Actual ppi, and when it was last updated or modified.

Check the Show Problems Only option to display missing and modified links exclusively. To relink or update a link, select it from the list and click the Relink or Update button. Click the Repair All button to update and/or relink all missing and modified links at once.

**Step 16.**
Press A to switch to the Direct Selection tool and then click inside any of the character outline letters to select the nested text frame. In the Transparency palette, lower the Opacity level to 40%.

**Step 17.**
Click the inner color layer in the Layers palette to select it and choose Duplicate Layer inner color layer from the Layers palette fly-out menu. In the dialog that appears, enter **white outline** in the Name field and click OK. Move the new white outline layer to the top of the list in the Layers palette. Option-click / Alt-click the new white outline layer to select the character outline.

**Step 18.**
Click the Swap Fill and Stroke arrows at the bottom of the Tools palette. In the Control palette, enter **1pt** in the Stroke Weight field.

**Step 19.**

In the Transparency palette, select Overlay from the Mode pop-up menu.

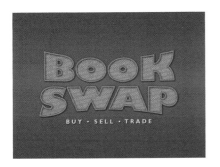

**Step 20.**

To complete the design, add some text below the book swap character outline. The example here uses the words "buy sell trade" in all uppercase yellow letters, using Gill Sans Bold 20pt, center-aligned, and the tracking set to 3. To make the type stand out even more, apply a slight drop shadow effect, as shown here.

## Preflighting Colors and Inks

The Summary panel lists the number of process and spot inks used in the document and whether a color management system (CMS) is being used. Because some print jobs require them, spot inks do not trigger a warning icon. If a preflight check reveals spot colors that should be process, click the Cancel button and convert them using the Ink Manager or Swatch Options dialog (both accessible through the Swatches palette).

Click the Colors And Inks category on the left to display the panel in the Preflight dialog. In the center of the panel, InDesign displays a list of all colors and inks used in the document as well as their halftone screen angles and lines per inch (if applicable).

# Inverted Text Wrap

Text wraps are generally used to push text away from an object. But you can get the opposite effect by applying InDesign's Invert Text Wrap option. When applied, it forces any neighboring text inside of a shape, rather than away from it.

Similar to Adobe Illustrator, InDesign also contains lots of tools for drawing custom shapes, including the Pen toolset, the Pencil toolset, the Scissors tool, the Pathfinder palette, and the Direct Selection tool. The guitar path shown in this example was created entirely in InDesign and exported as a snippet.

With these steps, we'll create a folk festival poster that features a guitar path made up of all of the names of the artists appearing at the event. By placing a paragraph of artist names over the guitar path with the Invert Text Wrap option applied, the text takes on the shape of the path. This is a great way to combine text with graphics.

## Make Your Paragraph Conform to Any Shape

To re-create this effect using the images and text shown here, download flag.psd, guitar.inds, and folk_artists.txt from *The InDesign Effects Book* website.

www.photospin.com © 2005

**Step 1.**
Create a new letter-sized document (8.5×11″). Press ⌘+D / Ctrl+D to display the Place dialog. Browse to the flag.psd file and click Open. Click anywhere on the page to place the photo at 100% of its size. Center the graphic frame on the page.

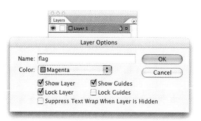

**Step 2.**
Choose Window ▷ Layers (or press F7) to display the Layers palette. Double-click Layer 1 to display the Layer Options dialog. Enter a name for the layer (e.g., **flag**), check the Lock Layer option, and click OK to close the dialog.

**Step 3.**
Option-click / Alt-click the Create New Layer button at the bottom of the Layers palette. In the Layer Options dialog, enter a name for it (e.g., **guitar path**) and click OK.

**Step 4.**

Press ⌘+D / Ctrl+D to display the Place dialog. Browse to the guitar.inds file and click Open. When the snippet appears in the center of your document, select it with the Selection tool. Choose Window ▷ Swatches (or press F5) to display the Swatches palette. Press X to bring the fill icon to the front. Enter **25%** in the Tint field.

**Step 5.**

To soften the edges of the shape, choose Object ▷ Feather. In the dialog that appears, check the Feather check box (at the top) to enable the effect, and the Preview check box (to the right) to see the settings applied as you enter them. Enter **1p3** in the Feather Width field and choose Diffused from the Corners pop-up menu. Keep the Noise setting at 0%. Click OK to apply.

**Step 6.**

Choose Object ▷ Drop Shadow. In the dialog that appears, click the Drop Shadow check box to enable the effect. Choose Multiply from the Mode pop-up menu and select the black swatch from the swatches list. Enter **50%** for Opacity, **0p11** for Blur, **0p4** for X Offset, and **1p1** for Y Offset. Enter **6%** for Spread and **5%** for Noise. Click OK to apply.

*continues on next page*

# Text Wrap Options

You can insert an image into a body of text by applying a text wrap to any custom shape or graphic frame. To place a text wrap, select an object and click one of the buttons located at the top of the Text Wrap palette:

**Wrap Around Bounding Box** allows you to apply a text wrap to the top, bottom, left, and right sides of a frame.

**Wrap Around Object Shape** applies one offset value around an entire object.

**Jump Object** applies a wrap that "jumps" text over an object, resulting in text above and below the offset, but not to the left or right.

**Jump To Next Column** applies a wrap that "jumps" text to the next column, stopping the text at the top of the offset.

To create an "inside-out" wrap, place a check in the Invert check box. This feature works well with the Wrap Around Object Shape option.

For objects set to Wrap Around Bounding Box, Jump Object, or Jump To Next Column, you can enter an offset distance amount in any of the top, bottom, left, and right offset fields of the palette. For objects set to Wrap Around Object Shape, you must enter a single offset distance amount in the Top Offset field.

# Inverted Text Wrap *continued*

## Text Wrap Contour Options

When applying the Wrap Around Object Shape option to a frame containing a placed image, InDesign activates the Contour Options portion of the palette. To access these options, choose Show Options from the palette menu.

The Type menu lets you choose a contour type (such as a clipping path) to base the text wrap on:

**Bounding Box** applies a text wrap to the outer edge of the placed graphic (this includes all areas cropped by a graphic frame).

**Detect Edges** applies a text wrap based on edges calculated by existing white areas in a placed graphic. Check the Include Inside Edges box to allow areas inside the clipping path to appear transparent.

**Alpha Channel or Photoshop Path** applies a text wrap to the contour of an embedded Photoshop path or alpha channel. If the placed image contains more than one Photoshop path or alpha channel, select select from the Path menu the one you'd like to apply.

**Graphic Frame** applies one offset value to all sides of the frame container.

**Same As Clipping** allows you to apply a text wrap based on a clipping path that is created in InDesign.

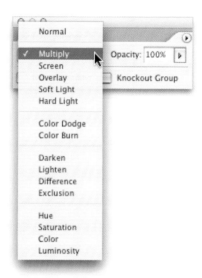

**Step 7.**
Choose Window ▷ Transparency (or press Shift+F10) to display the Transparency palette. Choose Multiply from the Mode pop-up menu. Doing so drops all of the white from the gray fill of the guitar. It also adds transparency so that you can see through to the soft shadow underneath.

**Step 8.**
Option-click / Alt-click the Create New Layer button at the bottom of the Layers palette. In the Layer Options dialog, enter a name for it (e.g., **text**) and click OK.

**Step 9.**
Choose Edit ▷ Deselect All and select the new text layer from the Layers palette. Press ⌘+D / Ctrl+D to display the Place dialog. Browse to the folk_artists.txt file and click Open. Click once on the page to place the text in a text frame. In the Control palette, enter **27p** in the X Location field and **33p** in the Y Location field. Enter **51p** in the Width field and **45p** in the Height field. Click the Formatting Affects Text button at the top of the Swatches palette and select the red swatch from the list.

### Step 10.

Press T to access the Type tool. In the Character Formatting Controls of the Control palette (or the Character palette), choose a script font set at a smaller point size. In the example shown here, it's Texas Hero at 8pt over 8pt leading, with Optical Kerning and -25 Tracking applied. Press ⌘+Shift+F / Ctrl+Shift+F to force-justify all lines of text in the frame.

### Step 11.

Press V to access the Selection tool and enter **12°** in the Rotation Angle field of the Control palette. Option-click / Alt-click the **guitar path** layer to select the path. Press Option+⌘+W / Alt+Ctrl+W to display the Text Wrap palette. Click the Wrap Around Object Shape button and enter **0p6** into the Top Offset field. Finally, check the Invert option.

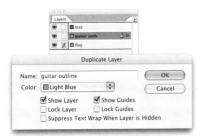

### Step 12.

Choose Duplicate Layer **guitar path** from the Layers palette fly-out menu. In the Duplicate Layer dialog that appears, enter **guitar outline** in the Name field and click OK. Move the new guitar outline layer to the top of the list in the Layers palette. Option-click / Alt-click the new guitar outline layer to select the path.

## Editing Text Wraps

You can edit a text wrap, by selecting and repositioning points on the boundary path with the Direct Selection tool. You can also add, delete, or convert points using the various Pen tools.

You cannot add points using the Pencil tool, erase points using the Erase tool, smooth points using the Smooth tool, or cut points and line segments using the Scissors tool.

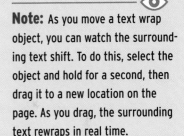

**Note:** As you move a text wrap object, you can watch the surrounding text shift. To do this, select the object and hold for a second, then drag it to a new location on the page. As you drag, the surrounding text rewraps in real time.

*continues on next page*

# Inverted Text Wrap *continued*

## Ignoring Text Wraps

In InDesign there are two ways that you can allow a text frame not to be affected by a neighboring text wrap object.

The first is to select the text frame and press ⌘+B / Ctrl+B to display the Text Frame Options dialog. At the bottom, check Ignore Text Wrap to enable this option.

The second is to press ⌘+K / Ctrl+K to display the Preferences dialog. Click Composition Preferences from the menu on the left to display the panel in the dialog. At the bottom, check Text Wrap Only Affects Text Beneath. Enabling this option allows a text frame to ignore a neighboring text wrap by bringing it to the front of the stacking order, as in QuarkXPress.

**Step 13.**
In the Transparency palette, choose Normal from the Mode pop-up menu. Press the forward slash key (/) to apply a fill of None. Press X to bring the stroke icon to the front and click the Paper (white) swatch. Choose Window ▷ Stroke (or press F10) to display the Stroke palette and enter **4pt** in the Stroke Weight field. Click the Align Stroke To Inside button. In the Text Wrap palette, click the No Text Wrap button.

**Step 14.**
Choose Object ▷ Drop Shadow and deselect the Drop Shadow check box to disable the effect. Click OK to close the dialog. Choose Object ▷ Feather to access the Feather dialog. Change the Feather Width amount to 0p4 and click OK to apply.

**Step 15.**
Choose Duplicate Layer guitar outline from the Layers palette fly-out menu. In the Duplicate Layer dialog that appears, enter **overlay layer** in the Name field and click OK. Option-click / Alt-click the new overlay layer to select the path.

**Step 16.**
Press the forward slash key (/) to apply a stroke of None. Press X to bring the fill icon to the front and click the black swatch in the Swatches palette list. Enter **40%** in the Tint field. Then in the Transparency palette, choose Overlay from the Mode pop-up menu. Doing so makes the outline of the guitar appear brighter so that it stands out against the darker colors used on the layers below.

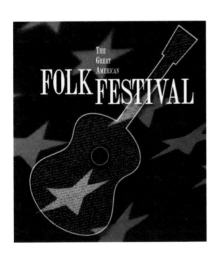

**Step 17.**
To complete the design, add some text above the body of the guitar. The example here uses the words "The Great American Folk Festival" in offset white letters, using the DJ WSJ font with the larger characters set at 92pt and the smaller ones at 19pt. To make the type stand out even more, apply a slight drop shadow effect as shown here on the words "Folk Festival."

## Text Wrap Composition Preferences

The Composition panel of the Preferences dialog contains several additional text wrap options:

**Text Wrap Justify Text Next To An Object** allows you to justify any text placed near an object that has a text wrap applied to it.

**Text Wrap Skip By Leading** allows you to force any wrapped text to apply the next available leading increment below a text-wrapped object, allowing the lines of text to line up evenly. Keeping this option off may cause lines of text to jump down below a wrapped object and not line up with neighboring columns or text frames.

**Text Wrap Only Affects Text Beneath** allows a text frame to ignore a neighboring text wrap by bringing it to the front of the stacking order.

# Angled Margins

InDesign allows you to change the shape of a paragraph by altering the points of its text frame container. As with any other path in InDesign, you can add, delete, cut, and convert points on a text frame. Doing so affects the way the text in the frame is aligned, thereby proving to be a valid alternative to applying a text wrap.

With these steps, we'll change the shape of a paragraph by altering its frame container with the Pencil tool. This is the quickest and easiest way to add points to a text frame. Ultimately, the new shape will realign the text to follow the contour of the placed image underneath. While we're at it, we'll also add a cool feather and outer glow effect to the text.

Once you get the hang of adjusting the shape of your paragraphs with the Pencil tool, be sure to experiment with this effect using different photographs and type treatments.

## No Need for Text Wraps

To re-create this effect using the image shown here, download skateboard.tif from *The InDesign Effects Book* website.

www.photospin.com © 2005

**Step 1.**

Create a new letter-sized document (8.5×11˝). Press ⌘+D / Ctrl+D to display the Place dialog. Browse to the skateboard.tif file and click Open. Draw a frame that covers the entire page to place the photo at 100% of its size. Press Shift+⌘+E / Shift+Ctrl+E to center the content.

**Step 2.**

Choose Window▷Layers (or press F7) to display the Layers palette. Double-click Layer 1 to display the Layer Options dialog. Enter a name for the layer (e.g., **skate photo**), check the Lock Layer option, and click OK to close the dialog.

**Step 3.**

Option-click / Alt-click the Create New Layer button at the bottom of the Layers palette. In the Layer Options dialog, enter a name for it (e.g., **type**) and click OK.

**Step 4.**

Press T to access the Type tool and draw a text frame surrounding the skater. In the Control palette, enter **22p9** in the X Location field and **29p4** in the Y Location field. Enter **28p5** in the Width field and **29p1.5** in the Height field. Press X to bring the fill icon to the front.

**Step 5.**

Choose Window ▷ Swatches (or press F5) to display the Swatches palette and choose New Color Swatch from the Swatches palette fly-out menu. Create a lime build using C=17, M=0, Y=100, K=0. Click OK to add the swatch.

**Step 6.**

Click the stroke icon at the top of the Swatches palette to bring it to the front. Click the magenta swatch in the Swatches palette list and enter **85%** in the Tint field. Choose Window ▷ Stroke (or press F10) to display the Stroke palette and enter **1.5pt** in the Stroke Weight field.

## Adjusting Frames

Clicking and dragging one of the boundary nodes of a single selected frame allows you to adjust the frame's dimensions but not scale the frame's contents. This same rule applies to all frames in a group.

To adjust a frame proportionately, be sure that the Constrain Proportions For Width & Height lock is secured in the Controls palette. You can also constrain proportions for width and height by holding down the Shift key as you drag a boundary node of a frame.

**Note:** Adjusting the frame dimensions can also move the frame's contents.

*continues on next page*

# Angled Margins *continued*

## Direct Selection Tool

InDesign's Direct Selection tool is designed to work like the one in Illustrator, but with a few twists. You can use it to select, move, or scale the contents of a graphic frame (such as a placed image) or to select and move points on a drawn path. You can also use it to change the shape of a frame by selecting and moving any of its corner nodes.

You can access the Direct Selection tool by clicking its icon in the Tools palette or by typing the letter A.

To select the contents of a graphic frame, just click anywhere on the contents with the Direct Selection tool. Once you do, the boundary frame of the placed content appears, indicating that you now have the item selected. You can then reposition the selected item within the frame by clicking and dragging with your mouse.

To select and reposition more than one item at a time, hold down the Shift key as you click. You can then move the selected items together. However, keep in mind that you are only moving the selected items within the boundaries of each item's container.

You can also make a selection by dragging with the Direct Selection tool over an area that includes the item(s) you want to select.

**Step 7.**

Press ⌘+Shift+R / Ctrl+Shift+R to Align Right and type some text (here, I used "Storm The Streets With The New Air Force"). Select the text and choose a dramatic font and size in the Control or Character palette. The example here uses Frantic Regular, 30pt over 40pt leading, with Optical Kerning and –50 Tracking, and 90% Horizontal Scaling applied.

**Step 8.**

To soften the edges of the text characters, switch to the Selection tool and choose Object ▷ Feather. In the dialog that appears, check the Feather check box to enable the effect. Enter 0p6 in the Feather Width field. Choose Diffused from the Corners pop-up menu and enter **12%** in the Noise field. Click OK to apply.

**Step 9.**

Press N to access the Pencil tool and draw from the top-right corner point of the text frame to the bottom-right corner point, following the contour of the skater's leg and skateboard. InDesign adds points to the text frame, changing its shape and realigning the text as shown here. If you need to, you can adjust the points with the Direct Selection tool.

**Step 10.**

To add a transparent outline to the text, choose Object ▷ Drop Shadow. In the dialog that appears, check the Drop Shadow check box to enable the effect. Choose Multiply from the Mode pop-up menu and CMYK from the Color pop-up menu. Create an orange build using C=6, M=52, Y=100, K=0. Enter 85% for Opacity, and 0 for all of the other settings. Click OK to apply. Click OK again when the high-resolution warning dialog appears. This warning dialog is telling you that applying a drop shadow that is under 0.5pt could add to the overall file size of the document and slow down printing. However, because this is a small graphic, it should not be a concern in this instance. But keep in mind that you should only apply shadows this way in moderation when creating layouts in InDesign.

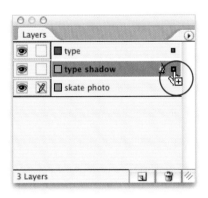

**Step 11.**

We can't add a drop shadow to the text because we've already used Drop Shadow to create a transparent outline. So what we'll have to do is duplicate the text and place it on a new layer underneath. In the Layers palette, press ⌘+Option / Ctrl+Alt and click the New Layer button to create a layer behind the type layer. Double-click the new layer to display the Layer Options dialog and enter type shadow in the Name field. Click OK to close the dialog. Then Option-click / Alt-click the small square icon on the type layer and drag it to the new type shadow layer.

# Position Tool

The Direct Selection toolset also includes a dynamic Position tool. This tool is used specifically for cropping placed images inside a graphic frame, not for altering points on a path. However, you can still position placed images with the Direct Selection tool if you prefer.

To crop images with the Position tool, select a graphic frame by clicking one of its edges. You can then select and move any of its corner or side nodes just as you would with the Selection tool. To select and move an image within a frame, hover the cursor over the image until it dynamically changes into a hand icon, then click and drag.

**Note:** With the Direct Selection or Position tool, you can scale a placed image proportionately within its frame by Shift-clicking and dragging any one of its boundary nodes.

*continues on next page*

# Angled Margins *continued*

## Pen Toolset

The Pen toolset in InDesign mirrors the one found in Illustrator. Although they appear differently in the Illustrator Tools palette, the tools have the same names and work in exactly the same ways. This means you can create custom vector drawings right in InDesign.

**Pen Tool** Choose the Pen tool to create a vector path. Click and drag to create a series of connecting points that result in a custom-drawn line or shape. Clicking with the Pen creates a point, and dragging with the mouse creates its curve in relation to the previous point and the next point placed on the path.

**Add Anchor Point Tool** This tool adds a point to an existing path, which lets you create intricate curves, corners, and bends to your custom-drawn line or shape. Simply click anywhere along the path to add a new point.

**Delete Anchor Point Tool** With this tool, click any existing point to delete it. Keep in mind that deleting points can drastically change the appearance of your custom-drawn line or shape.

**Convert Direction Point Tool** With this tool you can change the direction of a selected point's curve on an existing path. Click any existing point to reset the curve handles, allowing you to readjust it. Click and drag the handles to change the curve.

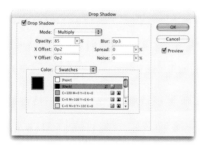

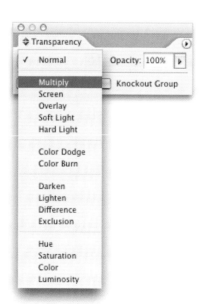

**Step 12.**
Click the Formatting Affects Text button and change the Stroke and Fill color to Paper (white). Click the Formatting Affects Container button and choose Object ▷ Feather. In the dialog that appears, change the Feather Width amount to 0p3 and the Noise amount to 5%. Click OK to apply.

**Step 13.**
Choose Object ▷ Drop Shadow. In the dialog that appears, choose Swatches from the Color pop-up menu and select black from the swatches list. Enter 0p3 for Blur, and 0p2 for X and Y Offsets. Keep Opacity set to 85% and the Spread and Noise settings at 0%. Click OK to apply.

**Step 14.**
Now all we need to do is drop the white fill color of the duplicate text and keep the shadow visible. To do so, choose Window ▷ Transparency (or press Shift+F10) to display the Transparency palette, and choose Multiply from the Mode pop-up menu. Remember, the Multiply blend mode always drops out any white from the selected object when it is applied.

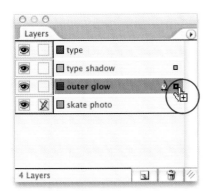

**Step 15.**

Now let's create one more duplicate text layer that we can add a soft, white outer glow to. In the Layers palette, press ⌘+Option / Ctrl+Alt and click the New Layer button to create a layer behind the type shadow layer. Double-click the new layer to display the Layer Options dialog and enter outer glow in the Name field. Click OK to close the dialog. Then Option-click / Alt-click the small square icon on the type shadow layer and drag it to the new outer glow layer.

**Step 16.**

Click the Formatting Affects Text button and press X to bring the stroke icon to the front. Press the backslash key to change the stroke to None. Click the Formatting Affects Container button and choose Object ▷ Feather. In the dialog that appears, change the Feather Width amount to 1p6 and the Noise amount to 0%. Click OK to apply.

**Step 17.**

Choose Object ▷ Drop Shadow. In the dialog that appears, choose Screen from the Mode pop-up menu and choose Paper (white) from the swatches list. Enter **100%** for Opacity, **2p8** for Blur, and **0p0** for X and Y Offsets. Enter **25%** for Spread and **0%** for Noise. Click OK to apply. Finally, in the Transparency palette, choose Screen from the Mode pop-up menu. Choose Edit ▷ Deselect All to view the finished project!

# Pencil Toolset

If trying to manipulate tiny little points and Bézier curves with the Pen toolset drives you nuts, you may want to try using the Pencil toolset instead. These tools allow you to draw freeform just as you would with a real pencil set. And if you use them along with a graphics pen and tablet, you can get a good feel for freeform drawing in InDesign.

**Pencil Tool** To create a freeform shape using the Pencil tool, just choose it from the Tools palette and begin drawing. As you draw, InDesign calculates where the points fall on the path and places them for you. You can then switch to the Pen toolset and manipulate the placed points, or you can try using the Smooth and Erase tools.

**Smooth Tool** If your drawing winds up a little too freeform, you can always clean it up by clicking and dragging over your points with the Smooth tool. Doing so removes any extraneous anchor points while maintaining the overall shape of the drawing. This is a great tool for smoothing out any harsh, jagged edges.

**Erase Tool** Sometimes it may just be easier to erase part of your drawing and redraw it. Just choose the Erase tool from the Tools palette and click and drag over any points you want to get rid of. Now you can redraw with the Pencil or Pen tool.

# Paragraph Rule Frame

Paragraph rule formatting is generally used to place a rule above or below a paragraph in a story. However, in the Paragraph Rules dialog, if you apply a solid rule set at an extremely large point size, you can add an inner stroke to the frame. By experimenting with the settings in the dialog, you can create an inner frame effect.

You have to have at least one text character placed in the frame in order to apply paragraph rule formatting and create the effect. To get around this, just add an invisible character, such as a space or a tab.

You will also want to access the Text Frame Options dialog and apply inset spacing to all sides of the frame. With inset spacing applied, you can set the paragraph rules to fill the column without applying any additional left/right indent amounts in the Paragraph Rules dialog.

## An Entirely Different Kind of Text Frame

To re-create this effect using the logotype shown here, download once.inds from *The InDesign Effects Book* website.

**Step 1.**
In a new document, press T to access the Type tool and create a text frame. Press V to switch to the Selection tool. In the Control palette, enter **37p6** in the Width field and **26p** in the Height field.

**Step 2.**
Press ⌘+B / Ctrl+B to display the Text Frame Options dialog. Enter **1p6** in the Top, Bottom, Left, and Right Inset Spacing fields. Click OK to apply.

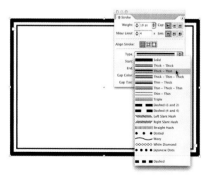

**Step 3.**
Choose Window ▷ Stroke (or press F10) to display the Stroke palette and enter **18pt** in the Weight field. Choose Thick – Thin from the Type pop-up menu.

**Step 4.**

Choose Window ▷ Swatches (or press F5) to display the Swatches palette and press X to bring the stroke icon to the front. Choose New Color Swatch from the Swatches palette fly-out menu. Create a purple build using C=72, M=100, Y=2, K=0. Click OK to add the swatch and close the dialog. Enter **50%** in the Tint field of the Swatches palette.

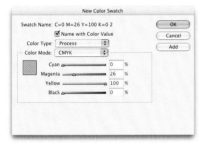

**Step 5.**

Deselect the text frame and choose New Color Swatch from the Swatches palette fly-out menu again. Create an orange build using C=0, M=26, Y=100, K=0. Click OK to add the swatch and close the dialog.

**Step 6.**

Press the spacebar to add a character to the text frame. Press Option+⌘+J / Alt+Ctrl+J to display the Paragraph Rules dialog. Choose Rule Above from the pop-up menu at the top and check the Rule On check box to enable the effect. Enter **251pt** in the Weight field and choose Solid from the Type pop-up menu. Choose Black from the Color pop-up menu and enter **60%** in the Tint field. Choose Column from the Width pop-up menu, then enter **-19p10** in the Offset field and **-0p5** in the Left and Right Indent fields. Don't click OK just yet.

## Underline

To apply an underline using paragraph formatting, select an area of text with the Type tool and choose Underline from the Character palette fly-out menu, or click the Underline toggle button in the Controls palette. To add an underline to all the text in a single, unthreaded frame, select the frame with either selection tool and apply the Underline command.

To customize an underline's appearance, access the Underline Options dialog by choosing Underline Options from the Character palette menu. When the dialog opens, click the Underline On option to access the settings. The rest of the dialog is set up like the Stroke palette, allowing you to choose an underline, weight, offset, type, color, and gap tint. You can also choose to overprint any applied underline or gap colors.

Although you cannot save these settings as an underline style, you can save them as part of a character or paragraph style.

The underline effect automatically applies itself to any selected spaces. If your design requires that word spaces not have underlines, you can always replace them using Find/Change.

*continues on next page*

# Paragraph Rule Frame *continued*

## Strikethrough

To apply the strikethrough effect using paragraph formatting, select an area of text with the Type tool and choose Strikethrough from the Character palette fly-out menu, or click the Strikethrough toggle button in the Controls palette. To add a strikethrough to all of the text in a single, unthreaded frame, select the frame with either selection tool and apply the Strikethrough command.

To customize a strikethrough's appearance, access the Strikethrough Options dialog by choosing Strikethrough Options from the Character palette menu. When the dialog opens, click the Strikethrough On option to access the settings. The rest of the dialog is set up exactly like the Underline Options dialog.

To avoid difficult registration on press, it is recommended that you enable the overprint option in this dialog when applying strikethrough or gap colors.

Unfortunately, just as with underlines, you cannot create and save a strikethrough style—but you can save these settings as part of a character or paragraph style.

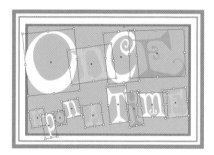

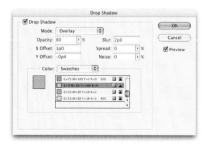

### Step 7.
Choose Rule Below from the pop-up menu at the top and check the Rule On check box to enable the effect. Enter **241pt** in the Weight field and choose Solid from the Type pop-up menu. Choose the orange swatch you created earlier from the Color pop-up menu and enter **80%** in the Tint field. Choose Column from the Width pop-up menu, then enter **-0p8** in the Offset field and **0p1** in the Left and Right Indent fields. Click OK.

### Step 8.
Press ⌘+D / Ctrl+D to display the Place dialog. Browse to the once.inds file and click Open. When the snippet appears in the center of your document, select it with the Selection tool and position it over the center of the frame as shown. Press Shift+⌘+G / Shift+Ctrl+G to ungroup the letters.

### Step 9.
Choose Object ▷ Drop Shadow. In the dialog that appears, check the Drop Shadow checkbox to enable the effect. To add a soft outer glow to the characters, choose Overlay from the Mode pop-up menu and choose the orange build from the swatches list. Enter **80%** for Opacity, **2p** for Blur, **1p** for X Offset, and **-0p4** for the Y Offset. Keep the Spread and Noise settings at 0% and click OK to apply.

**Step 10.**

Press ⌘+G / Ctrl+G to group the letters. You can now add an additional shadow to the group, even though the letters already have individual drop shadow settings applied. Choose Object ▷ Drop Shadow. In the dialog that appears, check the Drop Shadow check box to enable the effect. Choose Multiply from the Mode pop-up menu and black from the swatches list. Enter **65%** for Opacity, **0p3** for Blur, and **0p4** for X and Y Offsets. Enter **5%** for Spread and **0%** for Noise. Click OK to apply.

**Step 11.**

Deselect the grouped letters. If you'd like to adjust the Overlay drop shadow X and Y Offset settings for individual letters, select them with the Direct Selection tool and press Option+⌘+M / Alt+Ctrl+M to display the Drop Shadow dialog (or choose Object ▷ Drop Shadow). Make your adjustments and click OK.

**Step 12.**

Select the frame and choose Object ▷ Drop Shadow. In the dialog that appears, check the Drop Shadow check box to enable the effect. Choose Multiply from the Mode pop-up menu and black from the swatches list. Enter **60%** for Opacity, **0p3** for Blur, and **0p2** for X and Y Offsets. Enter **5%** for Spread and **0%** for Noise. Click OK to apply.

# Paragraph Rules

You can create and apply evenly spaced rules above and/or below selected paragraphs as part of their formatting, or as part of a paragraph style. To create a formatted paragraph rule, insert the Type tool cursor in a paragraph and choose Paragraph Rules from the Paragraph palette menu.

At the top of the Paragraph Rules dialog, select Rule Above or Rule Below from the menu and check the Rule On option. By default, InDesign places formatted rules behind the paragraph text.

Proceed to choose Weight, Type, Color, Tint, Gap Color, and Gap Tint settings for the rule stroke. You can also choose to overprint any applied stroke colors or gap colors. Check the Preview option at the bottom left of the dialog to see the settings applied as you adjust them. Use the Width menu to apply the rule across the width of the column or across the first line of text in the paragraph.

Enter a value in the Offset field to move the rule above or below the baseline. Enter higher values to move a Rule Above up or a Rule Below down. To apply a left/right indent to the rule, enter a value in the Left Indent and Right Indent fields.

# Vertical Side Heads

Generally, tables are used in InDesign to create organized lists of information, such as calendars or product listings. But they can also be used to organize design elements on a page, like the vertical side head in this example. With these steps, we'll use a simple two-column table to place a vertical side head next to some body text.

Tables can only be inserted into text frames—not graphic frames—which means that you can only work with them using the Type tool. Keep in mind that tables and table cells behave similarly to text frames, which means that any graphics placed in them are treated as nested inline objects.

With InDesign you can rotate text inside a table cell with the simple click of a button. If you then select the text from within the cell and convert it to outlines, it automatically becomes a nested inline object. You can the select the nested object and apply an effect such as a Feather or Drop Shadow.

## A Different Approach to Using Tables

To re-create this effect using the text shown here, download bio.txt from *The InDesign Effects Book* website.

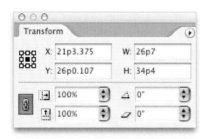

**Step 1.**
In a new document, press T to access the Type tool and create a Text Frame. Press V to switch to the Selection tool. In the Control or Transform palette, enter **26p7** in the Width field and **39p** in the Height field.

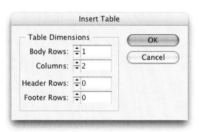

**Step 2.**
Press T to access the Type tool again and click inside the text frame. Choose Table▷Insert Table. In the Insert Table dialog that appears, enter **1** for Body Rows and **2** for Columns. Click OK.

The Threads came together by way of Tampa pop legends Barely Pink. After the Pink packed it up in the summer of 2004 (after a ten year run), founding members Ted Lukas and Brian Merrill decided to write and record some new songs together. The result—a new band with a new name, and an entirely new sound. The two former partners had not worked together since Lukas left Barely Pink in 1998 shortly after recording their second release, Ellie's Suitcase (Big Deal Records /USA, and JVC Victor/Japan). Lukas, who had spent the last six years playing in Hangtown and the Distractions (also featuring Barely Pink's Stan Arthur on drums) recommended bringing in his current guitar partner, Nashville transplant Sonny John Sundstrom. Along with Barely Pink's longest lasting rhythm section, Stan Arthur on drums and Michael Hoag on bass, recording sessions began and the Threads were born.

**Step 3.**
Insert the Type tool cursor into the right column of the table. Press ⌘+D / Ctrl+D to display the Place dialog. Browse to the bio.txt file and click Open.

### Step 4.

Press ⌘+A / Ctrl+A to select all of the text in the cell. In the Control or Character palette, choose a serif font. In the example here, I used Adobe Caslon Pro Regular, set at 12pt with Auto Leading and Optical Kerning applied. Press Shift+⌘+J / Shift+Ctrl+J to left-justify the text.

### Step 5.

Place the Type tool cursor anywhere in the first paragraph and choose Table ▷ Cell Options ▷ Rows And Columns. In the dialog that appears, enter **15p3** in the Column Width field. Click the Strokes and Fills button at the top of the dialog to access that panel. Enter 0 in the Weight field and click OK.

### Step 6.

Press Option+⌘+7 / Alt+Ctrl+7 (Windows), or click the Paragraph Formatting Controls icon in the Control palette. Enter **3** in the Drop Cap Number Of Lines field. If you like, highlight the drop cap with the Type tool and choose a slightly different font. The example here uses Bodoni Book with a 65% black tint applied.

*continues on next page*

## Creating Tables

A table in InDesign is treated like a very large inline character placed inside a text frame (not a graphic frame). This means that you must use the Type tool (not the Selection tools) to create a new table. Start out by inserting the Type tool into a text frame and choosing Table ▷ Insert Table.

When the Insert Table dialog appears, define the number of body rows, columns, header rows, and footer rows by entering values in the respective fields. You can also choose values by clicking the up/down arrows located next to each field.

Click OK for InDesign to insert the table into the frame. You can then place the Type tool cursor inside any cell and add text by typing. As you type, the table column expands vertically to fit the added text. Add text or inline graphics to a table cell by pasting from the Clipboard or importing with the Place command.

Any added text or inline graphics that do not fit into a table cell are stored as overset items. InDesign indicates overset text or graphics by displaying a red dot in the bottom-right corner of the cell.

# Vertical Side Heads *continued*

## Converting Text into Tables

You can convert text into tables by highlighting a range of text with the Type tool and choosing Table ▷ Convert Text To Table.

When the Convert Text To Table dialog appears, choose delimiter characters for table column and row separators from the respective menus. The Number Of Columns field becomes active only when the Paragraph option is chosen as the delimiter character for both column and row separators.

Click OK to convert the text into a table.

**Step 7.**

Place the Type tool cursor in the left column of the table and choose Table ▷ Cell Options ▷ Rows And Columns. In the dialog that appears, enter **9p** in the Column Width field. Click the Text button at the top of the dialog to access the Text panel and enter **0p10** in the Right Inset field. Click the Strokes and Fills button to access that panel. Enter **0** in the Weight field. Click OK to apply.

**Step 8.**

Choose Window ▷ Type & Tables ▷ Table (or press Shift+F9) to display the Table palette. Click the Align Bottom and Rotate text 270° buttons. In the Control or Character palette, choose a script font. I used Texas Hero at 126pt, with Optical Kerning and -30 Tracking applied.

**Step 9.**

Type the word **history** in the cell. Press ⌘+A / Ctrl+A to select all and choose Type ▷ Create Outlines.

The Threads came together by way of Tampa pop legends Barely Pink. After the Pink packed it up in the summer of 2004 (after a ten year run), founding members Ted Lukas and Brian Merrill decided to write and record some new songs together. The result—a new band with a new name, and an entirely new sound.

The two former partners had not worked together since Lukas left Barely Pink in 1998 shortly after recording their second release, Ellie's Suitcase (Big Deal Records /USA, and JVC Victor/Japan). Lukas, who had spent the last six years playing in Hangtown and the Distractions (also featuring Barely Pink's Stan Arthur on drums) recommended bringing in his current guitar partner, Nashville transplant Sonny John Sundstrom. Along with Barely Pink's longest lasting rhythm section, Stan Arthur on drums and Michael Hoag on bass, recording sessions began and the Threads were born.

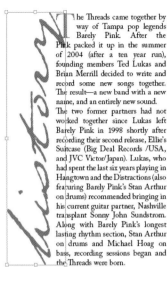

The Threads came together by way of Tampa pop legends Barely Pink. After the Pink packed it up in the summer of 2004 (after a ten year run), founding members Ted Lukas and Brian Merrill decided to write and record some new songs together. The result—a new band with a new name, and an entirely new sound. The two former partners had not worked together since Lukas left Barely Pink in 1998 shortly after recording their second release, Ellie's Suitcase (Big Deal Records /USA, and JVC Victor/Japan). Lukas, who had spent the last six years playing in Hangtown and the Distractions (also featuring Barely Pink's Stan Arthur on drums) recommended bringing in his current guitar partner, Nashville transplant Sonny John Sundstrom. Along with Barely Pink's longest lasting rhythm section, Stan Arthur on drums and Michael Hoag on bass, recording sessions began and the Threads were born.

**Step 10.**

Switch to the Selection tool and click the word history in the cell to select the nested frame. Choose Window ▷ Swatches (or press F5) to display the Swatches palette and press X to bring the fill icon to the front. Click the red swatch and enter **75%** in the Tint field.

## Resizing an Entire Table Interactively

To resize a table interactively, click the Type tool in any cell and then position the cursor over the bottom-right corner of the table.

When the cursor icon changes to display a diagonal, double-headed arrow, click and drag to scale. Hold down the Shift key as you drag to scale the table proportionately.

When resizing a table using this method, InDesign does not scale any existing cell contents along with the table. To resize a table and its contents together, you must scale the text frame using the Selection tool while holding down the ⌘ key (Mac) or Ctrl key (Windows).

**Step 11.**

Choose Object ▷ Feather. In the dialog that appears, check the Feather check box to enable the effect. Enter **0p3** in the Feather Width field and choose Diffused from the Corners pop-up menu. Keep the Noise setting at 0%. Click OK to apply.

**Step 12.**

Choose Object ▷ Drop Shadow. In the dialog that appears, check the Drop Shadow check box to enable the effect. Choose Multiply from the Mode pop-up menu and black from the swatches list. Enter **35%** for Opacity, **0p6** for Blur, **0p2** for X Offset, and **0p6** for Y Offset. Keep the Spread and Noise settings at 0%. Click OK to apply.

The Threads came together by way of Tampa pop legends Barely Pink. After the Pink packed it up in the summer of 2004 (after a ten year run), founding members Ted Lukas and Brian Merrill decided to write and record some new songs together. The result—a new band with a new name, and an entirely new sound. The two former partners had not worked together since Lukas left Barely Pink in 1998 shortly after recording their second release, Ellie's Suitcase (Big Deal Records /USA, and JVC Victor/Japan). Lukas, who had spent the last six years playing in Hangtown and the Distractions (also featuring Barely Pink's Stan Arthur on drums) recommended bringing in his current guitar partner, Nashville transplant Sonny John Sundstrom. Along with Barely Pink's longest lasting rhythm section, Stan Arthur on drums and Michael Hoag on bass, recording sessions began and the Threads were born.

# Feathered Drop Cap

Applying drop caps using paragraph formatting can sometimes limit your creativity. I'm sure you've seen and probably used the traditional serif drop cap that extends into three lines of text (yawn!). But not to worry—you can take drop caps to a whole other level by placing the character in its own text frame and applying cool effects such as feathers, drop shadows, blend modes, and of course, a text wrap.

With these steps, we'll import some tagged text, already styled and ready to apply a drop cap to. We'll then create a large script drop cap that has a gradient, feather, drop shadow, wrap around object text wrap, and overlay blend mode applied. It sounds like a lot just for one character, but sometimes a little extra effort is what it takes to make your layout or design really stand out.

## Get Creative with Your Drop Caps

To re-create this effect using the text shown here, download branded.txt from *The InDesign Effects Book* website.

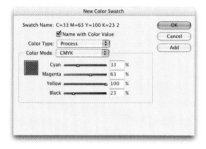

**Step 1.**
In a new document, Choose Window ▷ Swatches (or press F5) to display the Swatches palette. If it isn't already, press X to bring the fill icon to the front. Choose New Color Swatch from the Swatches palette fly-out menu. In the dialog that appears, create a brown build using C=33, M=63, Y=100, K=23. Click OK to add the swatch and close the dialog.

**Step 2.**
Press M to access the Rectangle tool and draw a rectangle to use as a background for the effect. Press X again to bring the stroke icon to the front. Press the backslash key (\) to apply a stroke of None.

**Step 3.**
Deselect the rectangle and press T to access the Type tool. Create a rectangle text frame over the background shape. Press V to switch to the Selection tool. In the Control or Transform palette, enter **25p11** in the Width field and **11p7** in the Height field.

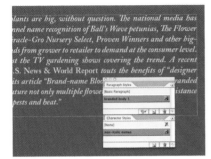

**Step 4.**

Press ⌘+D / Ctrl+D to display the Place dialog. Browse to the branded.txt file and click Open. The text should appear in the frame already styled because it is tagged with a paragraph style. Choose Window ▷ Type & Tables ▷ Paragraph Styles (or press F11) to display the Paragraph Styles palette and press Shift+F11 to display the Character Styles palette. If the palettes appear on your screen docked together, toggle between the two and notice the new styles listed in each one.

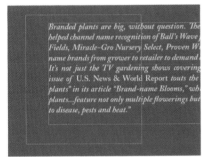

**Step 5.**

Press T to access the Type tool and select the first letter of the paragraph—B. Press ⌘+C / Ctrl+C to copy the character to the Clipboard. Create a new text frame that overlaps the right edge of the entire paragraph, as shown.

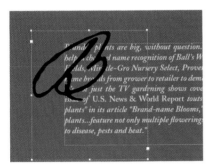

**Step 6.**

Press ⌘+V / Ctrl+V to paste the letter B into the new text frame. Press V to access the Selection tool and click the Formatting Affects Text button at the bottom of the Tools palette. Press T to access the Type tool. In the Control or Character palette, chose a script font. I used Texas Hero at 28pt.

*continues on next page*

## Importing Microsoft Word and RTF Text

To import text from a Word (.doc) or RTF (Rich Text Format) document, choose File ▷ Place and browse to the file's location on your system. Then check Show Import Options and click Open.

The Microsoft Word Import Options and RTF Import Options dialogs are divided into three sections: Include, Formatting, and Options

Under Include, check the items you'd like to import: Table Of Contents Text, Index Text, Footnotes, and Endnotes. It is also recommended that you check Use Typographer's Quotes under Options, as this is standard for most InDesign layouts.

Under Formatting you can choose to either remove or preserve text formatting on import. There are several additional options for preserving formatting, including Manual Page Breaks, Import Inline Graphics, Import Unused Styles, and Track Changes.

You can also choose to import styles automatically or by using a customized style import. When selecting automatic import, InDesign displays style conflicts according to the paragraph and character definitions chosen in the dialog menus. Options include Use InDesign Style Definition, Redefine InDesign Style, and Auto Rename.

# Feathered Drop Cap *continued*

## Importing Tagged Text

To import InDesign tagged text, choose File ▷ Place and browse to the file's location on your system. Once you've selected the file, check Show Import Options and click Open.

The Adobe InDesign Tagged Text Import Options dialog is much simpler to use and contains fewer options than the import dialogs for Word and RTF documents.

Under Formatting, you can choose to convert straight quotes to typographer's quotes (recommended) and also remove text formatting. To import tagged text formatting, leave the Remove Text Formatting option unchecked and choose a style conflict resolve option from the menu. When a style conflict occurs, you can choose to apply Publication Definition, which applies the InDesign document style, or Tagged File Definition, which applies the Tagged Text style.

To view a list of problem tags before placing imported tagged text, check the Show List option located at the bottom of the dialog.

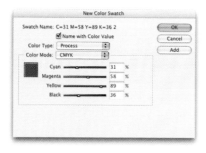

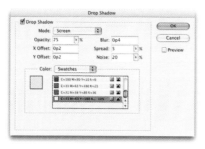

**Step 7.**

Choose Type ▷ Create Outlines. Then in the Swatches palette, choose New Color Swatch from the Swatches palette fly-out menu. In the dialog that appears, create a dark brown build using C=31, M=58, Y=89, K=36. Click OK to add the swatch and close the dialog.

**Step 8.**

Choose Object ▷ Drop Shadow. In the dialog that appears, check the Drop Shadow check box to enable the effect. Choose Screen from the Mode pop-up menu and select the 10% brown swatch from the swatches list. Enter **75%** for Opacity, **0p4** for Blur, and **0p2** for X and Y Offsets. Enter **5%** for Spread and **20%** for Noise, and click OK to apply.

**Step 9.**

Choose Object ▷ Feather. In the dialog that appears, check the Feather check box to enable the effect. Enter **0p3** in the Feather Width field and choose Sharp from the Corners pop-up menu. Keep the Noise setting at 0. Click OK to apply.

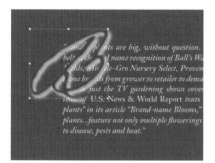

**Step 10.**

Press ⌘+C / Ctrl+C to copy the drop cap B to the Clipboard. Press Option+Shift+⌘+V / Alt+Shift+Ctrl+V to paste in place. Then press the Up Arrow key twice and the Left Arrow key twice to nudge the letter into position.

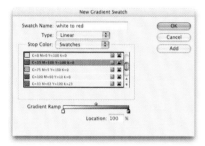

**Step 11.**

In the Swatches palette, choose New Gradient Swatch from the palette fly-out menu. In the dialog that appears, enter **white to red** in the Name field. Choose Linear from the Type pop-up menu and click the far-right color stop icon. Choose Swatches from the Color pop-up menu and select the red swatch from the list. Click OK to add the swatch and close the dialog.

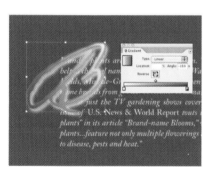

**Step 12.**

Choose Window ▷ Gradient to display the Gradient palette. Enter **-169** into the Angle field.

*continues on next page*

## Importing Other Text-Only Formats

To import text-only formats such as ASCII text, choose File ▷ Place and browse to the file's location on your system. Then check Show Import Options and click Open.

At the top of the Text Import Options dialog, choose a character set from the menu that matches the text-only file you are importing. Macintosh and PC platforms use different character sets. Therefore, to avoid importing strange characters, be sure and choose the platform that the file was originally created from the menu. You can also choose a dictionary to apply to the imported text from the pop-up menu.

In the center of the dialog, you have the option to remove any extra carriage returns placed at the ends of lines and between paragraphs. Having this option to remove unnecessary forced breaks upon text import can be extremely helpful—it can save you from having to spend an awful lot of time reformatting later!

At the bottom of the dialog are some basic import formatting options. You can choose to replace a specific number of spaces with a tab and also convert straight quotes into typographer's quotes.

# Feathered Drop Cap *continued*

## Importing XML

It is also possible to import XML text elements into a document. Choose File ▷ Import XML and browse to the file's location on your system. Once you select the file, check Show XML Import Options and click Open.

Enable the preferred import options and click OK to import. Choose View ▷ Structure ▷ Show Structure to view the imported XML. Upon import, the contents of all imported XML elements are applied to corresponding tagged frames and text objects.

To apply an XML element's contents to an existing untagged frame, click and drag it from the Structure window over the frame in the document layout. Release the mouse button to add the contents of the XML element to the frame.

To apply existing document Paragraph and Character Styles to imported XML tags, choose Map Tags To Styles from the Structure fly-out menu. Select the styles you'd like to map to each tag by clicking its name in the Style menu and choosing from the pop-up menu. If the tags and styles you'd like to map share the same name, click the Map By Name button and InDesign will assign them for you.

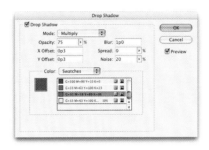

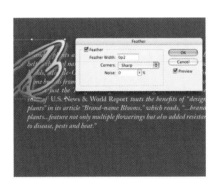

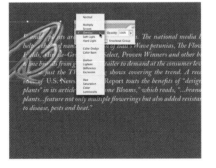

**Step 13.**
Choose Object ▷ Drop Shadow. In the dialog that appears, check the Drop Shadow check box to enable the effect. Choose Multiply from the Mode pop-up menu and select the dark brown swatch from the swatches list. Enter **75%** for Opacity, **1p** for Blur, and **0p3** for X and Y Offsets. Enter **0%** for Spread and **20%** for Noise, and click OK to apply.

**Step 14.**
Choose Object ▷ Feather. In the dialog that appears, change the Feather Width amount to **0p2**. Click OK to apply.

**Step 15.**
Choose Window ▷ Transparency (or press Shift+F10) to display the Transparency palette. Choose Overlay from the Mode pop-up menu.

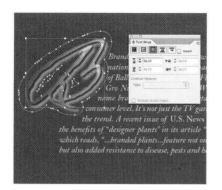

**Step 16.**
Press Option+⌘+W / Alt+Ctrl+W or choose Window▷Text Wrap to display the Text Wrap palette. Click the Wrap Around Object Shape button and enter **0p10** in all the Offset fields.

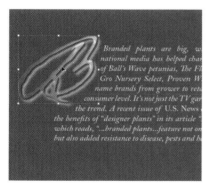

**Step 17.**
⌘+click / Ctrl+click the letter to select the drop cap underneath. Then hold down the Shift key and click again to add the topmost drop cap to the selection. Press ⌘+G / Ctrl+G to group the objects. You can then adjust the position of the drop cap by nudging it with the arrow keys or moving it with the Selection tool.

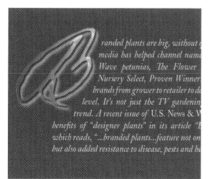

**Step 18.**
Highlight the first letter of the paragraph (the letter B) and press Delete (Mac) or Backspace (Windows). Choose Edit▷Deselect All to view your fancy, new, feathered drop cap!

# Filling with Placeholder Text

If you've ever had to wait until the last minute for an editor or client to submit text for a layout, you're not alone. This happens all the time. What most people don't realize is that text plays an important role in the look of your layout–and trying to design without it is like stumbling through the dark!

Thankfully with InDesign, you don't have to let late text submissions hold up your design work. While you're waiting for the real text to arrive in your inbox, go ahead and create a layout using text frames that are filled with placeholder text.

Click a frame with either selection tool or the Type tool, and choose Type▷Fill With Placeholder Text. InDesign immediately fills the entire text frame or series of threaded frames with fake-Latin gibberish.

The paragraphs are set up just like real text–perfect for use as placeholders in your layout. When zoomed out, the placeholder text appears normal–but a closer look reveals the fake-Latin gibberish.

You can also apply character and paragraph styles to placeholder text, if needed to complete a preliminary design. When the real text arrives, copy/paste it into the preexisting frames and it assumes the formatting already applied.

# Text Path Frame

By now we should all know how to create a text frame. And if you've been trying out the effects in this book, you should also know how to create a text path object. But what if we combined the two to create a *text path frame!*

With these steps we'll create a graphic frame that is also a text path object. Any image container in InDesign can also contain text that follows around the contour of its path. By doing this, you can surround a placed image with text, creating what I like to call a *text path frame.*

As you experiment with this effect, you'll soon come to realize that paragraphs make for really interesting graphic frames. Try placing some text around different shapes and then placing images inside them. You just might come up with a really cool design!

## Wrap Text Around the Outside of a Frame

To re-create this effect using the images and text shown here, download music.txt and record.psd from *The InDesign Effects Book* website.

**Step 1.**
In a new document, press D to set the default colors of None fill and black stroke. Then press F to access the Rectangle Frame tool. Hold down the Shift key and draw a square in the center of the document.

**Step 2.**
Choose Window ▷ Stroke (or press F10) to display the Stroke palette and enter **22pt** in the Weight field. Also, click the Align Stroke To Outside button. Then in the Control or Transform palette, enter **26p11** in the Width and Height fields.

**Step 3.**
Choose Object ▷ Corner Effects. In the dialog that appears, choose Rounded from the Effect pop-up menu, and enter **3p4** in the Size field. Click OK to close the dialog.

**Step 4.**
Press Shift+T to access the Type On A Path tool. Click on the frame edge and press ⌘+D / Ctrl+D to display the Place dialog. Browse to the music.txt file and click Open. Choose Window▷Swatches (or press F5) to display the Swatches palette. Press V to switch to the Selection tool and click the Formatting Affects Text button at the top of the Swatches palette. If it isn't already, press X to bring the fill icon to the front and then click the Paper (white) swatch in the palette.

**Step 5.**
Press ⌘+T / Ctrl+T to display the Character palette. Choose an extended sans serif font to apply to the text. I used Eurostile Extended 2, set at 12pt, with Optical Kerning and a Tracking amount of 30.

**Step 6.**
Click the Type tool icon in the Tools palette and choose the Type On A Path tool. Double-click the Type On A Path tool in the Tools palette to display the Type On A Path Options dialog. Enter 3 in the Spacing field and click OK.

*continues on next page*

## Threading Text Frames

In QuarkXPress this particular task is called "linking and unlinking text boxes." However, in InDesign it is referred to as "threading and unthreading text frames."

XPress requires that you use a special "linking or unlinking" tool to perform this task, but InDesign provides no special tools for "threading and unthreading." Instead, you must click the in or out "port" of a selected text frame with the Selection or Direct Selection tool.

The in port is located at the upper left of the text frame and the out port at the bottom right. Any frame containing text with an empty in and/or out port indicates the text is at the beginning or end of the story, respectively.

A port that contains a triangle indicates that the story is linked to another text frame. An out port containing a plus sign (+) indicates existing "overset" text, meaning that there is more copy to flow. To display the rest of the story, you can either make the current text frame larger, or thread the overset text into another frame.

To thread overset text, click the in or out "port" of a selected text frame with either Selection tool and the cursor changes into a loaded text place icon. Click the loaded cursor and a frame is drawn for you automatically using default text frame options.

# Text Path Frame *continued*

## Flowing Text

You can flow text into a document in several ways using the Place command:

**Manual Text Flow** Choose File ▷ Place and open the text document you'd like to import. With a loaded text place cursor, click anywhere in the document or draw a frame. InDesign creates a new frame using default text frame options and places the text into it. You can also place text by clicking an existing frame or a series of threaded frames. The Manual Text Flow icon changes its appearance when you hover the cursor over a frame or guide/grid snap point.

**Semi-Automatic Text Flow** This method reloads the text place cursor when a placed story does not end in a drawn or clicked frame (or series of frames). To flow placed text semi-automatically, hold down the Option or Alt key as you click or draw with the loaded text place cursor.

The Semi-Automatic Text Flow icon changes its appearance when you hover the cursor over a frame.

**Step 7.**
Click the Formatting Affects Container button at the bottom of the Tools palette. Press ⌘+D / Ctrl+D to display the Place dialog. Browse to the record.psd file and click Open.

**Step 8.**
Press Option+Shift+⌘+E / Alt+Shift+Ctrl+E to fit the content proportionately within the frame.

**Step 9.**
Press A to switch to the Direct Selection tool and click directly on the placed image to select it. Move the record over to the right until it appears centered at the top of the frame.

**Step 10.**

Press T to access the Type tool and create a text frame underneath the record. Click the red swatch in the Swatches palette. In the Control or Character palette, choose a condensed, bold, sans-serif font at a larger point size. I used Helvetica Ultra Compressed at 71pt, with Optical Kerning and -15 Tracking. Type the words **VINYL SOURCE** in all caps.

**Step 11.**

Switch to the Selection tool and choose Object ▷ Drop Shadow. In the dialog that appears, check the Drop Shadow check box to enable the effect. Choose Multiply from the Mode pop-up menu and select the black swatch from the swatches list. Enter **85%** for Opacity, **0p2** for Blur, **0p0** for X Offset, and **0p2** for Y Offset. Keep the Spread and Noise settings at 0%, and click OK to apply.

**Step 12.**

Choose Object ▷ Arrange ▷ Send To Back. Then choose Edit ▷ Deselect All to view the finished text path frame!

## Flowing Text *continued*

**Automatic Text Flow** This method adds as many threaded text frames as necessary to fit a story in the existing pages of a document. To flow placed text automatically, hold down Option+Shift (Mac) or Alt+Shift (Windows) as you click or draw with the loaded text place cursor.

**Super Autoflow** This method adds as many threaded text frames and pages as necessary to fit an entire story in a document. To Super Autoflow placed text, hold down Shift as you click or draw with the loaded text place cursor.

**Note:** Clicking a loaded text place cursor between column guides creates a text frame that fills the entire column.

# 4

## Shape Effects

*Next time you're faced with the challenge of designing a logo or creating a simple illustration, you might want to consider doing it in InDesign. Yes, you read that correctly—it says InDesign. I included this chapter to prove to all you nonbelievers out there that InDesign's drawing tools and built-in effects are the real deal! There's a lot more you can do here with shapes than you may realize. With these projects, we'll combine polygons with corner effects to create bursts and flower shapes. We'll also learn how to place custom shapes around a circle, and even try our hand at some photo-realistic illustration.*

**Spot Color Burst Gone Wild!**

**Interlocking Objects**

**Instant Flower Shapes**

**Getting in Gear**

**InDesign Snowflakes**

**Photo-realistic 3-D Sphere**

**Gel Buttons**

**Gel Sidebar Tabs**

**Object Silhouettes**

**Transparent Background Frames**

**Placing Shapes Around a Circle**

# Spot Color Burst Gone Wild!

I cringe every time an art director or client asks me to "put it in a burst." There's no doubt that the burst is probably the most overused design element in existence—yet you still see them everywhere. That's right. Any time the guy in marketing (you know the one I'm talking about) wants the price to stand out, you always have to "put it in a burst." Ugh!

Despite my distaste for bursts, I am still forced to use them on occasion, and I'm sure you will be too. I guess the burst has its purpose in life and we'll just have to accept it. However, just because we have to use a burst every now and again doesn't mean that we necessarily have to play by the rules—and I'm just the guy to show you how you can break them using InDesign.

You may also be asked to use a burst in a spot-color design, which poses even more of a challenge. With these steps we'll learn how you can add a little more excitement to a two-color sale tag design that includes a burst.

## From Polygon to Burst in Seconds Flat

Combining InDesign's corner effects with polygon star shapes can result in—believe it or not—*creative bursts!*

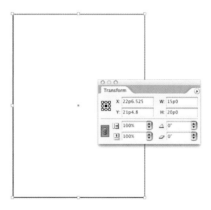

**Step 1.**
Create a new document and press D to select the default colors of None fill and black stroke. Then press M to access the Rectangle tool and draw a shape that is 15p wide and 20p high. To be precise, you can enter these values in the Width and Height fields of the Control or Transform palette once the shape is drawn.

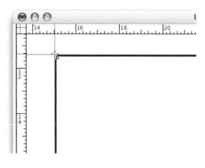

**Step 2.**
If they are not already visible, press ⌘+R / Ctrl+R to display the document window rulers. In the upper-left corner of the document window where the horizontal and vertical rulers intersect, click and drag to reset the zero point of the document to the upper-left corner of the rectangle, as shown. You can set your rulers to display picas by Control-clicking (Mac) or right-clicking on each ruler and selecting Picas from the contextual menu.

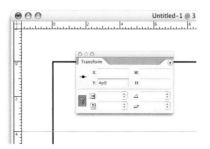

**Step 3.**
Click and drag a new ruler guide onto the page from the horizontal ruler above. With the guide still selected, enter **4p** in the Y Location field of the Control or Transform palette.

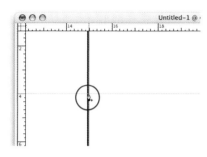

### Step 4.
Press P to access the Pen tool. Click to add a point where the new ruler guide intersects with the left side of the shape. Add a second point where the ruler guide intersects with right side of the shape.

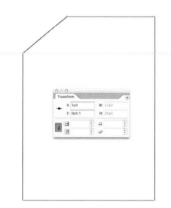

### Step 5.
Hold down the ⌘ or Ctrl key to temporarily access the Direct Selection tool. Click the upper-left corner point of the rectangle to select it. Enter **5p** in the X Location field of the Control or Transform palette.

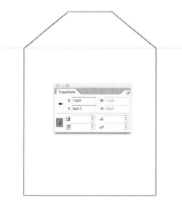

### Step 6.
Hold down the ⌘ or Ctrl key again and select the upper-right corner point. Enter **10p** in the X Location field of the Control or Transform palette. We now have an entirely new shape!

*continues on next page*

## Tooltips

These little guys can be really helpful if you're new to InDesign. Some of the visual label icons may be hard to decipher if you're new to the interface, in which case it's tooltips to the rescue! Just hover your mouse over any tool, control, or palette name and in a few seconds, a little yellow box appears with a description.

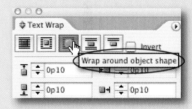

A few seconds not fast enough for you? Then open the InDesign General Preferences (⌘+K on Mac, Ctrl+K on Windows) and under Tool Tips, choose Fast.

Once you get used to the interface, tooltips may become more of a nuisance than a help. If this happens, you may just want to turn them off altogether. To do this, open the InDesign General Preferences panel (⌘+K / Ctrl+K) and under Tool Tips, choose None.

# Spot Color Burst Gone Wild! *continued*

## Adjusting Ruler Guides

Some designers find ruler guides extremely helpful when setting up initial page layouts and templates. You can use guides to line up page items evenly and snap them into place. Guides do not print by default—although they can be printed if you so choose. It is easy to move, lock, snap to, add, or delete guides, and you can even assign them different colors.

You can click and drag a new guide out from the horizontal or vertical rulers and onto the targeted page (or master page) at any time, no matter what tool you are using. Once the guide is placed, you can select it with either selection tool by hovering over it and clicking. To select multiple guides, Shift-click or marquee.

You can also choose to Hide/Show, Lock/Unlock, or Snap To guides under the View ▷ Grids & Guides submenu, or in the contextual menu (Control- or right-clicking anywhere on the Pasteboard). To access the Ruler Guides dialog, choose Layout ▷ Ruler Guides, or select a guide and choose it from the contextual menu.

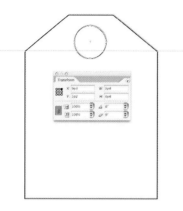

**Step 7.**
Press L to access the Ellipse tool. Center the cursor about 3p below the top line of the shape. Hold down Shift+Option (Mac) or Shift+Alt (Windows) and click and drag to draw a perfect circle. Enter **3p8** in the Width and Height fields of the Control or Transform palette.

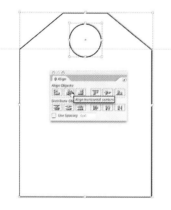

**Step 8.**
Press V to access the Selection tool. Hold down Shift and click the other shape to add it to your selection. Choose Window ▷ Object & Layout ▷ Align (or press Shift+F7) to display the Align palette, and click the Align Horizontal Centers button.

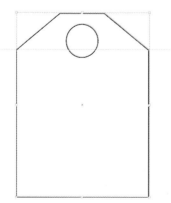

**Step 9.**
Press ⌘+8 / Ctrl+8 to create a compound path from the two selected shapes.

### Step 10.

Deselect the compound path. Click and hold the Ellipse tool icon in the Tools palette to reveal a list of shape tools. Select the Polygon tool from Shape tools list, and click the page. In the dialog that appears, enter **22p2** in the Polygon Width and Height fields, **20** in the Number Of Sides field, and **60%** in the Star Inset field. Click OK to apply.

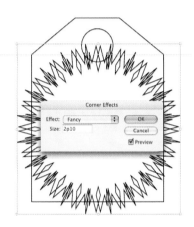

### Step 11.

Choose Object ▷ Corner Effects. In the dialog that appears, choose Fancy from the Effect pop-up menu and enter **2p10** in the Size field. Check the Preview check box to see the effect applied as you enter the settings in the dialog. Click OK to apply.

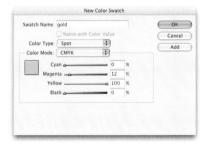

### Step 12.

Choose Window ▷ Swatches (or press F5) to display the Swatches palette. Select the yellow swatch in the palette list and choose New Color Swatch from the Swatches palette fly-out menu. In the dialog that appears, choose Spot from the Color Type pop-up menu and CMYK from the Mode pop-up menu. Create a gold build using C=0, M=12, Y=100, K=0. Enter a name into the field (e.g., **gold**) and click OK to add the swatch.

## Adjusting Margin and Column Guides

You can set margin and column guides in the New Document dialog when starting a new project, and you can edit them at any time while working in the document. To edit, choose Layout ▷ Margins And Columns.

Unlike in QuarkXPress, you can edit the margin and column settings for individual document pages–not just master pages. Margin and column guides are applied just like any other master page item, but they can also be edited in the document page using the Margin And Columns dialog.

**Note:** To allow InDesign to resize or reposition any object that is aligned to a margin, column, or ruler guide, enable the Layout Adjustment feature located under the Layout menu.

*continues on next page*

# Spot Color Burst Gone Wild! *continued*

## Aligning to Baseline Grid

Aligning multiple columns of body text to the baseline grid can greatly improve the overall appearance of a document. To display the baseline grid, choose View ▷ Grids & Guides ▷ Show Baseline Grid or press Option+⌘+' / Alt+Ctrl+'.

In Grids Preferences, enter the leading amount you're using for body text in the Increment Every data field, and click OK. Select the text frame and click the Align To Baseline Grid control in either the Paragraph palette or the Control palette.

To align just the first line of each paragraph to the baseline grid, select the text frame and choose Only Align First Line To Grid from the Paragraph palette menu.

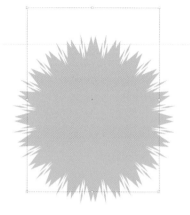

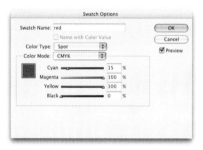

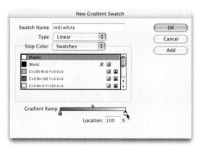

**Step 13.**

Press X to bring the stroke icon to the front, if necessary. Press the forward slash key (/) to apply a stroke of None to the burst. Press V to access the Selection tool and select the compound path. Press the forward slash key (/) again to apply a stroke of None to the compound path.

**Step 14.**

Press X to bring the fill icon to the front. Double-click the red swatch in the Swatches palette to display the Swatch Options dialog. Choose Spot from the Color Type pop-up menu. Enter a name into the field (e.g., **red**) and click OK.

**Step 15.**

Choose New Gradient Swatch from the Swatches palette fly-out menu. In the dialog that appears, choose Linear from the Type pop-up menu. Click the left color stop icon located beneath the Gradient Ramp at the bottom of the dialog. Choose Swatches from the Stop Color pop-up menu and select the red spot color swatch from the list. Click the right color stop icon and select Paper from the swatches list. Enter a name into the field (e.g., **red/white**) and click OK.

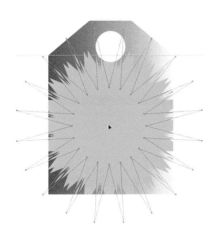

### Step 16.

Select the burst and press ⌘+X / Ctrl+X to cut the object from the page. Select the compound path and choose Edit ▷ Paste Into. Press A to switch to the Direct Selection tool and click the burst to select it. Click the center point of the burst path and drag to position it within the compound path as shown.

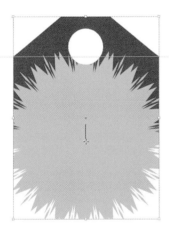

### Step 17.

Press V to switch to the Selection tool and select the compound path again. Press G to access the Gradient tool. Place the cursor directly beneath the center point of the compound path. Holding down Shift to constrain the angle, draw a vertical line that is approximately 2p in length. Doing so applies the red-to-white gradient behind the gold burst as shown.

### Step 18.

To complete the design, add some text as shown. I used 100pt Compacta ICG Bold, with a white fill and 1.5pt red (spot color) stroke. Optical Kerning is applied to the type and the text frame is rotated 7°. A drop shadow is also applied using the red spot color set to the Hard Light mode at 75% opacity.

## Snapping to Document Grid

You can align objects evenly on the page by snapping to the document grid. When shown, the document grid displays a series of both vertical and horizontal lines on the page, resulting in what looks like transparent graph paper placed over the top of your layout.

When made visible, the grid can be very distracting to work with–even when placed in back with a lighter color applied to it. Thankfully, you can still snap to the document grid even when it is hidden.

Document Grid color settings and gridline options are accessible in Grids Preferences. To align graphic frames and other objects to the top and bottom lines of paragraph text, enter gridline subdivision values that coincide with the baseline grid.

To snap to the document grid, select View ▷ Grids & Guides ▷ Snap To Document Grid, or Control- or right-click anywhere on the Pasteboard and select Snap To Document Grid from the contextual menu.

# Interlocking Objects

At first glance, you might guess that a common effect like this is really easy to pull off, right? Wrong! In fact, even in a more advanced application like Adobe Illustrator, which contains a lot more tools for combining and intersecting shapes, this trick is—well ... *tricky!*

All we're trying to do here is connect two shapes together, like a key ring or a chain link. A good example of this (that almost everyone is familiar with) is the Olympic rings.

Currently, there is no Divide command in the InDesign Pathfinder palette as there is in Illustrator. Therefore, in order to create the appearance of interlocking shapes in InDesign, we have to use the Scissors tool and the Arrange commands. Note that once a line segment is cut and sent to back, it must remain a separate element and cannot be grouped, or you will lose the effect.

## Not as Simple as It Looks

Although it's not as easy to create interlocking objects in InDesign as it is in Illustrator, it can be done. With these steps, we'll interlock two circle shapes together to create a logo.

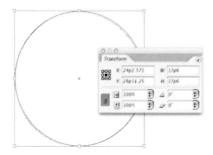

**Step 1.**

Create a new document and press L to access the Ellipse tool. Hold down Shift+Option (Mac) or Shift+Alt (Windows) and click and drag to draw a perfect circle. Enter **17p6** in the Width and Height fields of the Control or Transform palette.

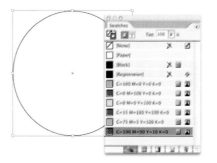

**Step 2.**

Choose Window ▷ Swatches (or press F5) to display the Swatches palette. Press X to bring the stroke icon to the front and select the blue swatch in the Swatches palette.

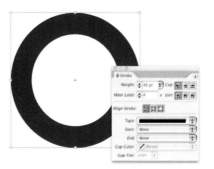

**Step 3.**

Choose Window ▷ Stroke (or press F10) to display the Stroke palette. Enter **40pt** in the Weight field.

**Step 4.**
Press V to access the Selection tool. Hover the cursor over the center point of the circle, hold down Option (Mac) or Alt (Windows), and click and drag to the right to make a copy of the object. Position the duplicate as shown.

## Measure Tool

The Measure tool goes hand in hand with the Info palette. Use this tool to calculate the size of a placed graphic or the angle of a drawn path to match sizes or angles among objects in a document layout.

You can access the Measure tool by clicking its icon in the Tools palette or by pressing K on the keyboard. To use the tool, click and drag along the area you want to measure. The Info palette opens automatically, providing you with specific measurements, including X and Y coordinates, width, height, and angle.

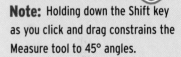

**Note:** Holding down the Shift key as you click and drag constrains the Measure tool to 45° angles.

**Step 5.**
With the duplicate circle still selected, click the red swatch in the Swatches palette to change its stroke color from blue to red.

**Step 6.**
Press C to switch to the Scissors tool. Hover the Scissors tool cursor over the upper left of the circle path as shown. When the cursor changes to display a target icon, click to cut the path. Then hover the Scissors tool cursor over the upper right of the circle path as shown. When the cursor changes to display a target icon, click to cut the path again.

*continues on next page*

# Interlocking Objects *continued*

## Button Tool

The Button tool is used for creating interactive behaviors that you can embed in an exported PDF document. Some of the behaviors you can attach to a button are Go To URL, Go To Anchor, Go To Page, Play Sound, and Play Movie.

You can access the Button tool by clicking its icon in the Tools palette or by pressing B.

To use the tool, click and drag over the area where you'd like to create an interactive button. Or you can click once in the upper-left corner of the interactive area and enter the width and height amount for the button in the dialog that appears.

You can then specify the General and Behaviors options for a selected button by choosing Object ▷ Interactive ▷ Button Options. Choose the Event (Mouse Up, Mouse Down, etc.) and the Behavior (Go To Anchor, Go To Page, Play Sound, etc.) settings for your new button, and click OK.

**Step 7.**

Press ⌘+Shift+[ / Ctrl+Shift+[ to send the path segment to the back. If you look closely, you will see two thin white lines appear where the path was cut, but these won't show up when you print. The lines will also not appear on screen if you export the logo as a JPEG (to potentially be used as a web graphic).

**Step 8.**

Press the forward slash key (\) to access the Line tool. Hold down Shift to constrain to a 45° angle and draw a diagonal line that is 7p7 in length. You can enter this amount in the Line Length field of the Control or Transform palette once the line is drawn. Press V to switch to the Selection tool and position the line to the upper left of the blue circle as shown.

**Step 9.**

Click the blue swatch in the Swatches palette to apply a blue stroke. Then in the Stroke palette, enter **25pt** in the Weight field and choose Triangle Wide from the Start pop-up menu.

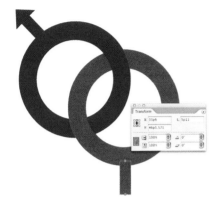

### Step 10.

Press the forward slash key (\) to access the Line tool again. Hold down Shift to constrain to a 45° angle and draw a vertical line that is 5p11 in length. You can enter this amount in the Line Length field of the Control or Transform palette once the line is drawn. Press V to switch to the Selection tool and position the line under the red circle as shown. Click the red swatch in the Swatches palette to apply a red stroke. Enter **25pt** in the Weight field of the Stroke palette.

### Step 11.

Double-click the Rotate tool icon in the Tools palette. In the dialog that appears, enter **90°** in the Angle field and click Copy. Enter **5p5.5** in the Line Length field of the Control or Transform palette.

**Don't stop now—Customize the Effect:**
To add to the design, try placing some images and adding some text as shown. The example here uses the ITC American Typewriter font, with a 75% black tint fill applied. Adding the images is a little trickier. You have to make duplicates of the circles, place the images inside them, and then place the duplicate circles behind the originals. Depending on where you cut the circle to create the interlocking effect, you may also have to place a duplicate image inside the open path and line it up with the crop of the adjacent photo.

## Scissors Tool

InDesign's Scissors tool is used for cutting points and lines on a path. You can divide symmetrical shapes, such as half-circles or diamonds, or remove pieces of a path to create interesting logo effects and design elements.

You can access the Scissors tool by clicking its icon in the Tools palette or by pressing C on the keyboard.

To cut points on a path, you must first select a shape with the Direct Selection tool, then switch to the Scissors tool. Hover your mouse over a specific point on the path until you see the cursor change to a target symbol. Click to cut the path. Continue clicking points until you've divided the shape the way you like. You can then separate the pieces with the Selection tool.

With the Scissors tool, you don't necessarily have to cut points on a path—you can also cut the connecting lines between points. Select a shape with the Direct Selection tool, then switch to the Scissors tool. Hover your mouse over a line on the path until you see the cursor change to a target symbol, then click to cut it. You'll see a new point added to the line. Keep clicking lines until you've divided the shape to your preference, then separate the pieces with the Selection tool.

# Instant Flower Shapes

As with the burst effect earlier in this chapter, you can combine stars that are created with the Polygon tool with InDesign's corner effects to create flower shapes. This just goes to show that you don't have to be a master illustrator to create cool shapes that can be used as logos or as design elements in a layout. In fact, you don't have to know how to draw at all!

With these steps, we'll create a logo design that uses a simple sunflower shape. Keep in mind, however, that this is just one way to use this effect. Once you get the hang of this, try combining polygons that contain different star inset amounts with other corner effects, all set at different sizes. To take it one step further, try creating different flower shapes and combining them in various ways with the Pathfinder.

## Combining Polygons with Inset Corner Effects

To re-create this effect using the text shown here, download summer_savings.inds from the *InDesign Effects Book* website.

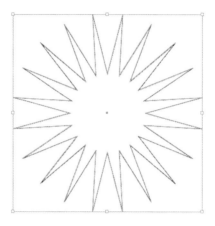

**Step 1.**
Create a new document. Select the Polygon tool from the Tools palette and click once anywhere on the page. In the dialog that appears, enter **24p5** in the Polygon Width and Polygon Height fields. Enter **20** in the Number Of Sides field and **60%** in the Star Inset field. Click OK.

**Step 2.**
Choose Object ▷ Corner Effects. In the dialog that appears, choose Inset from the Effect pop-up menu and enter **4p9** in the Size field. Click OK to apply.

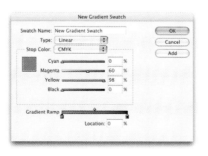

**Step 3.**
Choose Window ▷ Swatches (or press F5) to display the Swatches palette. Choose New Gradient Swatch from the Swatches palette fly-out menu. In the dialog that appears, click the left color stop icon located beneath the Gradient Ramp at the bottom of the dialog. Create a build that uses C=0, M=60, Y=98, K=0. Don't click OK just yet.

**Step 4.**
Click the right color stop icon and choose Swatches from the Stop Color pop-up menu. Select the yellow swatch from the list. Enter **sunflower** in the Swatch Name field and click OK.

# Gradient Tool

The Gradient tool allows you to apply various gradient styles to selected items within your layout. This tool works closely with the Gradient and Swatches palettes, allowing you to apply gradients to both fills and strokes on selected frames, shapes, paths, and text.

You can access the Gradient tool by clicking its icon in the Tools palette or by pressing G.

To apply a gradient, first select an object with the Selection tool or select some text with the Type tool (frames, shapes, paths, and text all work with the Gradient tool). Then activate the Gradient tool and click and drag in any direction to apply a gradient you've created in the Gradient palette or a gradient swatch that has been saved in the Swatches palette. To constrain the gradient in a certain direction, hold down the Shift key as you click and drag.

A single gradient can also be applied to multiple objects and grouped objects with the Gradient tool.

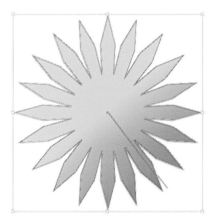

**Step 5.**
Press G to access the Gradient tool. Click and drag from the bottom-right corner of the sunflower shape to the center of the object. The gradient should appear in the sunflower shape as shown.

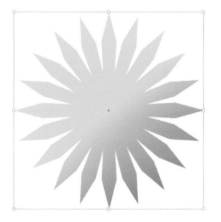

**Step 6.**
Press X to bring the stroke icon to the front and press the backslash key (/) to apply a stroke of None. If you like, press ⌘+H / Ctrl+H to hide frame edges and check out how your flower shape is starting to look.

*continues on next page*

# Instant Flower Shapes *continued*

## Creating Shapes with the Shape Tools

With the Shape tools, you can create rectangles, ellipses, and polygons.

You can access the Rectangle tool by clicking its icon in the Tools palette or pressing M. The shortcut key for the Ellipse tool is L. The Polygon tool has no default keyboard shortcut, but you can create one for it under Edit ▷ Keyboard Shortcuts.

To create a shape, choose the tool and click and drag. Hold down Shift as you click and drag to constrain your shape to its original proportions, making a rectangle a perfect square and an ellipse a perfect circle. Hold down Option (Mac) or Alt (Windows) as you click and drag to draw from the center.

InDesign applies default stroke settings to your shape, but you can adjust them in either the Stroke or Control palette. You can also add a fill and merge with other shapes.

Shapes created with the Shape tools can also be converted into graphic or text frames. To convert a shape into a graphic frame, simply place a graphic inside it. To convert a shape into a text frame, just click it with the Type tool and add text.

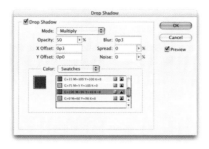

**Step 7.**

Choose Object ▷ Drop Shadow. In the dialog that appears, click the Drop Shadow check box to enable the effect, then turn on the Preview check box to see the shadow applied to your selected object. Select the blue swatch from the swatches list. Enter **50%** for Opacity, **0p3** for Blur, **0p3** for X Offset, and **0p0** for Y Offset. Keep the rest of the settings at their defaults. Click OK to apply.

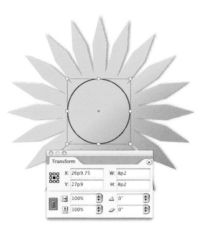

**Step 8.**

Press L to access the Ellipse tool. Position the cursor over the center point of the sunflower shape. Hold down Shift+Option / Shift+Alt and click and drag to draw a perfect circle. Enter **8p2** in the Width and Height fields of the Control or Transform palette.

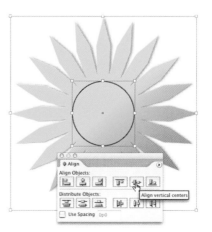

**Step 9.**

Choose Window ▷ Object & Layout ▷ Align (or press Shift+F7) to display the Align palette. Press V to access the Selection tool. Hold down Shift and click the sunflower shape to add it to the selection. In the Align palette, click the Align Horizontal Centers button, and then click the Align Vertical Centers Button.

**Step 10.**
Hold down Shift and click the sunflower shape to deselect it. Choose New Color Swatch from the Swatches palette fly-out menu. In the dialog that appears, create a brown building using C=29, M=87, Y=100, K=34. Click OK to add the swatch and close the dialog. The brown color is automatically applied to the selected circle.

**Step 11.**
Choose Window ▷ Stroke (or press F10) to display the Stroke palette. Enter **4pt** in the Weight field and choose Japanese Dots from the Type pop-up menu. If you prefer, you can also choose these settings in the Control palette.

**Step 12.**
To add a subtle outer glow to the center of the flower, choose Object ▷ Drop Shadow. In the dialog that appears, click the Drop Shadow check box to enable the effect. To get the glow effect, choose Hard Light from the Mode pop-up menu and select the red swatch from the swatches list. Enter **0p11** for Blur, **0p0** for both for X and Y Offset, and **5%** for Spread. Keep the rest of the settings at their defaults. Click OK to apply.

*continues on next page*

# The Polygon Dialog vs. the Polygon Settings Dialog

You can access the Polygon Settings dialog by double-clicking the Polygon Shape tool icon in the Tools palette, or access the Polygon dialog (containing additional width and height settings) by clicking once on the page with the Polygon Shape tool. Both dialogs let you choose the number of sides for your shape and also the percentage of inset to create a star shape.

The settings entered in the dialog remain the Polygon Tool defaults until you change them.

**Note:** You can add or subtract polygon sides by holding down the Up or Down arrow keys as you draw. The Up arrow adds sides and the Down arrow subtracts them.

# Instant Flower Shapes *continued*

## Transparency Palette

With the Transparency palette, InDesign allows you to adjust opacity levels and apply blend modes to selected fills and strokes, placed graphics, and editable text. Applied transparency and blend modes affect the entire object (fill and stroke), as well as all frame contents (placed graphic or text). It is not possible to apply different transparency effects or values to the fill and stroke of an object or to individual text characters or layers.

Enabling the Isolate Blending option in the palette allows items in a selected group with blend modes applied to them to affect only objects in the group.

Enabling the Knockout Group option allows transparent items in a selected group to block each other out visually.

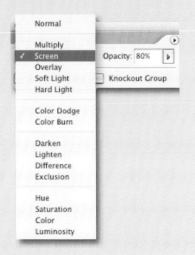

**Step 13.**

Double-click the Scale tool icon in the Tools palette. In the dialog that appears, enter **75%** in the Uniform Scale field and click Copy.

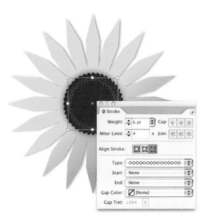

**Step 14.**

In the Stroke palette, enter **6pt** in the Weight field, click the Align Stroke To Outside button, and choose White Diamond from the Type pop-up menu.

**Step 15.**

Press X to bring the stroke icon to the front and click the yellow swatch in the Swatches palette list.

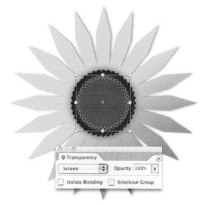

**Step 16.**
Choose Window ▷ Transparency
(or press Shift+F10) to display the
Transparency palette. Choose Screen
from the Mode pop-up menu.

## Scale Tool Options

**Scaling a frame's contents** To
scale a placed graphic within its
bounding frame, you must first select
it with the Direct Selection tool and
then switch to the Scale tool. You
can then scale the image within the
frame. You can also reposition the
scale-from point, just like with any
other object.

**Scaling a frame but not its
contents** Select an object, then
double-click the Scale tool's icon
in the Tools palette to bring up the
Scale dialog. Uncheck the Scale
Content box and enter values in the
appropriate data fields. Click the
Preview check box to see the effect,
and if you like what you see, click
OK to apply.

**Step 17.**
Press V to access the Selection tool and
deselect the circle. Press ⌘+D / Ctrl+D
to display the Place dialog. Locate
the summer_savings.inds image on
your system, and click Open. Use the
Selection tool to position the InDesign
snippet over the circle as shown.

**Don't stop now—customize the effect:**
Now try experimenting with this effect
by using different gradient colors and
applying different corner effect sizes
and styles to your polygon shape. The
example shown here uses the same
polygon as shown in the steps above,
but with a 5pt Fancy corner effect and
dark-red-to-magenta linear gradient
applied.

# Getting in Gear

I stumbled across this effect while experimenting with InDesign's corner effects. I discovered that by applying the Bevel corner effect to a star created with the Polygon tool, you can level off each point of the star. Doing so results in a perfect gear shape, like you'd find inside an old clock or wristwatch. You can use these gear shapes to create logos or simple illustrations, or to use as abstract design elements in a layout.

You can change the amount of gears in the shape by adding or subtracting sides of the initial polygon star. To add or subtract polygon sides quickly, hold down the Up/Down arrow keys as you draw the star with the Polygon tool. The Up arrow adds sides and the Down arrow subtracts them.

Once you create a gear shape, you can duplicate it and resize it—but before you do, make sure to choose Scale Strokes from the Transform palette fly-out menu. Otherwise, the applied stroke size will not scale along with the rest of the shape.

## Add Beveled Corner Effects to Star Shapes

With these steps, we'll create gear shapes by applying the Bevel corner effect to stars drawn with the Polygon tool.

**Step 1.**
Create a new document. Press M to access the Rectangle tool. Draw a large rectangle that covers the page. Press ⌘+L / Ctrl+L to lock the rectangle in position.

**Step 2.**
Choose Window ▷ Swatches (or press F5) to access the Swatches palette. Double-click the red swatch to display the Swatch Options dialog. Change the CMYK build to an orange color using C=17, M=63, Y=88, K=0. Click OK to close the dialog. Press X to bring the stroke icon to the front and then press the backslash key (/) to apply a stroke of None.

**Step 3.**
Select the Polygon tool from the Tools palette and click once anywhere on the page. In the dialog that appears, enter **16p** in the Polygon Width and Polygon Height fields. Enter **35** in the Number Of Sides field and **30%** in the Star Inset field. Click OK.

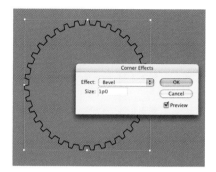

**Step 4.**

To turn the star into a gear shape, choose Object ▷ Corner Effects. In the dialog that appears, choose Bevel from the Effect pop-up menu and enter **1p** in the Size field. If you like, you can turn on the Preview check box to see the bevel applied to your selected object. Click OK to apply.

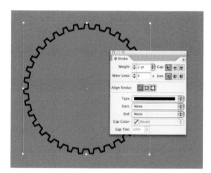

**Step 5.**

Choose Window ▷ Stroke (or press F10) to display the Stroke palette. Enter **2pt** in the Stroke Weight field and press Return (Mac) or Enter (Windows). If you prefer, you can also enter this setting in the Stroke Weight field of the Control palette.

**Step 6.**

In the Swatches palette, choose New Tint Swatch from the palette fly-out menu. In the dialog that appears, enter **30%** in the Tint field and click OK.

*continues on next page*

## The Tools Palette

The Tools palette contains all the different tools available to you–each one represented by a descriptive icon. However, if you're still not sure what tool you're viewing, hover your mouse over the icon until a small tooltip description appears.

You can activate a tool by clicking its icon or by typing its assigned keyboard shortcut (which is included in the tooltip). Any icon showing a small arrow in the bottom-right corner indicates an available toolset–more tools are "hidden" under the one shown. Clicking and holding the icon reveals a fly-out menu of additional tools.

There are three ways to display the free-floating Tools palette on your screen. The default preference displays it in Adobe's traditional double-column format. But in Preferences ▷ General, you can also change it to display in a single column (like QuarkXPress) or in a single, horizontal row.

# Getting in Gear *continued*

## Rotate Tool Options

**Rotating a frame's contents:** To rotate a placed graphic within its bounding frame, select it with the Direct Selection tool and switch to the Rotate tool. You can then rotate the image within the frame and reposition the rotation point, just as with any other object.

**Rotating a frame but not its contents:** To rotate a frame without rotating its contents, make your selection and then double-click the Rotate tool icon in the Tools palette to display the Rotate dialog. Uncheck the Rotate Content box and enter a value in the Angle field. Click the Preview check box to see the effect. Click OK to apply.

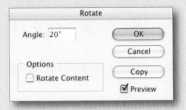

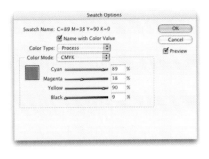

**Step 7.**
Press X to bring the fill icon to the front. Double-click the green swatch in the Swatches palette list to display the Swatch Options dialog. Change the CMYK build to a dark green color using C=89, M=38, Y=90, K=9. Click OK to close the dialog.

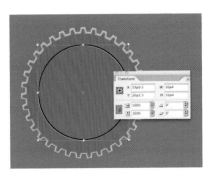

**Step 8.**
Press L to access the Ellipse tool. Hover the cursor over the center point of the gear shape. Hold down Shift+Option / Shift+Alt and click and drag to create a perfect circle. Enter **10p4** in the Width and Height fields of the Control or Transform palette.

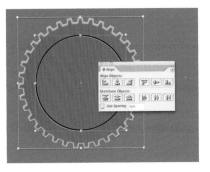

**Step 9.**
Choose Window ▷ Object & Layout ▷ Align (or press Shift+F7) to display the Align palette. Press V to access the Selection tool. Hold down Shift and click the gear shape to add it to the selection. In the Align palette, click the Align Horizontal Centers button, and then click the Align Vertical Centers Button.

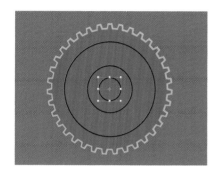

**Step 10.**

Shift-click the gear shape to deselect it. Double-click the Scale tool icon in the Tools palette. In the dialog that appears, enter **50%** in the Uniform Scale field and click Copy. Press Option+⌘+3 / Alt+Ctrl+3 to transform again, creating a third circle.

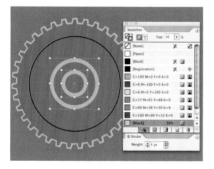

**Step 11.**

Press V to access the Selection tool. Shift-click the middle circle to add it to the selection. Enter **5pt** in the Stroke Weight field of the Stroke or Control palette and press Return (Mac) or Enter (Windows). Press X to bring the stroke icon to the front again. Click the 30% black tint swatch in the Swatches palette to apply it to the selected circles.

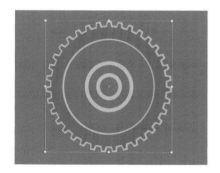

**Step 12.**

Select the gear shape. Shift-click the large inner circle (the only one without a gray stroke) to add it to the selection. Press ⌘+8 / Ctrl+8 to create a compound path from the two selected shapes.

*continues on next page*

## Shear Tool Options

**Shearing a frame's contents** To shear a placed graphic within its bounding frame, select it with the Direct Selection tool, and switch to the Shear tool. You can then shear the image within the frame. You can also reposition the shear-from point, just like with any other object.

**Shearing a frame but not its contents** To shear a frame without shearing its contents, make your selection and then double-click the tool's icon in the Tools palette to bring up the Shear dialog. Uncheck the Shear Content box and enter a value in one of the Angle data fields (overall shear angle or horizontal/vertical only). Click the Preview check box to see the effect. Click OK to apply.

# Getting in Gear *continued*

## Free Transform Tool

With the Free Transform tool you can move, rotate, and scale objects all at once. You can access this tool by clicking its icon in the Tools palette or by pressing E.

Select an object with the tool. To scale, click and drag any node. Clicking and dragging one of the corner nodes while holding down Shift constrains proportions in the direction that you scale. Clicking and dragging one of the side nodes while holding down Option (Mac) or Alt (Windows) constrains in both the direction that you scale and the opposite direction.

To rotate, place the cursor over any corner of the selected object until it changes to display a curved double-sided arrow. Click and drag to rotate the object. To move an object, click and drag as you would with the Selection tool.

Notice that a crosshair target does not appear indicating where the rotation or scale-from point is located. The default rotation/scale-from point is always in the absolute center of the object, and you cannot reposition it as you can with the Rotate, Scale, and Shear tools.

### Step 13.

Hold down Shift and click the two inner circles to add them to the selection. Choose Object ▷ Drop Shadow. In the dialog that appears, click the Drop Shadow check box to enable the effect, then turn on the Preview check box to see the shadow applied to your selected object. Enter **0p2** for Blur, **0p3** for X Offset, and **0p1** for Y Offset. Keep the rest of the settings at their defaults. Click OK to apply.

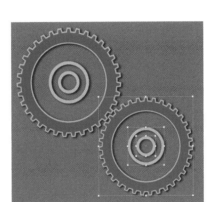

### Step 14.

Choose Window ▷ Object & Layout ▷ Transform (or press F9) to display the Transform palette. Choose Scale Strokes from the palette fly-out menu. Double-click the Scale tool icon in the Tools palette. In the dialog that appears, enter **90%** in the Uniform Scale field and click Copy. Press V to access the Selection tool and position the shapes as shown.

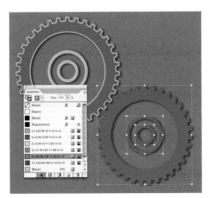

### Step 15.

Click the green swatch in the Swatches palette to change the stroke color of the selected objects. Enter **100%** in the Tint field of the Swatches palette and press Return (Mac) or Enter (Windows) to apply.

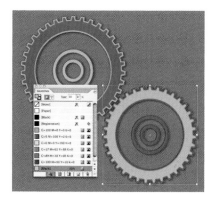

**Step 16.**

Shift-click the two inner circles to dese-lect them. Press X to bring the fill icon to the front. Click the 30% black tint swatch to change the fill color of the selected shape.

**Step 17.**

Select the original gear shape. Add the two inner circles to the selection by holding Shift and clicking each one. Double-click the Scale tool icon in the Tools palette. In the dialog that appears, enter **75%** in the Uniform Scale field and click Copy. Press V to access the Selection tool and position the shapes as shown.

**Step 18.**

To complete the design, add some text as shown. I used ITC Aachen Bold. Get creative! Try alternating the fill and stroke colors of the text, and playing with text frame arrangement and posi-tioning as you see here.

## Free Transform Tool Options

**Free transforming a frame's contents** To free transform a placed graphic within its bounding frame, select a placed graphic with the Direct Selection tool and switch to the Free Transform tool. You can then scale, move, or rotate the image within the frame.

**Free transforming text frames** Select any text frame with the tool and use it the same way as you would with a graphics frame. You can still edit the text after it has been transformed.

**Note:** You can also use the Free Transform tool to move, rotate, scale, and shear grouped objects.

# InDesign Snowflakes

InDesign CS2 contains a new Convert To Shape feature that allows you to instantly change the shape of selected objects. You can access these commands from the Transform palette menu.

In this example, we'll convert a rectangle into a triangle. We'll then proceed to rotate and copy the triangle several times around its center point using the Transform Again command. By selecting all the triangles, setting the transparency Mode pop-up to Screen, and reducing their opacity level, the fill colors of each shape will begin to interact with each other. Applying the Fancy Corner Effect takes it one step further, resulting in a pattern that resembles a snowflake.

Once you create a snowflake this way, you can group the triangles, duplicate the group, and then resize it to create a different pattern. However, before resizing, be sure to turn off the Scale Strokes option from the Transform palette menu. Otherwise, the applied stroke and corner effect size will scale along with the rest of the shape and the pattern will not change.

## Create Your Own Winter Wonderland

To re-create this effect using the text shown here, download snowflake_text.inds from the *InDesign Effects Book* website.

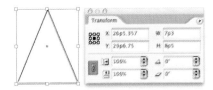

**Step 1.**
Create a new document. Press M to access the Rectangle tool, and draw a rectangle on the page. Choose Object ▷ Convert Shape ▷ Triangle. In the Control palette, enter **7p3** in the Width field and **8p5** in the Height field. If you prefer, you can also choose Window ▷ Object & Layout ▷ Transform (or press F9) to display the Transform palette and enter these values in the Width and Height fields located there.

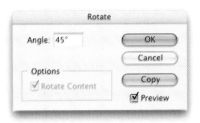

**Step 2.**
Double-click the Rotate Tool icon in the Tools palette. In the dialog that appears, enter **45°** in the Angle field and click Copy.

**Step 3.**
Press Option+⌘+3 / Alt+Ctrl+3 to transform again. Apply this command six more times until your screen matches what you see here.

**Step 4.**

Press ⌘+A / Ctrl+A to select all the shapes. Choose Window ▷ Swatches (or press F5) to display the Swatches palette. Click the Paper swatch to change the stroke color of the selected shapes to white.

**Step 5.**

Press X to bring the fill icon to the front. Click the blue swatch to apply a blue fill to the selected shapes.

**Step 6.**

Choose Window ▷ Transparency (or press Shift+F10) to display the Transparency palette. Choose Screen from the Mode pop-up menu. Enter 35% in the Opacity field and press Return (Mac) or Enter (Windows). Press ⌘+H / Ctrl+H to hide frame edges and preview the graphic. You can now see through the stack of transparent shapes!

*continues on next page*

# Targeting vs. Selecting Pages

By default, a targeted page or spread is the one you are working on in the document window; however, if you scroll to another page in the document, the page you were originally working on remains targeted.

You can *target* only one page or spread at a time; therefore, the page that you scrolled to does not become targeted until you actually click somewhere on the page with any tool except the Hand or Zoom tool.

InDesign identifies which page or spread is actually the targeted one by placing a black highlight over the page number in the Pages palette.

A page is *selected* when its page icon (not its page number) appears highlighted in the Pages palette. You can select a page by clicking its icon in the palette, and apply specific page editing commands to it (such as adjusting margins and columns, or moving the page), even when another page is targeted and centered in the document window.

# InDesign Snowflakes *continued*

## Creating Multipage Spreads

With InDesign, you can create what is known as a "gatefold" spread. Gatefolds contain more than two adjoining pages and are commonly used for large brochure or ad designs.

To create a multipage spread, select a page (single-sided document) or a spread (facing pages document), and click the palette menu button. Choose Keep Spread Together and notice the page number(s) for this page or spread appear in brackets in the Pages palette thumbnail display. In the Pages palette, click and drag a document or master page icon into the bracketed spread. Continue to add additional pages to the spread as needed.

To create a multipage master spread, select New Master from the Pages palette menu. In the dialog that appears, enter the number of pages to include (between 1 and 10). Click OK to close the dialog. InDesign displays the new gatefold master in the master pages portion of the Pages palette.

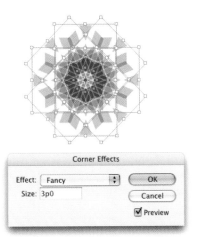

**Step 7.**
To create a snowflake, choose Object ▷ Corner Effects. In the dialog that appears, choose Fancy from the Effect pop-up menu. Enter **3p** in the Size field. If you like, click the Preview check box to see the effect applied as you increase the size with the Up arrow key. Click OK to apply.

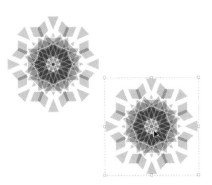

**Step 8.**
Press ⌘+G / Ctrl+G to group the selected objects. Press V to access the Selection tool. Hold down Option (Mac) or Alt (Windows), and click and drag to make a copy of the object.

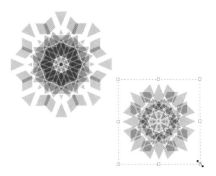

**Step 9.**
Click one of the grouped object's corner nodes. Hold down Shift and drag in or out to resize the object. As you resize, InDesign maintains the same Stroke and Corner Effect size settings. As a result, the snowflake's appearance changes each time you resize it.

**Step 10.**
Continue duplicating and resizing snowflakes on the page. They should all have a slightly different appearance, just like real snowflakes—except these won't melt!

**Step 11.**
Press ⌘+D / Ctrl+D to display the Place dialog. Locate the snowflake_text.inds image on your system, and click Open. Use the Selection tool to position the InDesign Snippet over the snowflakes as shown.

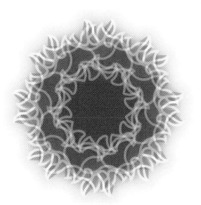

**Don't stop now—customize the effect:**
You can create interesting abstract design elements by experimenting with this effect. Try using different fill colors, different stroke styles, and applying different corner effect sizes and styles to the shapes. This example uses the same offset triangles as shown in the steps above, but with a dark red fill, a 1p6 Fancy corner effect, and a 5pt Wavy stroke style applied. It also uses a magenta drop shadow as an outer glow.

## Converting Document Pages to Master Pages

To convert a document page into a master page, select it from the Pages palette and then choose Save As Master from the palette menu. The converted master automatically appears at the bottom of the master page list with the next available prefix (A, B, C, etc.) applied to its name.

Here's an even easier way to convert a document page into a master page: Select it in the document pages portion of the Pages palette and drag it into the master pages portion.

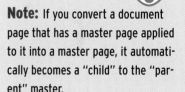

**Note:** If you convert a document page that has a master page applied to it into a master page, it automatically becomes a "child" to the "parent" master.

# Photo-realistic 3-D Sphere

I've always been a big fan of Adobe Illustrator and Photoshop. I especially like using both programs, together or separately, to create photo-realistic illustrations. There's just something really cool about being able to re-create the way light and color react in real life, *all on a computer screen!*

I can't tell you how excited I became when I discovered that this could also be done in InDesign. All the tools you need are here, including shapes, gradients, blur (the Feather effect), and masking (using nested objects).

With these steps we'll create a simple photo-realistic illustration, complete with shadows and highlights, just as you would with Illustrator or Photoshop.

## Add Some Life to Your Illustrations

By applying basic linear gradients, feathered highlights, and shadows, you can simulate realistic lighting conditions in your InDesign drawings.

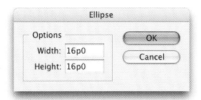

**Step 1.**
Create a new document. Press Shift+X to swap the default colors to a black fill and a None stroke. Press L to access the Ellipse tool and click once on the page. In the dialog that appears, enter **16p** in both the Width and Height fields and click OK.

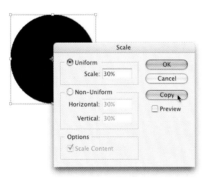

**Step 2.**
Double-click the Scale tool icon in the Tools palette. In the dialog that appears, enter **30%** in the Uniform Scale field and click Copy.

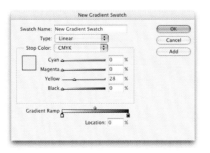

**Step 3.**
Choose Window ▷ Swatches (or press F5) to display the Swatches palette. Choose New Gradient Swatch from the Swatches palette fly-out menu. In the dialog that appears, click the left color stop icon located beneath the Gradient Ramp at the bottom of the dialog. Create a build that uses C=0, M=0, Y=28, K=0. Don't click OK just yet.

**Step 4.**

Click the right color stop icon and choose CMYK from the Stop Color pop-up menu. Create a build that uses C=7, M=13, Y=78, K=20. Enter **8-ball gradient** in the Swatch Name field. Click OK to add the swatch.

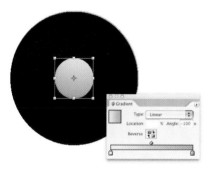

**Step 5.**

Choose Window ▷ Gradient to display the Gradient palette. Enter **-100°** in the Angle field and press Return (Mac) or Enter (Windows).

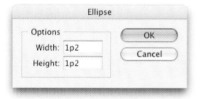

**Step 6.**

Choose Edit ▷ Deselect All. Press D to set the default colors back to None fill and Black stroke. Press L to access the Ellipse tool and click once near the top of the inner circle. In the dialog that appears, enter **1p2** in both the Width and Height fields and click OK.

*continues on next page*

# Applying Master Pages

To apply a master page, select the document pages you want to apply a master to in the Pages palette. You can do so by ⌘-clicking or Ctrl-clicking page icons in the Pages palette, or Shift-clicking to select contiguous pages. Once the pages are selected, choose Apply Master To Pages from the Layout ▷ Pages submenu or the Pages palette fly-out menu.

The page numbers automatically appear in the To Pages field of the dialog. If you choose not to select the pages first before opening the dialog, you can also enter the page numbers in the To Pages field, separated by commas. Click OK to apply the master.

You can also apply a master page by selecting it from the master pages portion of the Pages palette and dragging it over a document page icon. By positioning the cursor over the page icons until a thick black line appears around the entire spread, you can apply the master style to all pages in the spread when you release the mouse button.

One other fast way to apply a master style to several pages at once is to select the pages in the Pages palette and Option-click (Mac) or Alt-click (Windows) the Master page icon.

# Photo-realistic 3-D Sphere *continued*

## Deleting Master Pages

To delete a master page, select the master you want to delete from the master pages list in the Pages palette and choose Delete Master Spread from the Layout ▷ Pages submenu or the Pages palette fly-out menu.

You can also delete a master page by selecting it from the master pages list in the Pages palette and dragging it over the trash icon footer control. Or–if you like clicking better than dragging–select the master pages you want to delete and click the trash icon without having to drag the pages down.

InDesign displays a warning dialog if the master page you are deleting is applied to a page in the document. Click OK if you're sure you still want to delete the master. Upon deleting, all the page items that were placed on the master no longer appear in the document.

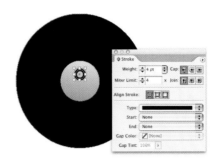

**Step 7.**

Choose Window ▷ Stroke (or press F10) to display the Stroke palette. Enter **4pt** in Stroke Weight field and press Return (Mac) or Enter (Windows). If you prefer, you can also enter this value in the Stroke Weight field of the Control palette.

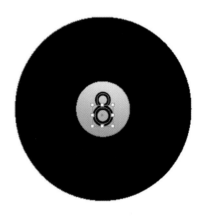

**Step 8.**

Double-click the Scale tool icon in the Tools palette. In the dialog that appears, enter **130%** in the Uniform Scale field and click Copy. Press V to switch to the Selection tool and position the duplicate circle directly beneath the original as shown. To be exact, hold down Shift to constrain the angle as you move it.

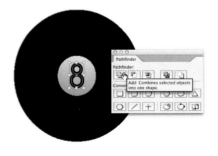

**Step 9.**

Shift-click the top circle to add it to the selection. To combine the two circles, choose Object ▷ Pathfinder ▷ Add, or Choose Window ▷ Object & Layout ▷ Pathfinder to display the Pathfinder palette, and click the Add button.

### Step 10.

Choose Window▷Object & Layout ▷Align (or press Shift+F7) to display the Align palette. Shift-click the inner circle (with the gradient fill) to add it to the selection. To center the objects, click the Align Horizontal Centers button and the Align Vertical Centers button. Use the arrow keys to nudge the selected objects slightly up and to the left, until they appear offset within the black circle as shown.

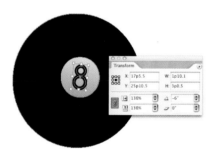

### Step 11.

Shift-click the inner circle again to remove it from the selection. Choose Window▷Object & Layout▷ Transform (or press F9) to display the Transform palette. Enter -6° in the Rotation Angle field and press Return (Mac) or Enter (Windows). If you prefer, you can also enter this value in the Rotation Angle field of the Control palette.

### Step 12.

Choose Object▷Drop Shadow. In the dialog that appears, click the Drop Shadow check box to enable the effect, then turn on the Preview check box to see the shadow applied to your selected object. Enter **85%** for Opacity, **0p3** for Blur, **0p0** for X and Y Offset, and **3%** for Spread. Keep the rest of the settings at their defaults. Click OK to apply.

## Creating and Applying Parent/ Child Master Pages

InDesign allows you to create master pages that are based on another master page. When you do this, all shared master page items change dynamically when the "parent" master is edited. Just as with document pages, all parent master page items applied to child masters cannot be edited unless overridden.

To create a new master that is based on an existing "parent" master, click the menu button on the Pages palette and choose New Master. When the dialog opens, choose a prefix, name, number of pages, and a parent master to base the new child master on from the menu. Click OK for the child master page to appear centered in the document window.

It's easy to identify parent/child masters in the Pages palette; the child master page icons always display the prefix letter of the parent master.

You can also create parent/child masters by selecting the master page icon of a chosen parent and dragging it over the page icon of a chosen child. This applies all parent master page items to the child master.

*continues on next page*

# Photo-realistic 3-D Sphere *continued*

## Overriding Master Page Items

Master page items that have been applied to a document page cannot be edited unless they are overridden. To override a master page item, press ⌘+Shift / Ctrl+Shift and click the item. This allows you to edit the item on the document page only. Any changes made do not affect the original item on the master page.

To override all master page items for a selected page or spread, choose Override All Master Page Items from the Pages palette fly-out menu, or press ⌘+Option+Shift+L / Ctrl+Alt+Shift+L.

To undo any overrides made to selected master page items on a page or spread, choose Remove All Local Overrides from the Pages palette fly-out menu.

**Note:** You do not need to override a master page text or graphic frame to place content in it. Clicking the frame with a loaded place icon activates it.

**Step 13.**
Click the large black circle to select it. Double-click the Scale tool icon in the Tools palette. In the dialog that appears, enter **94%** in the Uniform Scale field and click Copy. In the Swatches palette, click the Paper (white) swatch to change the fill color to white.

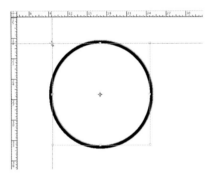

**Step 14.**
If they're not already visible, press ⌘+R / Ctrl+R to display the document window rulers. In the upper-left corner of the document window where the horizontal and vertical rulers intersect, click and drag to reset the zero point of the document to the upper-left corner node of the selected circle, as shown. You can set your rulers to display picas by Control-clicking/right-clicking on each ruler and selecting Picas from the contextual menu.

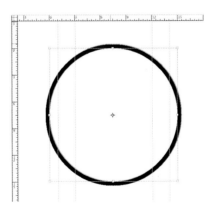

**Step 15.**
If they're not already visible, choose View ▷ Grids & Guides ▷ Show Guides. Double-click at 1p in the horizontal ruler to add a vertical ruler guide at that precise point on the page. Double-click again at 3p, 12p, and 14p. The four guides should appear on the page as shown. Sometimes it is hard to know exactly where your cursor is when hovering over the rulers because the X and Y Position fields only display values when you are moving the cursor on the page. If you need to make sure a guide that you have created is in a precise location, you can always double-click on a ruler guide on the page with the Selection tool to select the guide, and then enter the location value you want in the corresponding X or Y Location field in the Control palette.

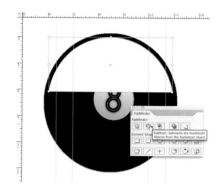

**Step 16.**

Press M to access the Rectangle tool. Draw a rectangle that covers the bottom half of the white circle. ⌘+Shift-click / Ctrl+Shift-click the white circle to add it to the selection. Choose Object ▷ Pathfinder ▷ Subtract, or click the Subtract button in the Pathfinder palette.

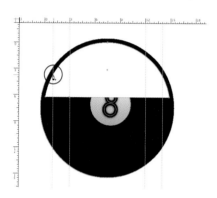

**Step 17.**

Press P to access the Pen tool. Hover the Pen tool cursor over the bottom-left edge of the path. When the cursor changes to display a plus sign (+), click to add a point where the path segment meets the 3p guide. Proceed to add another point to the upper-left curved path segment at 1p.

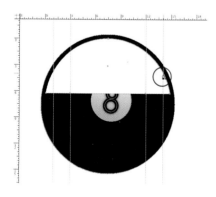

**Step 18.**

Now hover the Pen tool cursor over the bottom right edge of the path. When the cursor changes to display a plus sign (+), click to add a point where the path segment meets the 12p guide. Proceed to add another point to the upper-right curved path segment at 14p.

*continues on next page*

# Detach Selection From Master

Even though a master page item may be overridden on a document page, it is still linked to the item on the master page.

For example, if you were to change the fill color of a master page item on a document page by overriding it, any edits other than fill color that are made to the item on the master page are still applied. To unlink an overridden master page item from the original, select it on the document page and choose Detach Selection From Master from the Pages palette menu.

By default, frame contents (text or graphics) are always detached from the master page when overridden.

# Photo-realistic 3-D Sphere *continued*

## Auto Page Numbers

When you insert the special Auto Page Number character on applied master pages, the folios automatically number themselves. Learn to use this feature, and you'll never have to correct any page numbering when adding, deleting, and moving pages in a document.

On your master page or spread, create a text frame where you'd like the page numbers to appear and then choose Type ▷ Insert Special Character ▷ Auto Page Number, or press Option+Shift+⌘+N / Alt+Shift+Ctrl+N. Apply the master to your document and watch the pages number themselves. It's like magic!

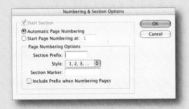

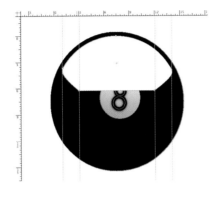

**Step 19.**

Hover the Pen tool cursor over the bottom-left corner point. When the cursor changes to display a minus sign (-), click to subtract the point from the path. Proceed to subtract the bottom-right corner point as well.

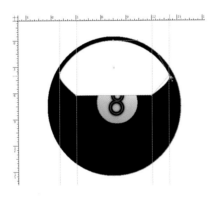

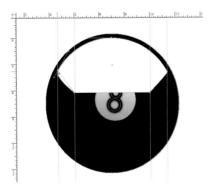

**Step 20.**

Hold down ⌘ (Mac) or Ctrl to temporarily access the Direct Selection tool. While holding down the key, click the point in the upper-right corner of the shape (at 14p) to select it. Hold down Option or Alt to temporarily access the Convert Direction Point tool. While holding down the key, click the right corner handle and move it to the left until it lines up vertically with the 14p ruler guide. Continue to hold down the key and drag the point up until the path segment is straight, as shown. Use the same method as described in the previous step to convert the point in the upper left of the shape at 1p.

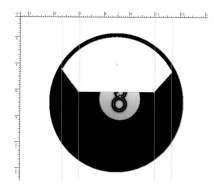

**Step 21.**
Hold down ⌘/Ctrl to temporarily access the Direct Selection tool, and click a blank area of the page to dese-lect the point. While holding down the key, click the white shape again. Let up on the key and hover the mouse over the center of the bottom path segment. When the cursor changes to display a plus sign (+), click to add a point.

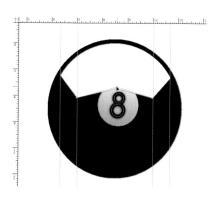

**Step 22.**
Hold down ⌘/Ctrl to temporarily access the Direct Selection tool again. While holding down the key, move the point upward about 1p toward the cen-ter of the shape. Once you start moving the point, you can hold down Shift to constrain the angle as you move it.

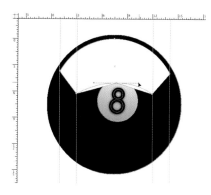

**Step 23.**
Hold down Option (Mac) or Alt (Windows) to temporarily access the Convert Direction Point tool. While holding down the key, click and drag outward until the curve of the bottom path segment is smooth. Once you start to drag outward, you can hold down Shift to constrain the angle of the curve.

*continues on next page*

## Numbered Sections

To start a new numbered section within a document, select a page in the Pages palette where you'd like it to start, and then choose Numbering & Section Options from the Layout menu or the Pages palette menu. Click the radio button for Start Page Numbering At, and enter a page num-ber in the data field. Once applied, Auto Page Numbering characters recognize any changes made in the Numbering & Section Options dialog.

Using this dialog, you can also apply a custom prefix, a numerical style (Arabic, Roman numeral, letters, etc.), or a section marker (section number, chapter name, etc.) to the page num-bering scheme.

**Note:** An InDesign document can contain more than one numbered section.

# Photo-realistic 3-D Sphere *continued*

## What Exactly Is an InDesign Library?

Libraries are great for storing objects that you know you will use repeatedly in your layouts. Common items such as logos, end marks, icons, formatted tables, and even style samples are all perfect candidates for storing in a library. Once the objects are saved in the library, you can place them into your layouts by dragging them from the Library palette.

A saved library can contain shapes, frames, text items, and even placed graphics. Placed graphics appear as links when dragged into a document from a library, and editable text items require that all live fonts be loaded on your system.

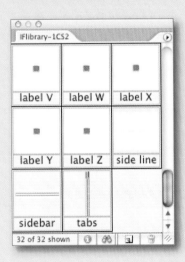

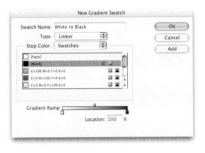

**Step 24.**
Choose New Gradient Swatch from the Swatches palette fly-out menu. In the dialog that appears, click the left color stop icon beneath the Gradient Ramp at the bottom of the dialog. Choose Swatches from the Stop Color pop-up menu. Select the Paper swatch from the list. Then click the right color stop icon, choose Swatches again from the Stop Color pop-up menu, and select the black swatch. Enter **White to Black** in the Swatch Name field and click OK to add the swatch.

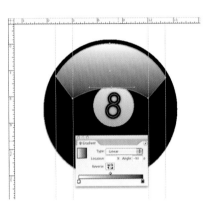

**Step 25.**
Choose Window▷Gradient to display the Gradient palette. Enter -90° in the Angle field and press Return (Mac) or Enter (Windows). The applied gradient simulates light that is reflecting off the black sphere.

**Step 26.**
To add to the lighting effect, choose Window▷Transparency (or press Shift+F10) to display the Transparency palette. Choose Screen from the Mode pop-up menu. Enter 90% in the Opacity field and press Return (Mac) or Enter (Windows).

**Step 27.**

Choose View ▷ Grids & Guides ▷ Hide Guides, then press ⌘+H / Ctrl+H to hide frame edges. To soften the highlight, choose Object ▷ Feather. In the dialog that appears, click the Feather check box to enable the effect, then turn on the Preview check box to see the feather applied to your selected object. Enter **1p6** in the Feather Width field. Leave the Corners pop-up menu setting at Diffused and the Noise setting at 0%. Click OK to apply.

**Step 28.**

To create a hard drop shadow directly beneath the 8 ball, press L to access the Ellipse tool. Click once on the page. In the dialog that appears, enter **7p9** in the Width field and **6p** in the Height field. Click OK.

**Step 29.**

Press Shift+X to swap the default colors, resulting in a black fill and a None stroke. Press V to access the Selection tool and position the ellipse at the bottom center of the 8 ball, as shown. Choose Object ▷ Arrange ▷ Send To Back.

*continues on next page*

## Saving Objects to a Library

To save objects into a library, you must first create one by choosing File ▷ New ▷ Library. Enter a name in the File Name field and then click the Save button. A new Library palette appears on your screen.

Add as many objects as you want to a saved library by dragging them into the palette.

You can also add items to a library by selecting an object on the page and choosing Add Item from the Library palette fly-out menu or clicking the New Library Item button. To save all the objects on a targeted page as one library item, choose Add Items On Page from the palette menu. To save all the objects on a targeted page as separate library items, choose Add Items On Page As Separate Objects.

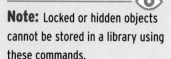

**Note:** Locked or hidden objects cannot be stored in a library using these commands.

# Photo-realistic 3-D Sphere *continued*

## Searching for Library Items

You can change a library item's name, specify an object type, or add an item description in the Item Information dialog. To access it, double-click the object in the library list or click the item information button located at the bottom of the Library palette.

To search for objects in the library by item name, creation date, object type, or description, click the Show Library Subset button at the bottom of the Library palette. When the dialog opens, enter your search parameters and click OK. Any found items appear in the Library palette by themselves.

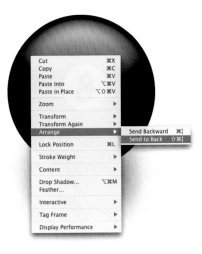

**Step 30.**

Choose Object ▷ Feather. In the dialog that appears, click the Feather check box to enable the effect. Enter **4p** in the Feather Width field. Leave the Corners pop-up menu setting at Diffused and enter **2%** in the Noise field. Click OK to apply.

**Step 31.**

Choose Object ▷ Drop Shadow. In the dialog that appears, click the Drop Shadow check box to enable the effect. Enter **85%** for Opacity, **4p5** for Blur, **0p0** for X Offset. and **0p9** for Y Offset. Enter **10%** for Spread and **3%** for Noise. Keep the rest of the settings at their defaults. Click OK to apply.

**Step 32.**

Now let's create a soft drop shadow that extends out further. Press ⌘+C / Ctrl+C to copy the object to the Clipboard. Choose Edit ▷ Paste In Place. Then choose Object ▷ Arrange ▷ Send To Back. You can also choose the Send To Back command from the contextual menu by Control-clicking/right-clicking.

**Step 33.**

Choose Object ▷ Drop Shadow. In the dialog that appears, change the Opacity setting to 75%, the Blur setting to 5p4, and the Spread setting to 40%. Keep the rest of the settings the same and click OK to apply.

**Step 34.**

Deselect the circle to view your illustration. Notice that the blend of the two feathered circles, each with slightly different drop shadow settings applied (one softer and not as spread out as the other), creates the illusion of real lighting. The feathered highlight at the top and the off-yellow gradient applied to the inner circle also contribute to the photo-realistic effect.

**Don't stop now—customize the effect:**
Now try experimenting with this effect. With this example, I placed a sky image inside of the sphere in order to create a crystal ball effect. The shadow colors are sampled from the dark blue colors in the sky image.

## Creating Drop Caps

To apply a drop cap, insert the Type tool cursor anywhere in the paragraph and enter a value in the Drop Cap Number Of Lines field in the Paragraph palette or Control palette. This number determines the size and baseline shift for the drop cap character. You can apply this effect to additional characters by entering a larger value in the Drop Cap One Or More Characters field.

Drop cap characters can be selected and formatted just like any other character. To enhance a drop cap's appearance, select it with the Type tool and change the applied font, type size, kerning, and baseline shift.

Drop caps can also be applied as part of a nested style.

**Note:** To place a drop cap outside a column, insert a hanging indent after it by pressing ⌘+\ or Ctrl+\. You can also insert a hanging indent by choosing Type ▷ Insert Special Character ▷ Indent To Here.

# Gel Buttons

One of my designer friends came by one day and asked if I would show him how to create a gel button in Photoshop. "Sure," I said, "but why not try doing it InDesign?" "InDesign?" he said. "I didn't know you could create something like that in InDesign?" "Yep, sure can," I said.

As I showed him how to create highlights and shadows in InDesign using layers, gradients, feathers, nesting, and transparency effects, my friend turned to me and said, "You know, you really should put this in your next book." So here it is!

Although this may seem like a lot of work for a simple effect, keep in mind that it's the close attention to detail that makes all the difference. You can use the basic principles covered here in these steps to create photo-realistic highlights and shadows in any design application, including InDesign, Illustrator, and Photoshop.

Also keep in mind that once you create one of these in InDesign, you can save it as a library item or snippet and use it over and over again in your layouts.

## Applying the "Gel-ly" Effect to Shapes

To re-create this effect using the background shown here, download brushed_metal.psd from the *InDesign Effects Book* website.

**Step 1.**
In a new document, press ⌘+D / Ctrl+D to display the Place dialog. Locate the brushed_metal.psd image on your system, and click Open. Click the loaded place cursor once anywhere on the page to place the image at 100% of its size.

**Step 2.**
Choose Window▷Layers (or press F7) to display the Layers palette. Double-click Layer 1 to display the Layer Options dialog. Enter a name for the background layer, check the Lock Layer option, and click OK to close the dialog.

**Step 3.**
Option-click / Alt-click the Create New Layer button at the bottom of the Layers palette. In the Layer Options dialog, enter a name for the layer (e.g., **triangle 1**) and click OK.

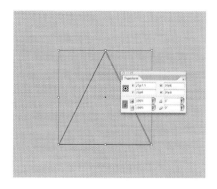

**Step 4.**

Press M to access the Rectangle tool, and draw a rectangle on the page. Choose Object ▷ Convert Shape ▷ Triangle. In the Control palette, enter **16p6** in the Width field and **16p** in the Height field. If you prefer, you can also choose Window ▷ Object & Layout ▷ Transform (or press F9) to display the Transform palette and enter these values in the Width and Height fields located there.

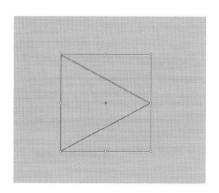

**Step 5.**

Press R to access the Rotate tool. Hold down Shift to constrain the rotation angle to 45° increments and rotate the triangle 90° clockwise, as shown.

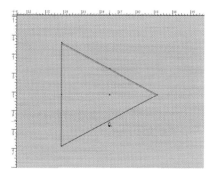

**Step 6.**

If they're not already visible, press ⌘+R / Ctrl+R to display the document window rulers. Drag two ruler guides out onto the page and position them so they intersect at the center point of the triangle as shown. Press P to access the Pen tool. Hover the Pen tool cursor over the left path segment where the guide intersects. When the cursor changes to display a plus sign (+), click to add a point. Use this same method to add two more points, one on the top path segment and one on the bottom segment where the vertical guide intersects.

## Hand Tool Scrolling and Display Performance

Depending on your system, you may notice a slow redraw when scrolling with the Hand tool—especially when the View ▷ Display Performance setting is set to High Quality Display. For faster Hand scrolling, press ⌘+K / Ctrl+K to open the Preferences dialog, and click the Display Performance tab on the left. Click and drag the Scrolling ▷ Hand Tool slider located at the bottom of the Display Performance Preferences panel all the way to the left, so that it is positioned just under the words "Better Performance." Click OK, and then zoom in to about 300%.

Now try scrolling with the Hand tool. Notice the images and text items become gray as you move around the page. As soon as you stop scrolling, the items return to their normal display setting.

*continues on next page*

# Gel Buttons *continued*

## Screen Modes

InDesign also features several screen modes in which you can view your document layout.

**Normal mode** is the default, which allows you to see all your guides, frame edges, and any items positioned off the page.

**Preview mode** hides all guides and frame edges and fills the entire area surrounding the page with gray.

**Bleed mode** also hides all guides and frame edges, but reveals any added bleed areas while filling the rest of the area surrounding the page with gray.

**Slug mode** previews your document in the same way as Bleed mode, but also allows you to view any additional slug areas.

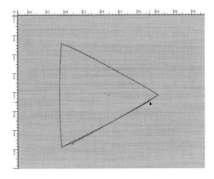

**Step 7.**

Hold down ⌘/Ctrl to temporarily access the Direct Selection tool. Click the background to deselect the shape. While holding down the key, click the triangle again, then click the new point added to the left side of the shape to select it. Use the Left arrow key to nudge the point over about four clicks. Hold down Option (Mac) or Alt (Windows) to temporarily access the Convert Direction Point tool. While holding down the key, click and drag outward until the curve of the path segment is smooth. Use the same method to adjust the curve for the other two path segments of the triangle (be sure to nudge the top point with the Up arrow key and the bottom point with Down arrow key).

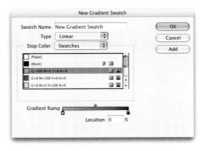

**Step 8.**

Choose Object ▷ Corner Effects. In the dialog that appears, select Rounded from the Effect pop-up menu. Enter 0p6 in the Size field and click OK to apply.

**Step 9.**

Choose Window ▷ Swatches or (press F5) to display the Swatches palette. Choose New Gradient Swatch from the Swatches palette fly-out menu. In the dialog that appears, click the left color stop icon located beneath the Gradient Ramp at the bottom of the dialog. Choose Swatches from the Stop Color pop-up menu and select the cyan swatch from the list. Don't click OK just yet.

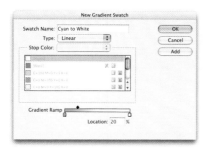

### Step 10.

Click the right color stop icon and select the Paper (white) swatch from the list. Click the midpoint slider above the Gradient Ramp and enter 20% in the Location field below. Enter **cyan to white** in the Swatch Name field. Click OK to add the swatch.

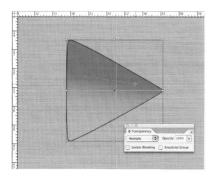

### Step 11.

Choose Window▷Transparency (or press Shift+F10) to display the Transparency palette. Choose Multiply from the Mode pop-up menu. Press G to access the Gradient tool. To apply the gradient, draw a line that extends from the middle of the upper-left quadrant to the middle of the upper-right quadrant using the angle shown here.

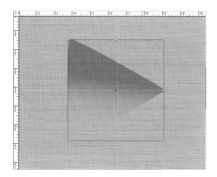

### Step 12.

Press X to bring the stroke icon to the front, and then press the backslash key (/) to apply a stroke of None. Press ⌘+H / Ctrl+H to hide frame edges and see the difference.

*continues on next page*

# Fill and Stroke Swatches

The Fill and Stroke swatches, located at the bottom of the Tools palette, the top of the Swatches palette, and in the Color palette, display either the default fill and stroke colors, or the colors of any currently selected object in your document. The forefront swatch, either Fill or Stroke, is the active control. All colors in InDesign are applied according to the active control.

You can switch between the Fill and Stroke controls by clicking either swatch, or by pressing X. Clicking the arrows located at the upper-right swaps colors between Fill and Stroke. You can reset the default Fill and Stroke colors by clicking the Default Fill And Stroke button at the lower left, or by just pressing D on your keyboard.

**Note:** Double-clicking the fill or stroke icon in the Tools palette or Color palette displays the Color Picker dialog.

# Gel Buttons *continued*

## Organizing Palettes

When you're in a creative mind-set, it's tough to stay organized. No one wants to stop work on a killer layout to create more design room on screen. Thankfully, InDesign understands that your creativity should always come first.

To help save screen real estate, you can dock together individual palettes as well as palette windows. And certain palettes can collapse vertically, allowing you to show or hide specific options. And if that's not enough to help you stay organized, you can also store individual and docked palettes into the stashed side tabs.

Every palette contains a title bar. You can click and drag the title bar to reposition the palette window on your screen. Double-click the title bar to collapse the window.

Each palette also contains a tab that displays the palette name. Click and drag the palette tab to group a palette with another palette or stash it to the side of the screen. Single-click the tab to bring a docked palette to the front of a group. Double-click the tab to collapse the palette.

Every palette window contains a well to dock other palettes in. Palette tabs are positioned side by side in the well for easy access.

**Step 13.**

Choose Object ▷ Drop Shadow. In the dialog that appears, click the Drop Shadow check box to enable the effect, then turn on the Preview check box to see the shadow applied to your selected object. Enter **80%** for Opacity, **0p7** for Blur, **-0p1** for X Offset, and **0p3** for Y Offset. Enter **5%** for Spread. Keep the rest of the settings at their defaults. Click OK to apply.

**Step 14.**

Press ⌘+; / Ctrl+; to hide guides. Option-click / Alt-click the Create New Layer button at the bottom of the Layers palette. In the Layer Options dialog, enter a name for the layer (e.g., **triangle 2**) and click OK.

**Step 15.**

In the Layers palette, Option-click / Alt-click the small square icon located on the triangle 1 layer below and drag it to the new triangle 2 layer above. Doing so creates a copy of the path and places it on the new triangle 2 layer.

**Step 16.**

Choose Object ▷ Drop Shadow. In the dialog that appears, click the Drop Shadow check box to disable the effect. Click OK to apply.

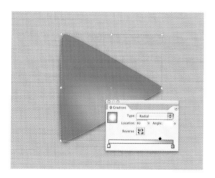

**Step 17.**

Press X to bring the fill icon to the front. Choose Window ▷ Gradient to display the Gradient palette. Choose Radial from the Type pop-up menu and click the Reverse button.

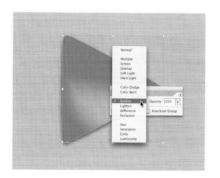

**Step 18.**

In the Transparency palette, choose Darken from the Mode pop-up menu. Darken causes the colors on this layer to react with the colors on the layers underneath like a less intense version of the Multiply blend mode; therefore, the radial gradient applied on this layer suggests a much softer, rounded shadow than the linear gradient applied on the layer below.

# Docking Palettes

To dock palettes together, simply click the tab of one palette and drag it into another. Hold the mouse button down until a thick black outline appears around the palette window you are dragging into, then release. The palettes will now be docked together inside the same window.

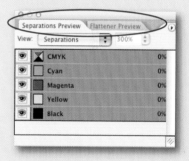

Clicking a docked palette's tab brings it to the front of the group and grays out all other docked palettes behind it.

To undock a palette, click the tab, hold the mouse button down, and drag it out of the well. Release the mouse button to place the free-floating palette somewhere else on your screen, or add it into another palette group or stashed palette group.

*continues on next page*

# Gel Buttons *continued*

## Docking Palette Windows

To dock palette windows together, click the tab of one palette, hold the mouse button down, and drag it over the bottom edge of another. Release the mouse button when a thick black line appears at the bottom edge of the window you're docking to. The palette windows dock together in a vertical column.

Click and drag the title bar of the top palette window to reposition the docked group on your screen. Double-click the title bar to collapse the docked windows, leaving only the tabs visible.

Windows with multiple palettes docked inside them can be docked together and collapsed to save space.

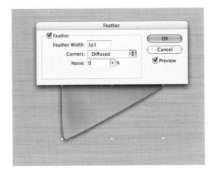

**Step 19.**

Choose Object ▷ Feather. In the dialog that appears, click the Feather check box to enable the effect, then turn on the Preview check box to see the feather applied to your selected object. Enter **3p3** in the Feather Width field. Leave the Corners pop-up menu setting at Diffused and the Noise setting at 0%. Click OK to apply.

**Step 20.**

Option-click / Alt-click the Create New Layer button at the bottom of the Layers palette. In the Layer Options dialog, enter a name for the layer (e.g., **highlights**) and click OK.

**Step 21.**

In the Layers palette, Option-click / Alt-click the small square icon located on the triangle 2 layer below and drag it to the new highlights layer above. Doing so creates a copy of the path and places it on the new highlights layer.

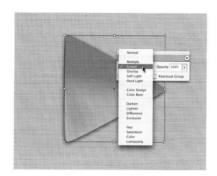

**Step 22.**

Choose Object ▷ Feather. In the dialog that appears, click the Feather check box to disable the effect. Click OK to apply. Press the backslash key (/) to apply a fill color of None. In the Transparency palette, choose Screen from the Mode pop-up menu.

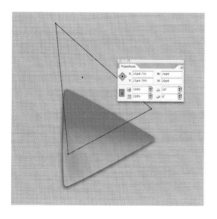

**Step 23.**

Now let's create some shapes to use as highlights. We can nest these shapes inside the triangle on this layer. Press M to access the Rectangle tool, and draw a rectangle. Choose Object ▷ Convert Shape ▷ Triangle. In the Control or Transform palette, enter **16p6** in the Width field and **20p6** in the Height field. Enter **28°** in the Rotation Angle field. Press V to access the Selection tool and position the triangle as shown.

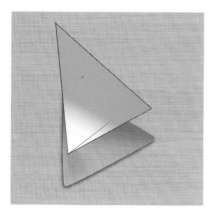

**Step 24.**

Click the Cyan to White gradient swatch in the Swatches palette to apply the gradient as a fill. Click the Reverse button in the Gradient palette. Press G to access the Gradient tool. To apply the gradient, draw a line using the angle shown here, that extends from the bottom-left corner of the triangle to the upper-right edge of the triangle underneath.

# Collapsing Palette Windows

InDesign offers four ways to collapse palette windows: double-click the title bar; double-click the palette tab; click the Collapse Window button; or click the up/down cycle arrows located next to the palette name (note: only certain palettes contain these arrows).

Click multiple times on the up/down cycle arrows or the palette tab to incrementally collapse or expand palettes that contain extra options or extensive item lists (e.g., Layers, Styles, Swatches).

One click on the up/down arrows (or one double-click on the tab) collapses the window to reveal only basic options.

Two clicks on the up/down arrows (or two double-clicks on the tab) fully collapses the window.

*continues on next page*

# Gel Buttons *continued*

## Stashing Individual Palettes to the Side of the Screen

To stash a palette, click the palette tab and drag it to either side of your screen. Hold the mouse button down until the horizontal palette outline changes to a vertical outline, then release the palette window to snap into place. You can then add more palettes to the window if you want.

When you stash a palette, it's collapsed on the side of your screen. Click once on the palette tab to expand the window. You can reposition the side tab by clicking in the gray palette well area and dragging up or down.

You can also expand the side tab vertically. First hover your mouse over the top (Windows only) or bottom edge (Mac and Windows) until the up/down arrow icon appears. Click and drag in either direction to lengthen the palette.

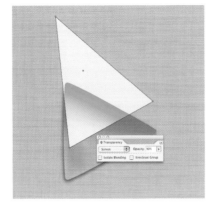

### Step 25.
Press X to bring the stroke icon to the front. Press the backslash key (/) to apply a stroke of None. In the Transparency palette, choose Screen from the Mode pop-up menu. Enter **90%** in the Opacity field and press Return (Mac) or Enter (Windows).

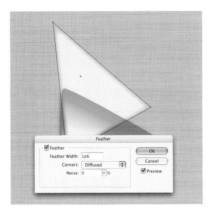

### Step 26.
Choose Object ▷ Feather. In the dialog that appears, click the Feather check box to enable the effect. Enter **1p6** in the Feather Width field. Leave the Corners pop-up menu setting at Diffused and the Noise setting at 0%. Click OK to apply.

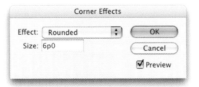

### Step 27.
Choose Object ▷ Corner Effects. In the dialog that appears, select Rounded from the Effect pop-up menu. Enter **6p** in the Size field and click OK to apply.

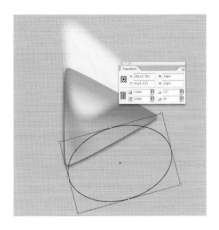

**Step 28.**

Press L to access the Ellipse tool and draw an oval. In the Control or Transform palette, enter **18p4** in the Width field and **12p3** in the Height field. Enter **15°** in the Rotation Angle field. Press V to access the Selection tool and position the triangle as shown.

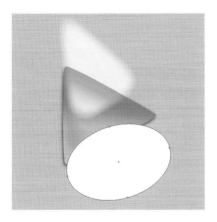

**Step 29.**

Press the backslash key (/) to apply a stroke of None. Press X to bring the fill icon to the front. Click the Paper swatch in the Swatches palette to apply a white fill.

**Step 30.**

Choose Object ▷ Feather. In the dialog that appears, click the Feather check box to enable the effect. Enter **1p6** in the Feather Width field. Leave the Corners pop-up menu setting at Diffused and the Noise setting at 0%. Click OK to apply.

## Docking Palette Windows to the Side Tabs

To stash a palette group that contains several palettes, Option-drag (Mac) or Alt-drag (Windows) on any of the palette tabs to either side of your screen. Hold the mouse button down until the horizontal palette outline changes to a vertical outline, then release. The palette window will snap into place. You can then add more palettes to the stashed window.

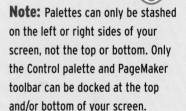

**Note:** Palettes can only be stashed on the left or right sides of your screen, not the top or bottom. Only the Control palette and PageMaker toolbar can be docked at the top and/or bottom of your screen.

*continues on next page*

# Gel Buttons *continued*

## Saving a Workspace

InDesign allows you to save your workspace environment so that you don't have to spend time repositioning palettes on the screen every time you launch the application. You can create and save a custom workspace for every type of layout work you do. For instance, a production-oriented job might require a totally different set of palettes than a design-oriented one. No problem! InDesign lets you save a workspace for each.

To save your preferred work environment, choose Window ▷ Workspace ▷ Save Workspace. When the dialog appears, enter a name for it and click OK. You can now restore your workspace whenever you like by selecting it under the Window ▷ Workspace submenu.

To save changes made to your custom environment, choose Window ▷ Workspace ▷ Save Workspace, and enter the name of the workspace you want to update. Click OK when the dialog asks you if you want to replace the workspace.

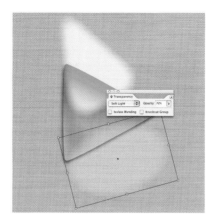

**Step 31.**
In the Transparency palette, choose Soft Light from the Mode pop-up menu. Enter **70%** in the Opacity field and press Return (Mac) or Enter (Windows). Shift-click the triangle shape above to add it to the selection. Press ⌘+G / Ctrl+G to group the objects.

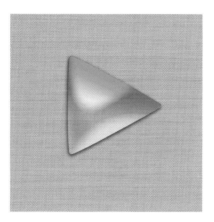

**Step 32.**
To nest the selected shapes, press ⌘+X / Ctrl+X. This cuts the objects to the Clipboard and removes them from the page. Option-click / Alt-click the highlights layer in the Layers palette to select the triangle. Choose Edit ▷ Paste Into. Choose Object ▷ Fitting ▷ Center Content. Press A to access the Direct Selection tool. Click the nested oval shape to select it. Shift-click the nested triangle to add it to the selection. Enter 90° in the Rotation Angle field of the Control or Transform palette. Press V to access the Selection tool, click one of the center points, and move the objects back into their original position.

**Step 33.**
Option-click / Alt-click the Create New Layer button at the bottom of the Layers palette. In the Layer Options dialog, enter a name for the layer (e.g., **top shadow**) and click OK.

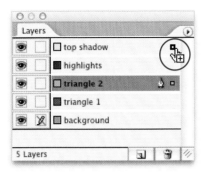

**Step 34.**

Option-click / Alt-click the triangle 2 layer to select the triangle that is on that layer. Option-click / Alt-click the small square icon located on the triangle 2 layer and drag it up to the new top shadow layer above. Doing so creates a copy of the selection and places it on the new layer.

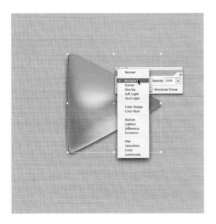

**Step 35.**

Choose Object ▷ Feather. In the dialog that appears, enter **0p9** in the Feather Width field. Leave the Corners pop-up menu setting at Diffused and the Noise setting at 0%. Click OK to apply. In the Transparency palette, change the Mode to Multiply.

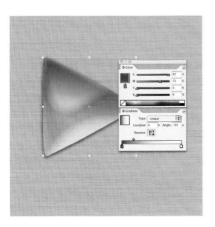

**Step 36.**

Click the Cyan to White gradient swatch in the Swatches palette to apply the gradient as a fill. In the Gradient palette, click the left color stop icon located beneath the Gradient Ramp. Choose Window ▷ Color (or press F6) to display the Color palette. Choose CMYK from the Color palette fly-out menu and create a build that uses C=97, M=72, Y=0, K=0.

## Attributes Palette

The Attributes palette is used to set overprint options that affect the color separation and output of your document. InDesign automatically overprints any solid black items by default; however, all other colors are set to automatically knock out (or replace all underlying inks). You can use the Attributes palette to overprint any colors instead by applying this option to the fills and strokes of any individual frames in your layout.

The Attributes palette also contains one other hidden feature: the ability to make selected items within your document or master pages nonprintable. This is particularly useful when you are in the early stages of a design and many of your page items are still FPO (for placement only). InDesign allows you to suppress printing of any individual placeholder items or extraneous screen notations.

*continues on next page*

# Gel Buttons *continued*

## Data Merge Palette

The Data Merge palette allows you to create standardized documents based on a data file (e.g., a form letter that you mail to a large list of clients).

To use the Data Merge palette, you must have a data file prepared to apply to an existing InDesign document. You can merge a .csv file (comma-separated value), or a simple .txt file with all the information separated by either commas or tabs (but not both). The first line of your data file must contain category names separated by either commas or tabs.

To merge, click the menu button and choose Select Data Source. Browse to the .csv or .txt file, make sure Show Import Options is checked at the bottom of the dialog, then click Open. When the dialog opens, choose either Comma Separated or Tab Delimited, depending on which type of data file you are merging, and click OK.

The named categories from the first line of your data file appear in the Data Merge palette and can then be applied to various text items in your InDesign document. Select the text you want the data applied to, and then click the appropriate category name in the Data Merge palette.

The Preview check box displays the data in the applied areas and the Create Merged Document button allows you to generate InDesign pages based on the applied data.

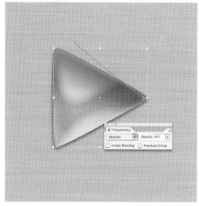

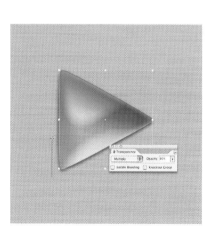

**Step 37.**

Press G to access the Gradient tool. To apply the gradient, draw a line using the angle shown here, which extends from just beyond the top point of the triangle to the tip of right point. In the Transparency palette, enter **60%** in the Opacity field and press Return (Mac) or Enter (Windows).

**Step 38.**

From the Layers palette fly-out menu, choose Duplicate Layer top shadow. In the dialog that appears, type **left shadow** in the Name field and click OK. Option-click / Alt-click the new left shadow layer in the palette to select the triangle. Choose Object▷ Feather. In the dialog that appears, click the Feather check box to disable the effect. Click OK to apply.

**Step 39.**

Change the gradient fill by clicking the Cyan to White gradient swatch from the Swatches palette list. Press G to access the Gradient tool. To apply the gradient, draw a line using the angle shown here, which extends from just outside the bottom point of the triangle up about 1p6. In the Transparency palette, enter **80%** in the Opacity field and press Return (Mac) or Enter (Windows).

**Step 40.**
Select the triangle 1 layer in the Layers palette. ⌘+Option-click / Ctrl+Alt-click the Create New Layer button at the bottom of the palette to create a new layer underneath it. Double-click the new layer to display the Swatch Options dialog. Enter **type** in the Name field and click OK.

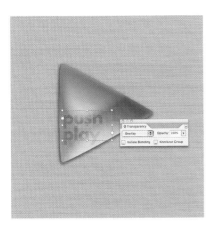

**Step 41.**
Add some text as shown. The "push play" text shown here uses the Futura Bold font set in all lowercase, 34pt, with 32pt leading, Optical Kerning, and -10 Tracking. In the Transparency palette, choose Overlay from the Mode pop-up menu.

**Step 42.**
From the Layers palette menu, choose Duplicate Layer type. Click OK to bypass the dialog that appears. Option-click / Alt-click the new type copy ▷ layer in the palette to select the text frame. In the Transparency palette, change the Mode to Soft Light. Enter **75%** in the Opacity field and press Return (Mac) or Enter (Windows). The word "PRODUCTIONS" in the example shown here was added on a separate layer at the top of the list using the Futura Medium font, 18pt with Optical Kerning and 310 Tracking. A Paper (white) fill and None stroke is applied.

## Scripts Palette

Wouldn't it be great if you could automate InDesign to do all the repetitive grunt work for you? Well, you can with scripting. And the best part is—*you don't have to know how to write scripts to use them.*

To run a script, just place the script file in the \Presets\Scripts folder located in the InDesign application folder. InDesign can run scripts written in Extend-Script (a cross-platform version of JavaScript), AppleScript (Mac only), or Virtual Basic Script, Virtual Basic for Applications, and Visual Basic (Windows only).

Double-click the script name in the Scripts palette to run the script. Hold down the Option or Alt key as you double-click to open in a script editor. Hold down the Shift key and double-click the script name to open in the JavaScript debugger.

To learn more about scripting in InDesign, or to try out some example scripts, check out the *Adobe InDesign CS2 Scripting Guide* found on the installer CD.

# Gel Sidebar Tabs

As a designer, it's not uncommon to include a small body of text that is offset from the rest of your layout. In magazine design, this is referred to as a "sidebar," but you don't necessarily have to be designing magazines to use them. In fact, small offset text items can be used in all types of page layout design, from catalogs to brochures to interactive PDFs (and just about anywhere else you can find a use for them!).

These "sidebars" usually contain headers or tabs of some sort, and it can be challenging to find a creative way to display them. Next time you're faced with this challenge, try creating a sidebar tab using the steps described here. All you have to do is add a little nesting, feathering, and transparency effects and your boring old sidebar headers will be rockin' in no time!

## Give Your Sidebars a Whole New Look

Add highlights to your sidebar tabs by applying gradient fills, transparency blend modes, and feather effects to nested shapes.

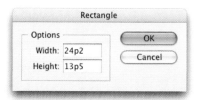

**Step 1.**
In a new document, press M to access the Rectangle tool. Click once anywhere on the page. In the dialog that appears, enter **24p2** in the Width field and **13p5** in the Height field. Click OK to apply.

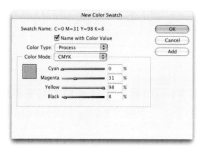

**Step 2.**
Choose Window ▷ Swatches (or press F5) to display the Swatches palette. Choose New Color Swatch from the palette fly-out menu. In the dialog that appears, create a gold build that uses C=0, M=31, Y=98, K=8. Click OK to add the swatch.

**Step 3.**
Press ⌘+H / Ctrl+H to hide frame edges. Choose Window ▷ Stroke (or press F10) to display the Stroke palette. Enter **3pt** in the Weight field and press Return (Mac) or Enter (Windows). If you prefer, you can also enter this value in the Stroke Weight field of the Control palette.

### Step 4.
Press X to bring the fill icon to the front. Click the Paper swatch in the Swatches palette to apply a white fill to the rectangle.

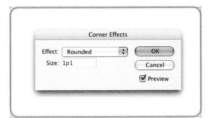

### Step 5.
Choose Object ▷ Corner Effects. In the dialog that appears, choose Rounded from the Effect pop-up menu. Enter **1p1** in the Size field and click OK to apply.

### Step 6.
Choose Object ▷ Drop Shadow. In the dialog that appears, click the Drop Shadow check box to enable the effect, then turn on the Preview check box to see the shadow applied to your selected object. Enter **65%** for Opacity and **0p3** for both X and Y Offset amounts. Keep the rest of the settings at their defaults. Click OK to apply.

*continues on next page*

## Info Palette

The items displayed in the Info palette vary depending on what you have selected and with what tool. You can use the Info palette to determine a placed object's color space and file size, or the color build of a specific fill or stroke. You can also access valuable information about text items that are selected with the Type tool, such as word and character count.

The Info palette also goes hand in hand with the Measure tool, allowing you to match the size and/or angle of different objects in a document layout.

**Note:** To determine the color space of a placed graphic (RGB, CMYK, Grayscale, or LAB), select it with the Selection tool (V) or Direct Selection tool (A), and refer to the Info palette.

# Gel Sidebar Tabs *continued*

## Bookmarks Palette

The Bookmarks palette allows you to create links to specific pages within your document. This is especially useful when you are creating a layout intended for PDF output. The links appear in the Bookmarks tab when you are viewing in Acrobat and let you navigate a large document much more easily.

To create a page bookmark, double-click a page in the Pages palette and then click the Create New Bookmark icon at the bottom of the Bookmarks palette. To create a text bookmark, highlight some text with the Type tool or click an insertion point and then click the New Bookmark icon. You can nest text bookmarks within page bookmarks to help keep them organized in the palette. Rearrange bookmarks in the palette by clicking and dragging them anywhere in the list, or choose Sort Bookmarks from the palette menu.

Double-click a bookmark in the palette to go to the link. To rename a bookmark, click once and wait for the data field to appear, or choose Rename Bookmark from the palette fly-out menu. To delete a bookmark, select it, then click the trash icon at the bottom of the palette.

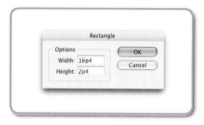

**Step 7.**
Click once on the page to create another rectangle. In the dialog that appears, enter **16p4** in the Width field and **2p4** in the Height field. Click OK to apply.

**Step 8.**
Press V to access the Selection tool and position the rectangle as shown. Click the gold swatch in the Swatches palette to apply a gold fill. Press X to bring the stroke icon to the front. Press the backslash key (/) to apply a stroke of None.

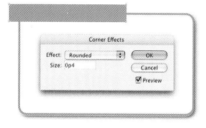

**Step 9.**
Choose Object ▷ Corner Effects. In the dialog that appears, choose Rounded from the Effect pop-up menu. Enter **0p4** in the Size field and click OK to apply.

**Step 10.**

Choose Object ▷ Drop Shadow. In the dialog that appears, click the Drop Shadow check box to enable the effect. Enter **65%** for Opacity, **0p1** for X Offset, and **0p2** for Y Offset. Keep the rest of the settings at their defaults. Click OK to apply.

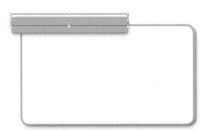

**Step 11.**

Press M to access the Rectangle tool again, and click once on the page. In the dialog that appears, enter **16p5** in the Width field and **1p9** in the Height field. Click OK to apply. Press V to access the Selection tool and position the rectangle as shown.

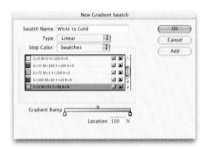

**Step 12.**

Press the backslash key (/) to apply a stroke of None. Press X to bring the fill icon to the front. Choose New Gradient Swatch from the Swatches palette fly-out menu. Click the right color stop icon located beneath the Gradient Ramp at the bottom of the dialog. Choose Swatches from the Stop Color pop-up menu and select the gold swatch you created in an earlier step from the list. Enter **White to Gold** in the Swatch Name field. Click OK to add the swatch.

*continues on next page*

## Hyperlinks Palette

Using the Hyperlinks palette, you can add interactive web and e-mail links to your InDesign documents and exported PDFs. To create a basic URL link, highlight the URL from the document with the Type tool and choose New Hyperlink From URL from the Hyperlinks palette menu.

To create all other types of hyperlinks, select a graphic or text item as the source and click the Create New Hyperlink button at the bottom of the Hyperlinks palette. When the dialog appears, choose a name, destination document and type, and appearance setting.

**Note:** To quickly access Hyperlink commands, try using contextual menus (Windows: right-click, Mac: Control-click).

# Gel Sidebar Tabs *continued*

## States Palette

The States palette allows you to apply different rollover states to an existing graphic button. Placed graphics can be converted into buttons containing Up, Rollover, and Down states. You can then export a PDF of your document, containing rollover buttons that work the same way as they would in a web browser.

You can apply preset or custom states to your buttons. Select a button and choose a preset from the menu; or to create a custom rollover, click the New State button at the bottom of the palette to create a Rollover state, and once more to create a Down state. By default, all InDesign buttons already contain an Up state.

With the button still selected, click a state in the palette to make a change to its appearance. You can switch out a placed graphic, edit text, and change the fill and stroke appearance of a button when creating custom states.

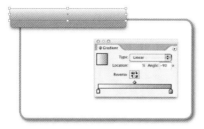

**Step 13.**
Choose Window ▷ Gradient to display the Gradient palette. Enter **-90°** in the Angle field and press Return (Mac) or Enter (Windows).

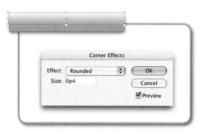

**Step 14.**
Choose Object ▷ Corner Effects. In the dialog that appears, choose Rounded from the Effect pop-up menu. Enter **0p4** in the Size field and click OK to apply.

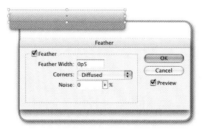

**Step 15.**
Choose Object ▷ Feather. In the dialog that appears, click the Feather check box to enable the effect, then turn on the Preview check box to see the feather applied to your selected object. Enter **0p5** in the Feather Width field. Leave the Corners pop-up menu setting at Diffused and the Noise setting at 0%. Click OK to apply.

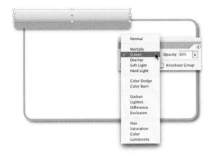

**Step 16.**

Choose Window ▷ Transparency (or press Shift+F10) to display the Transparency palette. Choose Screen from the Mode pop-up menu. Enter **80%** in the Opacity field and press Return (Mac) or Enter (Windows).

**Step 17.**

Press the forward slash key (\) to access the Line tool. Hold down Shift and draw a line that extends from the bottom-left side of the rectangle to the bottom-right side, as shown.

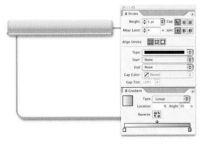

**Step 18.**

Enter **5pt** in the Weight field of the Stroke or Control palette. Press X to bring the stroke icon to the front. Click the White to Gold gradient swatch in the Swatches palette. Enter **90°** in the Angle field of the Gradient palette and press Return (Mac) or Enter (Windows).

*continues on next page*

# Trap Presets Palette

The Trap Presets palette can assist you in creating, saving, loading, and applying trap presets. You can apply the default preset, no preset, or a custom preset to any or all the pages in a document. You can also load trap presets from other InDesign documents.

To assign a saved trap preset, the default trap preset, or no trap preset at all to the document or to a page range, click the desired option and select Assign Trap Preset from the palette menu. If a Trap Preset is not applied manually to a page range using the Trap Presets palette, InDesign uses the default setting.

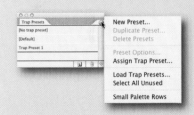

# Gel Sidebar Tabs *continued*

## Separations Preview Palette

The Separations Preview palette allows you to preview CMYK process plates individually on screen, before outputting. You can use the separations preview to check rich black builds, total ink coverage (to make sure it does not exceed press limitations), and overprinting (including transparency and blends).

Click a single process plate in the palette (C, M, Y, or K) to preview that separation. By default, the individual separations appear on screen as black. However, you can change the preview setting to reflect actual plate colors by disabling the Show Single Plates In Black option in the palette menu.

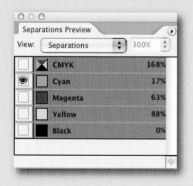

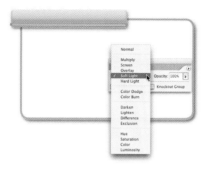

**Step 19.**
For a less intense blend than the one applied to the top highlight, choose Soft Light from the Transparency palette Mode pop-up menu.

**Step 20.**
Choose Object ▷ Feather. In the dialog that appears, enter **0p2** in the Feather Width field. Leave the Corners pop-up menu setting at Diffused and the Noise setting at 0%. Click OK to apply.

**Step 21.**
Press V to access the Selection tool. Shift-click the top highlight to add it to the selection. Press ⌘+G / Ctrl+G to group the objects. The dotted line that appears around the objects indicates that they are now grouped.

### Step 22.

To nest the selected group, press ⌘+X / Ctrl+X. This copies the group to the Clipboard and removes it from the page. Click the gold rectangle to select it. Choose Edit ▷ Paste Into.

### Step 23.

Add some text as shown. The text shown here uses the Myriad Pro Bold font set at 18pt, with Optical Kerning, and 10 Tracking. In the Transparency palette, choose Multiply from the Mode pop-up menu.

### Step 24.

Add some body text to your sidebar. Now that you've created one, you can save your gel sidebar tab as a library item or export it as an InDesign snippet to be used over and over again in your layouts.

# Flattener Preview Palette

The Flattener Preview palette allows you to highlight areas in a document that are affected by transparency flattening during output. It also allows you to apply the proper flattener preset.

You can apply different transparency flattener presets to all transparent items in your document when printing or exporting to PDF, SVG, or EPS. Choose from default Low, Medium, or High presets, or select a saved custom preset. You can create, save, and apply your own custom presets in the Transparency Flattener Presets dialog accessible through the Flattener Preview palette menu.

InDesign Help also contains a thorough list of output guidelines that you can refer to when creating or editing flattener presets.

**Note:** You can base a custom flattener preset on one of the default presets. Select the default preset from the Transparency Flattener Presets dialog and click the New button. The default settings appear in the Transparency Flattener Preset Options dialog that launches.

# Object Silhouettes

Sometimes less is more. When designing a logo or a graphic to be used in a layout, whether it's an advertisement, brochure, or any other number of projects, you may find that using a simple outline of a familiar shape can be more effective than using a four-color photo.

With these steps, we'll place an image containing an embedded Photoshop path into an InDesign document. We'll then convert the clipping path into a frame and delete the image. What we'll wind up with is an InDesign path in the shape of the image. This is a great way to create InDesign paths from preexisting Photoshop paths. Nowadays, most of the stock images available contain paths already embedded in them, so why not put them to good use in InDesign!

## Convert Clipping Paths into Silhouettes

To re-create this effect using the image shown here, download dog.tif from the *InDesign Effects Book* website.

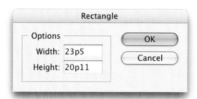

**Step 1.**
In a new document, press M to access the Rectangle tool. Click once anywhere on the page. In the dialog that appears, enter **23p5** in the Width field and **20p11** in the Height field. Click OK to apply.

**Step 2.**
Press Shift+X to swap the default fill and stroke colors. Doing so applies a black fill and None stroke to the rectangle.

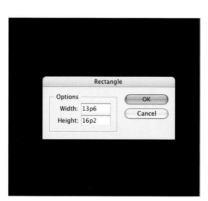

**Step 3.**
Click once on the page to create another rectangle. In the dialog that appears, enter **13p6** in the Width field and **16p2** in the Height field. Click OK to apply.

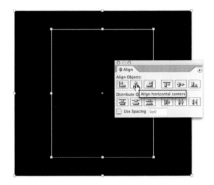

**Step 4.**

Choose Window ▷ Object & Layout ▷ Align (or press Shift+F7) to display the Align palette. Press V to access the Selection tool. Shift-click the black rectangle to add it to the selection. Click the Align Horizontal Centers button and the Align Vertical Centers button in the Align palette.

www.photospin.com © 2005

**Step 5.**

Shift-click the black rectangle to remove it from the selection. Press ⌘+D / Ctrl+D to display the Place dialog. Locate the dog.tif image on your system. Select the Show Import Options check box at the bottom of the dialog and click Open.

**Step 6.**

In the dialog that appears, click the Apply Photoshop Clipping Path check box and click OK. Choose Object ▷ Fitting ▷ Fit Content To Frame, then choose Object ▷ Fitting ▷ Center Content.

## Story Palette

The Story palette lets you adjust the optical margin alignment for selected text frames in a document. Enabling this option helps display large amounts of body text in an easy-to-read format by positioning punctuation marks (such as quotation marks) and other specific characters outside the column.

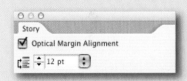

Click the Optical Margin Alignment box to apply optical margin alignment to selected text frames in the document. The second row (Align Based On Size) displays the amount of optical margin alignment for any currently selected text.

*continues on next page*

# Object Silhouettes *continued*

## Applying Keep Options

By applying InDesign's Keep Options feature, you can prevent widows and orphans from appearing throughout the text of your layout. A widow is the last line of a paragraph that ends up by itself at the top of a column, separated from the rest of the paragraph. An orphan is the first line of a paragraph that ends up on its own line at the end of a column. A word that gets separated from the rest of a paragraph and ends up on its own line is also considered a widow.

Not only do these little annoyances affect readability, but they are also a terrible eyesore! To ward off these typographical gremlins, select a paragraph (or multiple paragraphs) with the Type tool and choose Keep Options from the Paragraph palette menu, or press Option+⌘+K / Alt+Ctrl+K.

**Step 7.**

Control-click/right-click to access the contextual menu. Choose Convert Clipping Path To Frame. Press A to switch to the Direct Selection tool. Click the image to select it from within the frame. Press Delete/Backspace.

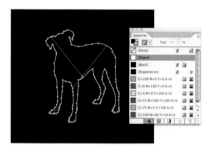

**Step 8.**

Press Shift+X to swap the default fill and stroke colors. Doing so applies a black fill and None stroke to the path. Choose Window ▷ Swatches (or press F5) to display the Swatches palette. Click the Paper swatch to apply a white stroke.

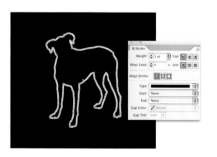

**Step 9.**

Choose Window ▷ Stroke (or press F10) to display the Stroke palette. Enter **3pt** in the Weight field and press Return (Mac) or Enter (Windows). If you prefer, you can also enter this value in the Stroke Weight field of the Control palette. Press ⌘+H or Ctrl+H to hide frame edges and view the silhouette.

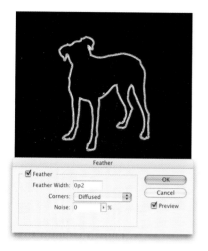

**Step 10.**

To soften the edge of the path just slightly, choose Object ▷ Feather. In the dialog that appears, check the Feather check box to enable the effect, then turn on the Preview check box to see the feather applied to the selected object. Enter **0p2** in the Feather Width field. Leave the Corners pop-up menu setting at Diffused and the Noise setting at 0. Click OK to apply.

**Step 11.**

To create a white outer glow around the path, choose Object ▷ Drop Shadow. In the dialog that appears, click the Drop Shadow check box to enable the effect, and then turn on the Preview check box to see the shadow applied to the selected object. Choose Screen from the Mode pop-up menu and select Paper (white) from the swatches list below. Enter **65%** for Opacity, **1p1** for Blur, and **0p0** for both X and Y Offset amounts. Enter **5%** for Spread and keep the Noise setting at 0%. Click OK to apply.

**Step 12.**

To complete the design, add some text as shown. The example here uses the Futura font.

## Applying Keep Options *continued*

**Keep With Next**  By entering a value of 1 in the Keep With Next field, you can ensure that headers always remain positioned above the paragraph that follows. Should any text or frame edits push the paragraph into a new column, new page, or a text wrap, the header will follow.

**Keep Lines Together**  To keep paragraphs together during editing, enter a value in the Start and End fields. These values tell InDesign the minimum number of lines allowed to separate at the start or end of a paragraph should it be pushed into a new column or page.

Choosing All Lines In Paragraph from the Keep Lines Together option does not allow for any lines to be separated from a paragraph should editing push it into a new column or page. Instead, the whole paragraph is moved.

**Start Paragraph**  The Start Paragraph menu contains options for forcing a column or page break before the selected paragraph. Choose one of these options to ensure the paragraph's position in the layout.

# Transparent Background Frames

Occasionally in a layout, you may want to place some text over a background image. In order to see the text clearly, you can apply a reverse fill color to the text (such as white). However, reversing the text can sometimes cause unwanted eyestrain for the reader, especially if a large amount of text is placed over the image.

One thing you can do to make the text easier to read is to place it over a screened frame. With these steps, we'll create some custom shapes using Pathfinder, then apply a white fill and reduce the opacity setting. In this example, the screened back frames resemble the type of computer interface you might see used in your favorite science-fiction television shows and movies.

You can also use this effect to create web page designs and mock-ups. If you have GoLive CS2 installed on your system, try utilizing the Package for GoLive feature available in InDesign CS2.

## Creating Custom Shapes with Pathfinder

To re-create this effect using the background image shown here, download planet.tif from the *InDesign Effects Book* website.

www.photospin.com © 2005

**Step 1.**
In a new document, press ⌘+D (Mac) or Ctrl+D to display the Place dialog. Locate the planet.tif image on your system, and click Open. Click the loaded place cursor once anywhere on the page to place the image at 100% of its size. Center the image on the page.

**Step 2.**
Choose Window ▷ Layers (or press F7) to display the Layers palette. Double-click Layer 1 to display the Layer Options dialog. Enter **background** in the Name field, check the Lock Layer option, and click OK to close the dialog.

**Step 3.**
Option-click / Alt-click the Create New Layer button at the bottom of the Layers palette. In the Layer Options dialog, enter a name for the layer (e.g., **shapes**) and click OK.

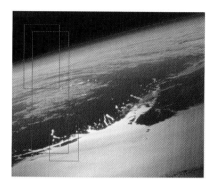

**Step 4.**

Press M to access the Rectangle tool. Draw three rectangles that overlap each other as shown.

**Step 5.**

Press V to access the Selection tool. Hold down Shift and click each shape to select them all. Choose Object ▷ Pathfinder ▷ Add. If you prefer, you can also choose Window ▷ Object & Layout ▷ Pathfinder to display the Pathfinder palette and click the Add button.

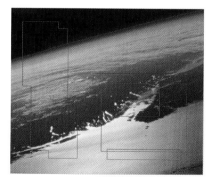

**Step 6.**

Press M to access the Rectangle tool. Draw three more rectangles that overlap each other as shown.

*continues on next page*

# Creating Hanging Indents with Indent Fields

Hanging indents are great for creating custom bulleted or number lists. By placing a hanging indent after a lead-in character (a bullet point, a number, etc.), you can force the subsequent lines of the paragraph to line up evenly with the indent.

To create a hanging indent using the Paragraph palette/Control palette indent fields, perform the following steps:

1. In the first line of each paragraph, insert a tab after the lead-in character.

2. Enter a positive value in the Left Indent field of the Paragraph palette or Control palette.

3. Enter the negative opposite of the value in the First Line Indent field of the Paragraph palette or Control palette.

# Transparent Background Frames *continued*

## Indent To Here Character

To create a hanging indent using the Indent To Here character, perform the following steps:

1. In the first line of each paragraph, insert a tab after the lead-in character.

2. Place the Type tool cursor just after the tab in each paragraph and choose Type ▷ Insert Special Character ▷ Indent To Here.

3. If necessary, select the paragraphs with the Type tool and adjust the tab indents using the Tabs palette.

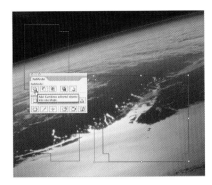

**Step 7.**
Press V to access the Selection tool. Hold down Shift and click the three new shapes to select them all. Choose Object ▷ Pathfinder ▷ Add, or click the Add button in the Pathfinder palette.

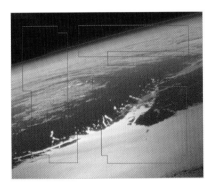

**Step 8.**
Press M to access the Rectangle tool. Draw two more rectangles that overlap each other as shown.

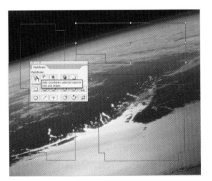

**Step 9.**
Press V to access the Selection tool. Hold down Shift and click the two new shapes to select them both. Choose Object ▷ Pathfinder ▷ Add, or click the Add button in the Pathfinder palette.

**Step 10.**
In the Layers palette, Option-click / Alt-click the shapes layer to select everything on it. Choose Object ▷ Corner Effects. In the dialog that appears, choose Bevel from the Effect pop-up menu. Check the Preview check box to see the effect applied to the selected objects. Enter **0p5** in the Size field and click OK.

**Step 11.**
Press the backslash key to apply a stroke of None. Press X to bring the fill icon to the front. Choose Window ▷ Swatches (or press F5) to display the Swatches palette. Click the Paper swatch in the Swatches palette list to apply a white fill.

**Step 12.**
Choose Window ▷ Transparency (or press Shift+F10) to display the Transparency palette. Enter **70%** in the Opacity field and press Return (Mac) or Enter (Windows).

*continues on next page*

# Hanging Punctuation

You can greatly improve the "look" of your text by hanging punctuation marks outside the column edge. You can do this by applying the Optical Margin Alignment option located in the Story palette. When you enable this feature, InDesign not only adjusts the punctuation, but also makes a slight adjustment to the edges of any characters extending outside the column edge as well (a common occurrence with capital serifs).

Select a text frame with either Selection tool and then open the Story palette by choosing Window ▷ Type ▷ Tables ▷ Story. Click the Optical Margin Alignment check box to allow InDesign to instantly adjust the punctuation and extended character alignment. Optical Margin Alignment carries through to all linked frames in a story.

To adjust the applied "hang" amount, increase or decrease the value entered in the Align Based On Size field.

# Transparent Background Frames *continued*

## Packaging for GoLive

The Package For GoLive feature allows you to create web versions of InDesign print or PDF documents. A GoLive package includes a document preview as well as all of the text and graphic files needed to create a web version of the document in GoLive. You can open the package in GoLive CS2 and drag objects from the preview into a GoLive web page. Note that the InDesign CS2 Package for GoLive feature is compatible only with Adobe GoLive CS2 and not CS.

When packaging for GoLive, all InDesign stories are converted to XML files with the .incd filename extension (threaded text frames are converted into a single XML file). All applied paragraph and character styles are converted to Cascading Style Sheets (CSS) in GoLive.

All placed images and graphics are converted to TIFF for faster web display. You can also save applied graphic transformations such as scaling, shearing, and rotating. Native and custom drawn InDesign shapes can be dragged into a GoLive web page from the InDesign Layout tab in GoLive InDesign shapes are converted to GIF but are not added to the Assets folder.

**Step 13.**
From the Layers palette menu, choose Duplicate Layer shapes. In the dialog that appears, enter **outlines** in the Name field and click OK. Option-click / Alt-click the new outlines layer in the palette to select the duplicate shapes.

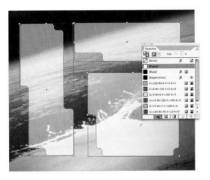

**Step 14.**
Press the backslash key to apply a fill of None. Press X to bring the stroke icon to the front. Click the Paper swatch in the Swatches palette list to apply a white stroke.

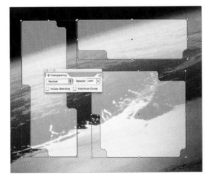

**Step 15.**
In the Transparency palette, enter **100%** in the Opacity field and press Return (Mac) or Enter (Windows).

**Step 16.**

To make the outlines "pop," choose Object ▷ Drop Shadow. In the dialog that appears, click the Drop Shadow check box to enable the effect, then turn on the Preview check box to see the shadow applied to the selected object. Enter **100%** for Opacity, **0p2** for Blur, and **0p1** for both X and Y Offset amounts. Keep the rest of the settings at their defaults. Click OK to apply.

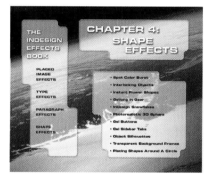

**Step 17.**

To complete the design, create a new layer and add some text over the transparent background frames as shown. The example here uses the Eurostile Extended 2 font with a dark blue drop shadow applied on the headline text. Press ⌘+H / Ctrl+H to hide frame edges and view your transparent background frames in action!

## Packaging for GoLive *continued*

To create a GoLive package of an InDesign document, choose File ▷ Package For GoLive. In the first dialog (Package Publication For GoLive), choose a name and system location and click Package. InDesign will launch the Package For GoLive dialog.

In the Pages section of the Package For GoLive dialog, choose All, Range, or Selection. Check the Include Hidden Layers option to package linked objects on hidden layers.

In the Options portion of the dialog, check the View Package When Complete option to open the package in GoLive CS2 immediately after. You can also select an encoding format from the menu.

In the Images, Movies & Sounds portion of the dialog, choose how you would like to package these file types. Check the Original Images option to copy the original graphics files and format the images later in GoLive. Check the Formatted Images option to copy the images as they appear in InDesign (such as cropped images). Check the Movies And Sounds option to copy the original movie and sound files.

When you're ready, click Package. You can then open the .idpk file in GoLive and re-create the layout for web display.

# Placing Shapes Around a Circle

With InDesign's Stroke Styles option, you can create custom strokes based on a dot, dash, or a line. You can then apply the stroke style to an ellipse, rectangle, polygon, or any InDesign path. But what if you'd like to create a style that uses a shape other than a dot, dash, or line?

There is a way to get around this. First, create (or import) the shape you'd like to use, then copy/paste it around the path as an inline object. You can do this using the Copy/Paste commands and the Type On A Path tool. InDesign treats the pasted inline objects like text characters, which means that you can space them around the shape by adjusting kerning and tracking values.

With these steps, we'll create an illustration of a dinner plate using this method of placing shapes around a circle. While we're at it, we'll add some shadows and highlights to our layers to add a more realistic effect to the illustration.

## Using Type On A Path with Inline Objects

To re-create this effect using the shapes shown here, download shape1.inds and shape2.inds from the *InDesign Effects Book* website.

**Step 1.**
In a new document, press L to access the Ellipse tool. Click once anywhere on the page. In the dialog that appears, enter **28p1** in the Width and Height fields. Click OK to apply. Press V to access the Selection tool and center the circle on the page.

Press ⌘+D / Ctrl+D to display the Place dialog. Locate shape1.inds on your system, and click Open. The shape will appear on the page at 100% of its size. Click the shape to select it. Choose Window ▷ Swatches (or press F5) to display the Swatches palette. Click the Paper swatch to apply a white fill to the shape.

**Step 2.**
Choose Object ▷ Drop Shadow. In the dialog that appears, click the Drop Shadow check box to enable the effect, then turn on the Preview check box to see the effect applied to the selected object. Choose Screen from the Mode pop-up menu and select Paper (White) from the Swatches list below. Enter **0p10** for Blur, and **0p0** for both X and Y Offset amounts. Keep the rest of the settings at their defaults. Click OK to apply. You won't see a change in the object, but that's okay. You will in the steps ahead.

**Step 3.**
Press ⌘+X / Ctrl+X to copy the shape to the Clipboard and remove it from the page. Press Shift+T to access the Type On A Path tool. Click on the circle and press ⌘+V / Ctrl+V to paste the shape as an inline object. You won't see it because of the white fill, but it's there! Just focus on the blinking Type cursor.

## Quick Apply

If you have so many styles saved in your document that it takes a long time to scroll through the style palettes to find the one you need, try using Quick Apply.

Click the Quick Apply button in the Control palette, or choose Edit ▷ Quick Apply to open the Quick Edit list. Type the name (or even just the first two letters) of the style you're trying to locate in the search field. Quick Apply then displays any characters that match your search in the Quick Edit list below.

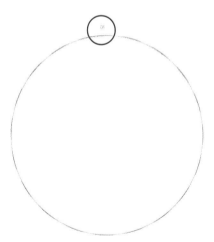

**Step 4.**
Continue pressing ⌘+V / Ctrl+V until you see a red + appear at the top of the circle. The red + indicates that the last shape you placed is overset.

Once you locate the style, press Return (Mac) or Enter (Windows) to apply it to your selection. The Quick Edit list automatically closes once a style is applied. If you can't find the style you're looking for, press Esc, or click the Quick Apply button to close the Quick Edit list.

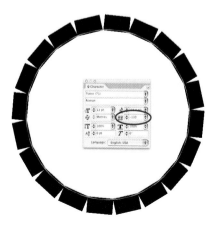

**Step 5.**
Press ⌘+A / Ctrl+A to select all the shapes around the circle. To fix the overset shape, enter **-130** in the Tracking field of the Control palette. If you prefer, you can also choose Window ▷ Type & Tables ▷ Character, and enter this value into the Tracking field of the Character palette. Notice the red + disappear.

*continues on next page*

# Placing Shapes Around a Circle *continued*

## Change/Apply Hyphenation Settings

InDesign allows you to apply specific hyphenation settings to a document or selected paragraph. You can do this using the Hyphenation Settings dialog, which you access by choosing Hyphenation from the Paragraph palette menu.

To set document-wide hyphenation settings, choose Edit ▷ Deselect All. In the resulting dialog, the settings you specify are applied to all added and imported text (untagged and unformatted), while preexisting paragraphs retain their applied hyphenation settings.

To adjust hyphenation settings for a specific paragraph (or paragraphs), insert the Type tool cursor anywhere in the paragraph (or highlight multiple paragraphs) and access the Hyphenation Settings dialog.

To set customized application-wide default hyphenation settings, make your adjustments in the dialog without any documents open. These settings are then applied to all added and imported text (untagged and unformatted, of course) in all your documents. Preexisting paragraphs will retain their applied hyphenation settings.

**Step 6.**
Double-click the Type On A Path tool icon in the Tools palette. In the dialog that appears, click the Flip check box and click OK.

**Step 7.**
Click the Selection tool icon in the Tools palette. Press X to bring the stroke icon to the front. In the Swatches palette, select the Paper swatch to apply a white stroke. Choose Window ▷ Stroke (or press F10) to display the Stroke palette. Enter **4pt** in the Weight field and press Return (Mac) or Enter (Windows). If you prefer, you can also enter this value in the Weight field of the Control palette.

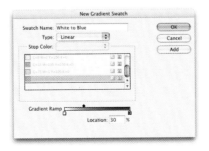

**Step 8.**
Press X to bring the fill icon to the front. Choose New Gradient Swatch from the Swatches palette fly-out menu. In the dialog that appears, click the right color stop icon located beneath the Gradient Ramp at the bottom of the dialog. Select the blue swatch from the swatches list. Click the center midpoint slider and enter **30%** in the Location field. Enter **White to Blue** in the Swatch Name field. Click OK to add the swatch.

**Step 9.**

Choose Window ▷ Gradient to display the Gradient palette. Enter –45° in the Angle field and press Return (Mac) or Enter (Windows). Choose Window ▷ Transparency (or press Shift+F10) to display the Transparency palette. Choose Lighten from the Mode pop-up menu.

**Step 10.**

Choose Object ▷ Drop Shadow. In the dialog that appears, click the Drop Shadow check box to enable the effect. Choose CMYK from the Color pop-up menu and create a build that uses C=100, M=90, Y=10, K=40. Enter **1p4** for Blur, **0p8** for X offset, and **1p** for Y Offset amounts. Keep the rest of the settings at their defaults. Click OK to apply.

**Step 11.**

Choose Window ▷ Layers (or press F7) to display the Layers palette. Double-click Layer 1 to display the Layer Options dialog. Enter **outer pattern** in the Name field, and click OK to close the dialog.

# Change/Apply Justification Settings

The Justification dialog, which you can access by choosing Justification from the Paragraph palette menu, allows you to control how InDesign handles word and letter spacing. The values entered in the Minimum, Desired, and Maximum fields of this dialog are percentages of the standard word and letter spaces embedded in the font by its designer.

The Justification dialog also lets you adjust the default Auto Leading percentage, specify a Single-Line or Paragraph Composer, and choose from available Single Word Justification options.

To set application-wide default justification settings, make your adjustments in the dialog without any documents open. These settings are then applied to all added and imported text (untagged and unformatted, of course) in all your documents. Preexisting paragraphs retain their applied justification settings.

*continues on next page*

# Placing Shapes Around a Circle *continued*

## Bullets and Numbering

InDesign CS2 allows you to place a bullet or number before each paragraph in a list using paragraph formatting. You can also save bulleted and numbered list attributes as part of a paragraph style.

To set and apply bullet and numbering attributes, select the list with the Type tool and choose Bullets and Numbering from the Paragraph palette menu. InDesign launches the Bullets and Numbering dialog. In the dialog, choose Bullets or Numbers from the List Type menu.

When you select the Bullets option, the dialog displays a glyphs icon grid that allows you to select a character to place before each paragraph in the selected list. You can also choose a font family and style, point size, and color to apply to the selected bullet character. At the bottom of the dialog, define the bullet position by choosing Hanging or Flush Left from the Position menu, or by entering values in the Left Indent, First Line Indent, and Tab Position fields. Check the Preview option to see the settings applied as you enter them.

**Step 12.**
Option-click / Alt-click the Create New Layer button at the bottom of the Layers palette. In the Layer Options dialog, enter **outer ring** in the Name field and click OK.

**Step 13.**
Press L to access the Ellipse tool. Hover the cursor over the center point of the circle. Option-drag / Alt-drag to draw a circle from the center point. Add the Shift key to constrain width and height amounts and create a perfect circle. Enter **22p6** in the Width and Height fields of the Control or Transform palette.

**Step 14.**
Press X to bring the stroke icon to the front. Select the Paper swatch in the Swatches palette to apply a white stroke. Enter **2pt** in the Weight field of the Stroke or Control palette. Enter **90%** in the Opacity field of the Transparency palette and press Return (Mac) or Enter (Windows).

**Step 15.**

Choose Object ▷ Drop Shadow. In the dialog that appears, click the Drop Shadow check box to enable the effect. Enter **90%** for Opacity, **1p1** for Blur, and **0p0** for both X and Y Offset amounts. Keep the rest of the settings at their defaults. Click OK to apply.

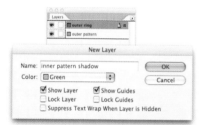

**Step 16.**

Option-click / Alt-click the Create New Layer button at the bottom of the Layers palette. In the Layer Options dialog, enter **inner pattern shadow** in the Name field and click OK.

**Step 17.**

Hover the cursor over the center point of the circle. Option-drag or Alt-drag to draw a second circle from the center point on the new layer. Add the Shift key to constrain width and height amounts and create a perfect circle. Enter **20p2** in the Width and Height fields of the Control or Transform palette.

*continues on next page*

# Adding Bullet Characters

You can add characters to the bullet glyph set by clicking the Add button. InDesign launches the Add Bullets dialog, which allows you to select characters from a chosen font and add them to the bullet glyph set.

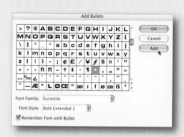

To ensure that an added bullet character is applied using the selected font, check the Remember Font With Bullet option. Click OK to add the selected character to the bullet glyph set and close the dialog.

Click the Add button to add the selected character and keep the dialog open.

# Placing Shapes Around a Circle *continued*

## Creating Jump Lines

You may run into an instance, especially in book or magazine publishing, where you need to indicate what page a story continues on. Thankfully, InDesign has special characters devoted to creating auto jump lines. Using these characters, InDesign automatically identifies the page you are jumping to or from.

In a separate text frame that overlaps the main story, type a jump line followed by the Next Page Number or Previous Page Number character. To insert either character, choose Type ▷ Insert Special Character ▷ Next/Previous Page Number. You can also insert these characters using the contextual menu by Control/right-clicking.

**Step 18.**
Press ⌘+D / Ctrl+D to display the Place dialog. Locate shape2.inds on your system, and click Open. Press V to access the Selection tool and click the imported shape to select it. Press X to bring the fill icon to the front. Click the blue swatch in the Swatches palette to apply a blue fill.

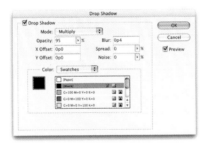

**Step 19.**
Choose Object ▷ Drop Shadow. In the dialog that appears, click the Drop Shadow check box to enable the effect. Enter **95%** for Opacity, **0p4** for Blur, and **0p0** for both X and Y Offset amounts. Keep the rest of the settings at their defaults. Click OK to apply.

**Step 20.**
Hold down Option or Alt and click and drag to create a duplicate of the shape. Press ⌘+X / Ctrl+X to copy the shape to the Clipboard and remove it from the page. Press Shift+T to access the Type On A Path tool. Click the circle and press ⌘+V / Ctrl+V to paste the shape as an inline object.

**Step 21.**

Continue pressing ⌘+V / Ctrl+V until the circle is surrounded by the repeated shape. Stop applying the Paste command when there is not enough room to fit any more shapes on the path. The image should look like the image shown here.

**Step 22.**

Press ⌘+A / Ctrl+A to select all the shapes around the circle. To space the shapes evenly, enter **63** in the Tracking field of the Control or Character palette.

**Step 23.**

In the Layers palette, choose Duplicate Layer inner pattern shadow from the palette menu. In the dialog that appears, enter **inner pattern** in the Name field and click OK. Click the eye icon to turn the new layer's visibility off.

*continues on next page*

# Glyphs Palette

You can access and insert special characters through the Glyphs palette. These characters (called glyphs) are actually built into the selected font and can be previewed and applied using the palette. You can open it by choosing Type ▷ Glyphs or Window ▷ Type & Tables ▷ Glyphs.

The palette Show menu allows you to display available glyph characters for an entire font or alternates for a type selection. You can also choose to display additional glyph subsets such as Small Capitals, Discretionary Ligatures, or Slashed Zeros, for OpenType fonts that contain them.

To insert a glyph, position the Type tool cursor anywhere you'd like the glyph to appear and double-click the character in the palette.

# Placing Shapes Around a Circle *continued*

## Glyph Sets

The Glyphs palette allows you to create and save all your favorite glyph characters in a custom glyph set. To create a set, choose New Glyph Set from the palette menu, enter a name for it, and click OK. Choose a font from the menu at the bottom of the palette and then select a glyph to add to the set. Choose Add To Glyph Set from the palette menu and select your set's name from the submenu list. You can continue to select and add as many glyphs as you like.

To edit a set, choose Edit Glyph Set from the palette menu and select a set from the submenu. To remove a glyph from the set, select it from the Edit Glyph Set dialog display and click the Delete From Set button. You can also apply a different font and style to a selected glyph character in this dialog.

**Step 24.**
Press Delete (Mac) or Backspace (Windows) to remove the shapes from the selected circle. Click the Selection tool icon in the Tools palette. Click the duplicate shape that you created earlier to select it. Select the Paper swatch in the Swatches palette to apply a white fill.

**Step 25.**
Press ⌘+X / Ctrl+X to copy the shape to the Clipboard and remove it from the page. Press Shift+T to access the Type On A Path tool. Click on the circle and press ⌘+V / Ctrl+V to paste the shape as an inline object.

**Step 26.**
Continue pressing ⌘+V / Ctrl+V until the circle is surrounded by the repeated shape. Double-click the Type On A Path tool icon in the Tools palette. In the dialog that appears, click the Flip check box and click OK.

### Step 27.

Click the Selection tool icon in the Tools palette. Select the Paper swatch in the Swatches palette to apply a white fill to the circle. Press X to bring the stroke icon to the Enter **2pt** in the Weight field of the Stroke palette and press Return (Mac) or Enter (Windows).

### Step 28.

Choose Multiply from the Transparency palette Mode pop-up menu. Enter **80%** in the Opacity field and press Return or Enter.

### Step 29.

To soften the edges just slightly, choose Object ▷ Feather. In the dialog that appears, check the Feather check box to enable the effect, then turn on the Preview check box to see the feather applied to the selected object. Enter **0p5** in the Feather Width field. Leave the Corners pop-up menu setting at Diffused and the Noise setting at 0%. Click OK to apply.

*continues on next page*

# OpenType Special Characters

Certain OpenType fonts also contain special characters (such as fractions and discretionary ligatures) that can be applied automatically through the Character palette menu. You can turn these automatic special character options on and off by selecting them from the OpenType submenu.

An option that appears in brackets, such as [Contextual Alternates], indicates that it is not available for the currently selected font. When available, you can also apply a Stylistic Set from the OpenType submenu. When chosen, set glyphs are applied over the font's default glyphs.

# Placing Shapes Around a Circle *continued*

## Inserting Footnotes

InDesign CS2 allows you to create footnote references that automatically number themselves. To insert a footnote, position the Type tool cursor at the end of a word and choose Type ▷ Insert Footnote. InDesign creates a superscript number and places the corresponding reference at the bottom of the column for you to enter footnote text.

As you type, the footnote text area automatically expands up the column as needed, but not past the footnote reference number. If you allow it to split, overset footnote text carries over to the next text frame column or threaded frame. If not, the footnote reference is either moved to the next column or an overset icon appears. When this happens, you can either resize the frame or change the text formatting.

Footnote numbering restarts with each story. You can change footnote numbering, formatting, and layout in the Footnote Options dialog. To access the dialog, choose Type ▷ Document Footnote Options.

**Step 30.**
Click the eye icon next to the inner pattern layer in the Layers palette to make it visible again. Click the duplicate shape to select it and press Delete or Backspace. Option-click / Alt-click the inner pattern layer to select everything on it. Press X to bring the fill icon to the front. Select the Paper swatch to apply a white fill to the circle. Press X to bring the stroke icon to the front and click the blue swatch in the Swatches palette. Enter **2pt** in the Weight field of the Stroke or Control palette and press Return or Enter.

**Step 31.**
Double-click the Type On A Path tool icon in the Tools palette. In the dialog that appears, click the Flip check box and then click OK. Reposition the inner pattern shadow layer at the bottom of the list in the Layers palette.

**Step 32.**
⌘-click / Ctrl-click the Create New Layer button at the bottom of the Layers palette to create a layer directly above the one you currently have selected. Double-click the new layer. In the Layer Options dialog that appears, enter **center ring** in the Name field, and click OK.

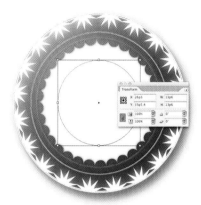

**Step 33.**

Press L to access the Ellipse tool. Hover the cursor over the center point of the circle. Option-drag or Alt-drag to draw a circle from the center point. Add the Shift key to constrain width and height amounts and create a perfect circle. Enter **13p6** in the Width and Height fields of the Control or Transform palette.

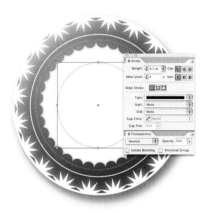

**Step 34.**

Click the blue swatch in the Swatches palette to apply a blue stroke. Enter **0.5 pt** in the Weight field of the Stroke or Control palette and press Return or Enter. Enter **50%** in the Opacity field of the Transparency palette and press Return or Enter. Press ⌘+H / Ctrl+H to hide frame edges and see the image better.

**Step 35.**

Option-click or Alt-click the Create New Layer button at the bottom of the Layers palette. In the Layer Options dialog, enter **top shadow** in the Name field and click OK.

*continues on next page*

# Applying and Editing a Photoshop Clipping Path

If the image you are importing contains a Photoshop clipping path, you can apply it via the Image panel of the Image Import Options dialog or the Clipping Path dialog. You can then edit the Photoshop path using InDesign's path editing tools. Any edits made to a Photoshop clipping path in InDesign are not applied to the original file–they only affect the image as it appears in InDesign. InDesign does not allow you to edit Photoshop clipping paths applied to EPS files.

To apply a Photoshop path when placing an image, check the Apply Photoshop Clipping Path box in the Image Import Options dialog.

To apply a Photoshop path after the image has been placed, select it with either Selection tool and choose Object ▷ Clipping Path. At the top of the Clipping Path dialog, choose Photoshop Path from the Type menu. If the image contains more than one Photoshop path, you can select which one to apply in the Path menu below. To see the path as you are applying it, click the Preview check box. To remove any extraneous black or white edges from the path, contract it by entering a value in the Inset Frame field. You can also invert a Photoshop path by clicking the Invert check box.

# Placing Shapes Around a Circle *continued*

## Creating and Editing an InDesign Clipping Path

One way to extract an image from a photograph is to create a clipping path. To create an InDesign clipping path, select a placed image with either selection tool and choose Object ⊳ Clipping Path. At the top of the Clipping Path dialog, choose Detect Edges from the Type menu. You can then adjust the Threshold and Tolerance settings by entering values in the respective fields or dragging the sliders. To see the path as you are applying it, click the Preview check box.

The Threshold slider determines how close a color must be to white before it is removed. Apply lower values to drop a light color background and higher values to drop a dark one. The Tolerance slider determines how close a pixel must be to the Threshold value in order to be removed by the clipping path. Once the Threshold and Tolerance values are set, you can contract the resulting path and remove any black or white edges by entering a value in the Inset Frame field.

**Step 36.**
Hover the cursor over the center point of the circle. Option-click and drag (or Alt-click and drag) to draw a circle from the center point. Add the Shift key to constrain width and height amounts and create a perfect circle. Enter **28p4** in the Width and Height fields of the Control or Transform palette.

**Step 37.**
Option+Shift-click / Alt+Shift-click the outer pattern layer in the Layers palette to add what's on that layer to the selection. Choose Window ⊳ Object & Layout ⊳ Align (or press Shift+F7) to display the Align palette. To line both selected objects up evenly, click the Align Horizontal Centers button and the Align Vertical Centers button.

**Step 38.**
Option-click or Alt-click the top shadow layer to select just what's on that layer. Press the backslash key to apply a stroke of None. Press X to bring the fill icon to the front. Press the period key (.) to apply the last used gradient. In the gradient palette, click the bottom-right color stop icon under the Gradient Ramp. Click and drag the black swatch from the Swatches palette directly over the selected color stop icon. Let go of the mouse button when you see a + sign appear over the hand icon.

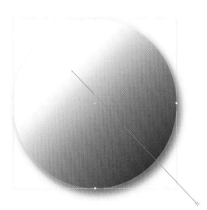

**Step 39.**

Press G to access the Gradient tool. Using the angle shown here, click and drag from inside the upper-left edge of the circle to well outside the bottom-right edge. The angle does not have to be exact.

**Step 40.**

In the Transparency palette, choose Multiply from the Mode pop-up menu. Type **18%** in the Opacity field and press Return or Enter.

**Step 41.**

To complete the design, create a new layer and add some text over the image as shown. I used the Bickley Script font at 110pt with a drop shadow applied. Choose Edit ▷ Deselect All to view your design!

## Updating Missing and Modified Links

The Links palette is similar to the Picture Usage feature in QuarkXPress in that it allows you to update and relink modified and missing links. When a link is edited outside InDesign, it is considered "modified." When a link is moved from its previous location on your system, it is considered "missing." In either scenario, InDesign displays a missing or modified icon next to the link name in the palette.

When the Sort By Status option is enabled in the Links palette menu, missing and modified links always appear at the top of the palette list. You can also choose to sort by name or by page.

To update a modified link, select it in the Links palette and click the Update Link button located in the palette footer controls, or choose Update Link from the palette menu. You can also select and update several modified links at once.

To relink a missing item, select it in the palette and click the Relink button, or choose Relink from the palette menu. When the Locate File dialog opens, browse to the link on your system and then click Open. It is also possible to select and relink several missing items at once.

# Index